Report on the Condition of the South "1865"

by
Carl Schurz

Civil War Classic Library

MESSAGE OF THE PRESIDENT OF THE UNITED STATES,

COMMUNICATING,

In compliance with a resolution of the Senate of the 12th instant, information in relation to the States of the Union lately in rebellion, accompanied by a report of Carl Schurz on the States of South Carolina, Georgia, Alabama, Mississippi, and Louisiana; also a report of Lieutenant General Grant, on the same subject.

DECEMBER 19, 1865.—Read and ordered to be printed, with the reports   of
Carl Schurz and Lieutenant General Grant.

To the Senate of the United States:

In reply to the resolution adopted by the Senate on the 12th instant, I have the honor to state, that the rebellion waged by a portion of the people against the properly constituted authorities of the government of the United States has been suppressed; that the United States are in possession of every State in which the insurrection existed; and that, as far as could be done, the courts of the United States have been restored, post offices re-established, and steps taken to put into effective operation the revenue laws of the country.

As the result of the measures instituted by the Executive, with the view of inducing a resumption of the functions of the States comprehended in the inquiry of the Senate, the people in North Carolina, South Carolina, Georgia, Alabama, Mississippi, Louisiana, Arkansas, and Tennessee, have reorganized their respective State governments, and "are yielding obedience to the laws and government of the United States," with more willingness and greater promptitude than, under the circumstances, could reasonably have been anticipated. The proposed amendment to the Constitution, providing for the abolition of slavery forever within the limits of the country, has been ratified by each one of those States, with the exception of Mississippi, from which no official information has yet been received; and in nearly all of them measures have been adopted or are now pending to confer upon freedmen rights and privileges which are essential to their comfort, protection, and security. In Florida and Texas the people are making commendable progress in restoring their State governments, and no doubt is entertained that they will at an early period be in a condition to resume all of their practical relations with the federal government.

In "that portion of the Union lately in rebellion" the aspect of affairs is more promising than, in view of all the circumstances, could well have been expected. The people throughout the entire south evince a laudable desire to renew their allegiance to the government, and to repair the devastations of war by a prompt and cheerful return to peaceful pursuits. An abiding faith is entertained that their actions will conform to their professions, and that, in acknowledging the supremacy of the Constitution and the laws of the United States, their loyalty will be unreservedly given to the government, whose leniency they cannot fail to appreciate, and whose fostering care will soon restore them to a condition of prosperity. It is true, that in some of the States the demoralizing effects of war are to be seen in occasional disorders, but these are local in character, not frequent in occurrence, and are rapidly disappearing as the authority of civil law is extended and sustained. Perplexing questions were naturally to be expected from the great and sudden change in the relations between the two races, but systems are gradually developing themselves under which the freedman will receive the protection to which he is justly entitled, and, by means of his labor, make himself a useful and independent member of the community in which he has his home. From all the information in my possession, and from that which I have recently derived from the most reliable authority, I am induced to cherish the belief that sectional animosity is surely and rapidly merging itself into a spirit of nationality, and that representation, connected with a properly adjusted system of taxation, will result in a harmonious restoration of the relations of the States to the national Union.

The report of Carl Schurz is herewith transmitted, as requested by the Senate. No reports from the honorable John Covode have been received by the President. The attention of the Senate is invited to the accompanying report of Lieutenant General Grant, who recently made a tour of inspection through several of the States whose inhabitants participated in the rebellion.

ANDREW JOHNSON

Washington, D.C., *December* 18, 1865.

REPORT OF CARL SCHURZ ON THE STATES OF SOUTH CAROLINA, GEORGIA, ALABAMA, MISSISSIPPI, AND LOUISIANA.

Sir: When you did me the honor of selecting me for a mission to the States lately in rebellion, for the purpose of inquiring into the existing condition of things, of laying before you whatever information of importance I might gather, and of suggesting to you such measures as my observations would lead me to believe advisable, I accepted the trust with a profound sense of the responsibility connected with the performance of the task. The views I entertained at the time, I had communicated to you in frequent letters and conversations. I would not have accepted the mission, had I not felt that whatever preconceived opinions I might carry with me to the south, I should be ready to abandon or modify, as my perception of facts and circumstances might command their abandonment or modification. You informed me that your "policy of reconstruction" was merely experimental, and that you would change it if the experiment did not lead to satisfactory results. To aid you in forming your conclusions upon this point I understood to be the object of my mission, and this understanding was in perfect accordance with the written instructions I received through the Secretary of War.

These instructions confined my mission to the States of South Carolina, Georgia, Alabama, Mississippi, and the department of the Gulf. I informed you, before leaving the north, that I could not well devote more than three months to the duties imposed upon me, and that space of time proved sufficient for me to visit all the States above enumerated, except Texas. I landed at Hilton Head, South Carolina, on July 15, visited Beaufort, Charleston, Orangeburg, and Columbia, returned to Charleston and Hilton Head; thence I went to Savannah, traversed the State of Georgia, visiting Augusta, Atlanta, Macon, Milledgeville, and Columbus; went through Alabama, by way of Opelika, Montgomery, Selma, and Demopolis, and through Mississippi, by way of Meridian, Jackson, and Vicksburg; then descended the Mississippi to New Orleans, touching at Natchez; from New Orleans I visited Mobile, Alabama, and the Teche country, in Louisiana, and then spent again some days at Natchez and Vicksburg, on my way to the north. These are the outlines of my journey.

Before laying the results of my observations before you, it is proper that I should state the *modus operandi* by which I obtained information and formed my conclusions. Wherever I went I sought interviews with persons who might be presumed to represent the opinions, or to have influence upon the conduct, of their neighbors; I had thus frequent meetings with individuals belonging to the different classes of society from the highest to the lowest; in the cities as well as on the roads and steamboats I had many opportunities to converse not only with inhabitants of the adjacent country, but with persons coming from districts which I was not able to visit; and finally I compared the impressions thus received with the experience of the military and civil officers of the government stationed in that country, as well as of other reliable Union men to whom a longer residence on the spot and a more varied intercourse with the people had given better facilities of local observation than my circumstances permitted me to enjoy. When practicable I procured statements of their views and experience in writing as well as copies of official or private reports they had received from their subordinates or other persons. It was not expected of me that I should take formal testimony, and, indeed, such an operation would have required more time than I was able to devote to it.

My facilities for obtaining information were not equally extensive in the different States I visited. As they naturally depended somewhat upon the time the military had had to occupy and explore the country, as well as upon the progressive development of things generally, they improved from day to day as I went on, and were best in the States I visited last. It is owing to this circumstance that I cannot give as detailed an account of the condition of things in South Carolina and Georgia as I am able to give with regard to Louisiana and Mississippi.

Instead of describing the experiences of my journey in chronological order, which would lead to endless repetitions and a confused mingling of the different subjects under consideration, I propose to arrange my observations under different heads according to the subject matter. It is true, not all that can be said of the people of one State will apply with equal force to the people of another; but it will be easy to make the necessary distinctions when in the course of this report they become of any importance. I beg to be understood when using, for the sake of brevity, the term "the southern people," as meaning only the people of the States I have visited.

CONDITION OF THINGS IMMEDIATELY AFTER THE CLOSE OF THE WAR.

In the development of the popular spirit in the south since the close of the war two well-marked periods can be distinguished. The first commences with the sudden collapse of the confederacy and the dispersion of its armies, and the second with the first proclamation indicating the "reconstruction policy" of the government. Of the first period I can state the characteristic features only from the accounts I received, partly from Unionists who were then living in the south, partly from persons that had participated in the rebellion. When the news of Lee's and Johnston's surrenders burst upon the southern country the general consternation was extreme. People held their breath, indulging in the wildest apprehensions as to what was now to come. Men who had occupied positions under the confederate government, or were otherwise compromised in the rebellion, run before the federal columns as they advanced and spread out to occupy the country, from village to village, from plantation to plantation, hardly knowing whether they wanted to escape or not.

Others remained at their homes yielding themselves up to their fate. Prominent Unionists told me that persons who for four years had scorned to recognize them on the street approached them with smiling faces and both hands extended. Men of standing in the political world expressed serious doubts as to whether the rebel States would ever again occupy their position as States in the Union, or be governed as conquered provinces. The public mind was so despondent that if readmission at some future time under whatever conditions had been promised, it would then have been looked upon as a favor. The most uncompromising rebels prepared for leaving the country. The masses remained in a state of fearful expectancy.

This applies especially to those parts of the country which were within immediate reach of our armies or had previously been touched by the war. Where Union soldiers had never been seen and none were near, people were at first hardly aware of the magnitude of the catastrophe, and strove to continue in their old ways of living.

Such was, according to the accounts I received, the character of that first period. The worst apprehensions were gradually relieved as day after day went by without bringing the disasters and inflictions which had been vaguely anticipated, until at last the appearance of the North Carolina proclamation substituted new hopes for them. The development of this second period I was called upon to observe on the spot, and it forms the main subject of this report.

RETURNING LOYALTY.

It is a well-known fact that in the States south of Tennessee and North Carolina the number of white Unionists who during the war actively aided the government, or at least openly professed their attachment to the cause of the Union, was very small. In none of those States were they strong enough to exercise any decisive influence upon the action of the people, not even in Louisiana, unless vigorously supported by the power of the general government. But the white people at large being, under certain conditions, charged with taking the preliminaries of "reconstruction" into their hands, the success of the experiment depends upon the spirit and attitude of those who either attached themselves to the secession cause from the beginning, or, entertaining originally opposite views, at least followed its fortunes from the time that their States had declared their separation from the Union.

The first southern men of this class with whom I came into contact immediately after my arrival in South Carolina expressed their sentiments almost literally in the following language: "We acknowledge ourselves beaten, and we are ready to submit to the results of the war. The war has practically decided that no State shall secede and that the slaves are emancipated. We cannot be expected at once to give up our principles and convictions of right, but we accept facts as they are, and desire to be reinstated as soon as possible in the enjoyment and exercise of our political rights." This declaration was repeated to me hundreds of times in every State I visited, with some variations of language, according to the different ways of thinking or the frankness or reserve of the different speakers. Some said nothing of adhering to their old principles and convictions of right; others still argued against the constitutionality of coercion and of the emancipation proclamation; others expressed their determination to become good citizens, in strong language, and urged with equal emphasis the necessity of their home institutions being at once left to their own control; others would go so far as to say they were glad that the war was ended, and they had never had any confidence in the confederacy; others protested that they had been opposed to secession until their States went out, and then yielded to the current of events; some would give me to understand that they had always been good Union men at heart, and rejoiced that the war had terminated in favor of the national cause, but in most cases such a sentiment was expressed only in a whisper; others again would grumblingly insist upon the restoration of their "rights," as if they had done no wrong, and indicated plainly that they would submit only to what they could not resist and as long as they could not resist it. Such were the definitions of "returning loyalty" I received from the mouths of a large number of individuals intelligent enough to appreciate the meaning of the expressions they used. I found a great many whose manner of speaking showed that they did not understand the circumstances under which they lived, and had no settled opinions at all except on matters immediately touching their nearest interests.

Upon the ground of these declarations, and other evidence gathered in the course of my observations, I may group the southern people into four classes, each of which exercises an influence upon the development of things in that section:

1. Those who, although having yielded submission to the nationalgovernment only when obliged to do so, have a clear perception of the irreversible changes produced by the war, and honestly endeavor to accommodate themselves to the new order of things. Many of them are not free from traditional prejudice but open to conviction, and may be expected to act in good faith whatever they do. This class is composed, in its majority, of persons of mature age—

planters, merchants, and professional men; some of them are active in the reconstruction movement, but boldness and energy are, with a few individual exceptions, not among their distinguishing qualities.

2. Those whose principal object is to have the States without delay restored to their position and influence in the Union and the people of the States to the absolute control of their home concerns. They are ready, in order to attain that object, to make any ostensible concession that will not prevent them from arranging things to suit their taste as soon as that object is attained. This class comprises a considerable number, probably a large majority, of the professional politicians who are extremely active in the reconstruction movement. They are loud in their praise of the President's reconstruction policy, and clamorous for the withdrawal of the federal troops and the abolition of the Freedmen's Bureau.

3. The incorrigibles, who still indulge in the swagger which was so customary before and during the war, and still hope for a time when the southern confederacy will achieve its independence. This class consists mostly of young men, and comprises the loiterers of the towns and the idlers of the country. They persecute Union men and negroes whenever they can do so with impunity, insist clamorously upon their "rights," and are extremely impatient of the presence of the federal soldiers. A good many of them have taken the oaths of allegiance and amnesty, and associated themselves with the second class in their political operations. This element is by no means unimportant; it is strong in numbers, deals in brave talk, addresses itself directly and incessantly to the passions and prejudices of the masses, and commands the admiration of the women.

4. The multitude of people who have no definite ideas about the circumstances under which they live and about the course they have to follow; whose intellects are weak, but whose prejudices and impulses are strong, and who are apt to be carried along by those who know how to appeal to the latter.

Much depends upon the relative strength and influence of these classes. In the course of this report you will find statements of facts which may furnish a basis for an estimate. But whatever their differences may be, on one point they are agreed: further resistance to the power of the national government is useless, and submission to its authority a matter of necessity. It is true, the right of secession in theory is still believed in by most of those who formerly believed in it; some are still entertaining a vague hope of seeing it realized at some future time, but all give it up as a practical impossibility for the present. All movements in favor of separation from the Union have, therefore, been practically abandoned, and resistance to our military forces, on that score, has ceased. The demonstrations of hostility to the troops and other agents of the government, which are still occurring in some localities, and of which I shall speak hereafter, spring from another class of motives. This kind of loyalty, however, which is produced by the irresistible pressure of force, and consists merely in the non-commission of acts of rebellion, is of a negative character, and might, as such, hardly be considered independent of circumstances and contingencies.

OATH-TAKING.

A demonstration of "returning loyalty" of a more positive character is the taking of the oaths of allegiance and amnesty prescribed by the general government. At first the number of persons who availed themselves of the opportunities offered for abjuring their adhesion to the cause of the rebellion was not very large, but it increased considerably when the obtaining of a pardon and the right of voting were made dependent upon the previous performance of that act. Persons falling under any of the exceptions of the amnesty proclamation made haste to avert the impending danger; and politicians used every means of persuasion to induce people to swell the number of voters by clearing themselves of all disabilities. The great argument that this was necessary to the end of reconstructing their State governments, and of regaining the control of their home affairs and their influence in the Union, was copiously enlarged upon in the letters and speeches of prominent individuals, which are before the country and need no further comment. In some cases the taking of the oath was publicly recommended in newspapers and addresses with sneering remarks, and I have listened to many private conversations in which it was treated with contempt and ridicule. While it was not generally looked upon in the State I visited as a very serious matter, except as to the benefits and privileges it confers, I have no doubt that a great many persons took it fully conscious of the obligations it imposes, and honestly intending to fulfil them.

The aggregate number of those who thus had qualified themselves for voting previous to the election for the State conventions was not as large as might have been expected. The vote obtained at these elections was generally reported as very light—in some localities surprisingly so. It would, perhaps, be worth while for the government to order up reports about the number of oaths administered by the officers authorized to do so, previous to the elections for the State conventions; such reports would serve to indicate how large a proportion of the people participated in the reconstruction movement at that time, and to what extent the masses were represented in the conventions.

Of those who have not yet taken the oath of allegiance, most belong to the class of indifferent people who "do not care one way or the other." There are still some individuals who find the oath to be a confession of defeat and a declaration of submission too humiliating and too repugnant to their feelings. It is to be expected that the former will gradually overcome their apathy, and the latter their sensitiveness, and that, at a not remote day, all will have qualified themselves, in point of form, to resume the right of citizenship. On the whole, it may be said that the value of the oaths taken in the southern States is neither above nor below the value of the political oaths taken in other countries. A historical examination of the subject of political oaths will lead to the conclusion that they can be very serviceable in certain emergencies and for certain objects, but that they have never insured the stability of a government, and never improved the morals of a people.

FEELING TOWARDS THE SOLDIERS AND THE PEOPLE OF THE NORTH.

A more substantial evidence of "returning loyalty" would be a favorable change of feeling with regard to the government's friends and agents, and the people of the loyal States generally. I mentioned above that all organized attacks upon our military forces stationed in the south have ceased; but there are still localities where it is unsafe for a man wearing the federal uniform or known as an officer of the government to be abroad outside of the immediate reach of our garrisons. The shooting of single soldiers and government couriers was not unfrequently reported while I was in the south, and even as late as the middle of September, Major Miller, assistant adjutant general of the commissioner of the Freedmen's Bureau in Alabama, while on an inspecting tour in the southern counties of that State, found it difficult to prevent a collision between the menacing populace and his escort. His wagon-master was brutally murdered while remaining but a short distance behind the command. The murders of agents of the Freedmen's Bureau have been noticed in the public papers. These, and similar occurrences, however, may be looked upon as isolated cases, and ought to be charged, perhaps, only to the account of the lawless persons who committed them.

But no instance has come to my notice in which the people of a city or a rural district cordially fraternized with the army. Here and there the soldiers were welcomed as protectors against apprehended dangers; but general exhibitions of cordiality on the part of the population I have not heard of. There are, indeed, honorable individual exceptions to this rule. Many persons, mostly belonging to the first of the four classes above enumerated, are honestly striving to soften down the bitter feelings and traditional antipathies of their neighbors; others, who are acting more upon motives of policy than inclination, maintain pleasant relations with the officers of the government. But, upon the whole, the soldier of the Union is still looked upon as a stranger, an intruder—as the "Yankee," "the enemy." It would be superfluous to enumerate instances of insult offered to our soldiers, and even to officers high in command; the existence and intensity of this aversion is too well known to those who have served or are now serving in the south to require proof. In this matter the exceptions were, when I was there, not numerous enough to affect the rule. In the documents accompanying this report you will find allusions confirming this statement. I would invite special attention to the letter of General Kirby Smith, (accompanying document No. 9.)

This feeling of aversion and resentment with regard to our soldiers may, perhaps, be called natural. The animosities inflamed by a four years' war, and its distressing incidents, cannot be easily overcome. But they extend beyond the limits of the army, to the people of the north. I have read in southern papers bitter complaints about the unfriendly spirit exhibited by the northern people—complaints not unfrequently flavored with an admixture of vigorous vituperation. But, as far as my experience goes, the "unfriendly spirit" exhibited in the north is all mildness and affection compared with the popular temper which in the south vents itself in a variety of ways and on all possible occasions. No observing northern man can come into contact with the different classes composing southern society without noticing it. He may be received in social circles with great politeness, even with apparent cordiality; but soon he will become aware that, although he may be esteemed as a man, he is detested as a "Yankee," and, as the conversation becomes a little more confidential and throws off ordinary restraint, he is not unfrequently told so; the word "Yankee" still signifies to them those traits of character which the southern press has been so long in the habit of attributing to the northern people; and whenever they look around them upon the traces of the war, they see in them, not the consequences of their own folly, but the evidences of "Yankee wickedness." In making these general statements, I beg to be understood as always excluding the individual exceptions above mentioned.

It is by no means surprising that prejudices and resentments, which for years were so assiduously cultivated and so violently inflamed, should not have been turned into affection by a defeat; nor are they likely to disappear as long as the southern people continue to brood over their losses and misfortunes. They will gradually subside when those who entertain them cut resolutely loose from the past and embark in a career of new activity on a common field with those whom they have so long considered their enemies. Of this I shall say more in another part of this report. But while we are certainly inclined to put upon such things the most charitable construction, it remains nevertheless true, that as long as these feelings exist in their present strength, they will hinder the growth of that reliable kind of loyalty which springs from the heart and clings to the country in good and evil fortune.

SITUATION OF UNIONISTS.

It would have been a promising indication of returning loyalty if the old, consistent, uncompromising Unionists of the south, and those northern men who during the war settled down there to contribute to the prosperity of the country with their capital and enterprise, had received that measure of consideration to which their identification with the new order of things entitled them. It would seem natural that the victory of the national cause should have given those who during the struggle had remained the firm friends of the Union, a higher standing in society and an enlarged political influence. This appears to have been the case during that "first period" of anxious uncertainty when known Unionists were looked up to as men whose protection and favor might be of high value. At least it appears to have been so in some individual instances. But the close of that "first period" changed the aspect of things.

It struck me soon after my arrival in the south that the known Unionists—I mean those who during the war had been to a certain extent identified with the national cause—were not in communion with the leading social and political circles; and the further my observations extended the clearer it became to me that their existence in the south was of a rather precarious nature. Already in Charleston my attention was called to the current talk among the people, that, when they had the control of things once more in their own hands and were no longer restrained by the presence of "Yankee" soldiers, men of Dr. Mackey's stamp would not be permitted to live there. At first I did not attach much importance to such reports; but as I proceeded through the country, I heard the same thing so frequently repeated, at so many different places, and by so many different persons, that I could no longer look upon the apprehensions expressed to me by Unionists as entirely groundless. I found the same opinion entertained by most of our military commanders. Even

Governor Sharkey, in the course of a conversation I had with him in the presence of Major General Osterhaus, admitted that, if our troops were then withdrawn, the lives of northern men in Mississippi would not be safe. To show that such anticipations were not extravagant, I would refer to the letter addressed to me by General Osterhaus. (Accompanying document No. 10.) He states that he was compelled to withdraw the garrison from Attala county, Mississippi, the regiment to which that garrison belonged being mustered out, and that when the troops had been taken away, four murders occurred, two of white Union men, and two of negroes. (He informed me subsequently that the perpetrators were in custody.) He goes on to say: "There is no doubt whatever that the state of affairs would be intolerable for all Union men, all recent immigrants from the north, and all negroes, the moment the protection of the United States troops were withdrawn." General Osterhaus informed me of another murder of a Union man by a gang of lawless persons, in Jackson, about the end of June. General Slocum, in his order prohibiting the organization of the State militia in Mississippi, speaks of the "outrages committed against northern men, government couriers, and negroes." (Accompanying document No. 12.) He communicated to me an official report from Lieutenant Colonel Yorke, commanding at Port Gibson, to General Davidson, pointing in the same direction. General Canby stated to me that he was obliged to disband and prohibit certain patrol organizations in Louisiana because they indulged in the gratification of private vengeance. Lieutenant Hickney, assistant commissioner of the Freedmen's Bureau, at Shreveport, Louisiana, in a report addressed to Assistant Commissioner Conway, says: "The life of a northern man who is true to his country and the spirit and genius of its institutions, and frankly enunciates his principles, is not secure where there is not a military force to protect him." (Accompanying document No. 32.) Mr. William King, a citizen of Georgia, well known in that State, stated to me in conversation: "There are a great many bad characters in the country, who would make it for some time unsafe for known Union people and northerners who may settle down here to live in this country without the protection of the military." The affair of Scottsborough, in the military district of northern Alabama, where a sheriff arrested and attempted to bring to trial for murder Union soldiers who had served against the guerillas in that part of the country, an attempt which was frustrated only by the prompt interference of the district commander, has become generally known through the newspapers. (Accompanying document No. 19.) It is not improbable that many cases similar to those above mentioned have occurred in other parts of the south without coming to the notice of the authorities.

It is true these are mere isolated cases, for which it would be wrong to hold anybody responsible who was not connected with them; but it is also true that the apprehensions so widely spread among the Unionists and northern men were based upon the spirit exhibited by the people among whom they lived. I found a good many thinking of removing themselves and their families to the northern States, and if our troops should be soon withdrawn the exodus will probably become quite extensive unless things meanwhile change for the better.

ASPECT OF THE POLITICAL FIELD.

The status of this class of Unionists in the political field corresponds with what I have said above. In this respect I have observed practical results more closely in Mississippi than in any other State. I had already left South Carolina and Georgia when the elections for the State conventions took place. Of Alabama, I saw only Mobile after the election. In Louisiana, a convention, a legislature, and a State government had already been elected, during and under the influence of the war, and I left before the nominating party conventions were held; but I was in Mississippi immediately after the adjournment of the State convention, and while the canvass preparatory to the election of the legislature and of the State and county officers was going on. Events have since sufficiently developed themselves in the other States to permit us to judge how far Mississippi can be regarded as a representative of the rest. Besides, I found the general spirit animating the people to be essentially the same in all the States above mentioned.

The election for the State convention in Mississippi was, according to the accounts I have received, not preceded by a very vigorous and searching canvass of the views and principles of the candidates. As I stated before, the vote was very far from being full, and in most cases the members were elected not upon strictly defined party issues, but upon their individual merits as to character, intelligence, and standing in society. Only in a few places the contest between rival candidates was somewhat animated. It was probably the same in Alabama, Georgia, and South Carolina.

The Mississippi convention was, in its majority, composed of men belonging to the first two of the four classes above mentioned. There were several Union men in it of the inoffensive, compromising kind— men who had been opposed to secession in the beginning, and had abstained from taking a prominent part in the rebellion unless obliged to do so, but who had, at least, readily acquiesced in what was going on. But there was, as far as I have been able to ascertain, only one man there who, like the Unionists of East Tennessee, had offered active resistance to the rebel authorities. This was Mr. Crawford, of Jones county; he was elected by the poor people of that region, his old followers, as their acknowledged leader, and his may justly be looked upon as an exceptional case. How he looked upon his situation appears from a speech he delivered in that convention, and especially from the amended version of it placed into my hands by a trustworthy gentleman of my acquaintance who had listened to its delivery. (Accompanying document No. 13.) But several instances have come to my knowledge, in which Union men of a sterner cast than those described as acquiescing compromisers were defeated in the election, and, aside from Mr. Crawford's case, none in which they succeeded.

The impulses by which voters were actuated in making their choice appeared more clearly in the canvass for State officers, Congressmen, and members of the legislature, when the antecedents and political views of candidates were more closely scrutinized and a warmer contest took place. The population of those places in the south which have been longest in the possession of our armies is generally the most accommodating as to the new order of things; at least the better elements are there in greater relative strength. A Union meeting at Vicksburg may, therefore, be produced as a not unfavorable exponent of Mississippi Unionism. Among the documents attached to this report you will find three speeches delivered before such a meeting—one by Mr. Richard Cooper, candidate for the attorney generalship of the State; one by Hon. Sylvanus Evans, candidate for Congress; and one by Colonel Partridge, candidate for a seat in the legislature. (Accompanying document No. 14.) The speakers represented themselves as Union men, and I have learned nothing about them that would cast suspicion upon the sincerity of their declarations as far as they go; but all there qualified their Unionism by the same important statement. Mr. Cooper: "In 1850 I opposed an attempt to break up the United States government, and in 1860 I did the same. I travelled in Alabama and Mississippi to oppose the measure. (Applause.) But after the State did secede, I did all in my power to sustain it." (Heavy applause.) Mr. Evans: "In 1861 I was a delegate from Lauderdale county to the State convention, then and in 1860 being opposed to the act of secession, and fought against it with all my powers. But when the State had seceded, I went with it as a matter of duty, and I sustained it until the day of the surrender with all my body and heart and mind." (Great applause.) Colonel Partridge: "He was a Union man before the war and a soldier in the war. He had performed his duty as a private and an officer on the battle-field and on the staff."

These speeches, fair specimens of a majority of those delivered by the better class of politicians before the better class of audiences, furnish an indication of the kind of Unionism which, by candidates, is considered palatable to the people of that region. And candidates are generally good judges as to what style of argument is best calculated to captivate the popular mind. In some isolated localities there may be some chance of success for a candidate who, proclaiming himself a Union man, is not able to add, "but after the State had seceded I did all in my power to sustain it," although such localities are certainly scarce and difficult to find.

It is not so difficult to find places in which a different style of argument is considered most serviceable. Your attention is respectfully invited to a card addressed to the voters of the sixth judicial district of Mississippi by Mr. John T. Hogan, candidate for the office of district attorney. (Accompanying document No. 15.) When, at the commencement of the war, Kentucky resolved to remain in the Union, Mr. Hogan, so he informs the constituency, was a citizen of Kentucky; because Kentucky refused to leave the Union Mr. Hogan left Kentucky. He went to Mississippi, joined the rebel army, and was wounded in battle; and because he left his native State to fight against the Union, "therefore," Mr. Hogan tells his Mississippian constituency, "he cannot feel that he is an alien in their midst, and, with something of confidence in the result, appeals to them for their suffrages." Such is Mr. Hogan's estimate of the loyalty of the sixth judicial district of Mississippi.

A candidate relying for success upon nothing but his identification with the rebellion might be considered as an extreme case. But, in fact, Mr. Hogan only speaks out bluntly what other candidates wrap up in lengthy qualifications. It is needless to accumulate specimens. I am sure no Mississippian will deny that if a candidate there based his claims upon the ground of his having left Mississippi when the State seceded, in order to fight for the Union, his pretensions would be treated as a piece of impudence. I feel warranted in saying that Unionism absolutely untinctured by any connexion with, or at least acquiescence in the rebellion, would have but little chance of political preferment anywhere, unless favored by very extraordinary circumstances; while men who, during the war, followed the example of the Union leaders of East Tennessee, would in most places have to depend upon the protection of our military forces for safety, while nowhere within the range of my observation would they, under present circumstances, be considered eligible to any position of trust, honor, or influence, unless it be in the county of Jones, as long as the bayonets of the United States are still there.

The tendency of which in the preceding remarks I have endeavored to indicate the character and direction, appeared to prevail in all the States that came under my observation with equal force, some isolated localities excepted. None of the provisional governments adopted the policy followed by the late "military government" of Tennessee: to select in every locality the most reliable and most capable Union men for the purpose of placing into their hands the positions of official influence. Those who had held the local offices before and during the rebellion were generally reappointed, and hardly any discrimination made. If such wholesale re-appointments were the only thing that could be done in a hurry, it may be asked whether the hurry was necessary. Even in Louisiana, where a State government was organized during the war and under the influence of the sentiments which radiated from the camps and headquarters of the Union army, and where there is a Union element far stronger than in any other of the States I visited, even there, men who have aided the rebellion by word and act are crowding into places of trust and power. Governor Wells, when he was elected lieutenant governor of Louisiana, was looked upon and voted for as a thorough Unionist; but hardly had he the patronage of the State government in his hands, when he was carried along by the seemingly irresistible current. Even members of the "Conservative Union party," and friends of Governor Wells, expressed their dissatisfaction with the remarkable "liberality" with which he placed men into official positions who had hardly returned from the rebel army, or some other place where they had taken refuge to avoid living under the flag of the United States. The apprehension was natural that such elements would soon obtain a power and influence which the governor would not be able to control even if he wished. Taking these things into consideration, the re-nomination of Governor Wells for the governorship can certainly not be called a victory of that Union sentiment to which he owed his first election. While I was in New Orleans an occurrence took place which may be quoted as an illustration of the sweep of what I might call the *reactionary movement*. When General Shepley was military governor of Louisiana, under General Butler's regime, a school board was appointed for the purpose of reorganizing the public schools of New Orleans. A corps of loyal teachers was appointed, and the education of the children was conducted with a view to make them loyal citizens. The national airs were frequently sung in the schools, and other exercises introduced, calculated to impregnate the youthful minds of the pupils with affection for their country. It appears that this feature of the public schools was distasteful to that class of people with whose feelings they did not accord.

Mr. H. Kennedy, acting mayor of New Orleans, early in September last, disbanded the school board which so far had conducted the educational affairs of the city, and appointed a new one. The composition of this new school board was such as to induce General Canby to suspend its functions until he could inquire into the loyalty of its members. The report of the officer intrusted with the investigation is among the documents annexed hereto. (Accompanying document No. 16.) It shows that a large majority of the members had sympathized with the rebellion, and aided the confederate government in a variety of ways. But as no evidence was elicited proving the members legally incapable of holding office, General Canby considered himself obliged to remove the prohibition, and the new school board entered upon its functions.

Without offering any comment of my own, I annex an editorial taken from the "New Orleans Times," of September 12, evidently written in defence of the measure. (Accompanying document No. 17.) Its real substance, stripped of all circumlocutions, can be expressed in a few words: "The schools of New Orleans have been institutions so intensely and demonstratively loyal as to become unpopular with those of our fellow-citizens to whom such demonstrations are distasteful, and they must be brought back under 'popular control' so as to make them cease to be obnoxious in that particular." It was generally understood, when the new school board was appointed, that a Mr. Rodgers was to be made superintendent of public schools. In Major Lowell's report to General Canby (Accompanying document No. 16) this Mr. Rodgers figures as follows: "Mr. Rodgers, the candidate for the position of superintendent of public schools, held the same office at the commencement of the war. His conduct at that time was imbued with extreme bitterness and hate towards the United States, and, in his capacity as superintendent, he introduced the 'Bonnie Blue Flag' and other rebel songs into the exercises of the schools under his charge. In histories and other books where the initials 'U.S.' occurred he had the same erased, and 'C.S.' substituted. He used all means in his power to imbue the minds of the youth intrusted to his care with hate and malignity towards the Union. He has just returned from the late confederacy, where he has resided during the war. At the time he left the city to join the army he left his property in the care of one Finley, who claims to be a British subject, but held the position of sergeant in a confederate regiment of militia."

No sooner was the above-mentioned prohibition by General Canby removed when Mr. Rodgers was actually appointed, and he now presides over the educational interests of New Orleans. There is something like system in such proceedings.

Similar occurrences, such as the filling with rebel officers of professorships in the Military Institute of Louisiana, where formerly General Sherman held a position, have already become known to the country, and it is unnecessary to go into further details. Many cases of this description are not of much importance in themselves, but serve as significant indications of the tendency of things in the south.

It is easily understood that, under such circumstances, Unionists of the consistent, uncompromising kind do not play an enviable part. It is a sad fact that the victory of the national arms has, to a great extent, resulted in something like a political ostracism of the most loyal men in that part of the country. More than once have I heard some of them complain of having been taunted by late rebels with their ill fortune; and it is, indeed, melancholy for them to reflect that, if they had yielded to the current of public sentiment in the rebel States instead of resisting it, their present situation and prospects would be much more pleasing. Nor is such a reflection calculated to encourage them, or others, to follow a similar course if similar emergencies should again arise.

WHAT HAS BEEN ACCOMPLISHED.

While the generosity and toleration shown by the government to the people lately in rebellion has not met with a corresponding generosity shown by those people to the government's friends, it has brought forth some results which, if properly developed, will become of value. It has facilitated the re-establishment of the forms of civil government, and led many of those who had been active in the rebellion to take part in the act of bringing back the States to their constitutional relations; and if nothing else were necessary than the mere putting in operation of the mere machinery of government in point of form, and not also the acceptance of the results of the war and their development in point of spirit, these results, although as yet incomplete, might be called a satisfactory advance in the right direction. There is, at present, no danger of another insurrection against the authority of the United States on a large scale, and the people are willing to reconstruct their State governments, and to send their senators and representatives to Congress.

But as to the moral value of these results, we must not indulge in any delusions. There are two principal points to which I beg to call your attention. In the first place, the rapid return to power and influence of so many of those who but recently were engaged in a bitter war against the Union, has had one effect which was certainly not originally contemplated by the government. Treason does, under existing circumstances, not appear odious in the south. The people are not impressed with any sense of its criminality. And, secondly, there is, as yet, among the southern people an *utter absence of national feeling*. I made it a business, while in the south, to watch the symptoms of "returning loyalty" as they appeared not only in private conversation, but in the public press and in the speeches delivered and the resolutions passed at Union meetings. Hardly ever was there an expression of hearty attachment to the great republic, or an appeal to the impulses of patriotism; but whenever submission to the national authority was declared and advocated, it was almost uniformly placed upon two principal grounds: That, under present circumstances, the southern people could "do no better;" and then that submission was the only means by which they could rid themselves of the federal soldiers and obtain once more control of their own affairs. Some of the speakers may have been inspired by higher motives, but upon these two arguments they had principally to rely whenever they wanted to make an impression upon the popular mind. If any exception is to be made to this rule it is Louisiana, in whose metropolis a different spirit was cultivated for some time; but even there, the return in mass of those who followed the fortunes of the confederate flag during the war does not appear to have a favorable influence upon the growth of that sentiment. (See Gen. Canby's letter, accompanying document No. 8.) While admitting that, at present, we have perhaps no right to expect anything better than this submission—loyalty which springs from necessity and calculation—I do not consider it safe for the government to base expectations upon it, which the manner in which it manifests itself does not justify.

The reorganization of civil government is relieving the military, to a great extent, of its police duties and judicial functions; but at the time I left the south it was still very far from showing a satisfactory efficiency in the maintenance of order and security.—In many districts robbing and plundering was going on with perfect impunity; the roads were infested by bands of highwaymen; numerous assaults occurred, and several stage lines were considered unsafe. The statements of Major General Woods, Brigadier General Kilby Smith and Colonel Gilchrist, (accompanying documents Nos. 11, 9 and 18,) give a terrible picture of the state of things in the localities they refer to. It is stated that civil officers are either unwilling or unable to enforce the laws; that one man does not dare to testify against another for fear of being murdered, and that the better elements of society are kept down by lawless characters under a system of terrorism. From my own observation I know that these things are not confined to the districts mentioned in the documents above referred to. Both the governors of Alabama and Mississippi complained of it in official proclamations. Cotton, horse and cattle stealing was going on in all the States I visited on an extensive scale. Such a state of demoralization would call for extraordinary measures in any country, and it is difficult to conceive how, in the face of the inefficiency of the civil authorities, the removal of the troops can be thought of.

In speaking above of the improbability of an insurrectionary movement on a large scale, I did not mean to say that I considered resistance in detail to the execution of the laws of Congress and the measures of the government impossible. Of all subjects connected with the negro question I shall speak in another part of this report. But there is another matter claiming the attention and foresight of the government. It is well known that the levying of taxes for the payment of the interest on our national debt is, and will continue to be, very unpopular in the south. It is true, no striking demonstrations have as yet been made of any decided unwillingness on the part of the people to contribute to the discharge of our national obligations. But most of the conversations I had with southerners upon this subject led me to apprehend that they, politicians and people, are rather inclined to ask money of the government as compensation for their emancipated slaves, for the rebuilding of the levees on the Mississippi, and various kinds of damage done by our armies for military purposes, than, as the current expression is, to "help paying the expenses of the whipping they have received." In fact, there are abundant indications in newspaper articles, public speeches, and electioneering documents of candidates, which render it eminently probable that on the claim of compensation for their emancipated slaves the southern States, as soon as readmitted to representation in Congress, will be almost a unit. In the Mississippi convention the idea was broached by Mr. Potter, in an elaborate speech, to have the late slave States relieved from taxation "for years to come," in consideration of "debt due them" for the emancipated slaves; and this plea I have frequently heard advocated in private conversations. I need not go into details as to the efforts made in some of the southern States in favor of the assumption by those States of their debts contracted during the rebellion. It may be assumed with certainty that those who want to have the southern people, poor as they are, taxed for the payment of rebel debts, do not mean to have them taxed for the purpose of meeting our national obligations. But whatever devices may be resorted to, present indications justify the apprehension that the enforcement of our revenue laws will meet with a refractory spirit, and may require sterner measures than the mere sending of revenue officers into that part of the country.

I have annexed to this report numerous letters addressed to me by gentlemen whose views on the loyalty of the southern people and kindred topics, formed as they are upon an extended observation and long experience, are entitled to consideration. (Letter of General Gillmore, accompanying document No. 1; letter of Dr. Mackey, No. 2; letter of Mr. Sawyer, No. 3; letter of General Hatch, No. 4; letter of Mr. Pilsbury, No. 5; statement of General Steedman, No. 6; letter of General Croxton, No. 7; letter of General Canby, No. 8; letter of General Kirby Smith, No. 9, &c.) In these papers a variety of opinions is expressed, some to a certain extent sanguine, others based upon a less favorable experience. I offer them to you, without exception, as they came to me. Many of the gentlemen who wrote them have never been in any way connected with party politics, and their utterances may be looked upon as coming from unbiassed and impartial observers.

THE NEGRO QUESTION—FIRST ASPECTS.

The principal cause of that want of national spirit which has existed in the south so long, and at last gave birth to the rebellion, was, that the southern people cherished, cultivated, idolized their peculiar interests and institutions in preference to those which they had in common with the rest of the American people. Hence the importance of the negro question as an integral part of the question of union in general, and the question of reconstruction in particular.

When the war came to a close, the labor system of the south was already much disturbed. During the progress of military operations large numbers of slaves had left their masters and followed the columns of our armies; others had taken refuge in our camps; many thousands had enlisted in the service of the national government. Extensive settlements of negroes had been formed along the seaboard and the banks of the Mississippi, under the supervision of army officers and treasury agents, and the government was feeding the colored refugees, who could not be advantageously employed, in the so-called contraband camps. Many slaves had also been removed by their masters, as our armies penetrated the country, either to Texas or to the interior of Georgia and Alabama. Thus a considerable portion of the laboring force had been withdrawn from its former employments. But a majority of the slaves remained on the plantations to which they belonged, especially in those parts of the country which were not touched by the war, and where, consequently, the emancipation proclamation was not enforced by the military power. Although not ignorant of the stake they had in the result of the contest, the patient bondmen waited quietly for the development of things. But as soon as the struggle was finally decided, and our forces were scattered about in detachments to occupy the country, the so far unmoved masses began to stir. The report went among them that their liberation was no longer a mere contingency, but a fixed fact. Large numbers of colored people left the plantations; many flocked to our military posts and camps to obtain the certainty of their freedom, and others walked away merely for the purpose of leaving the places on which they had been held in slavery, and because they could now go with impunity. Still others, and their number was by no means inconsiderable, remained with their former masters and continued their work on the field, but under new and as yet unsettled conditions, and under the agitating influence of a feeling of restlessness. In some localities, however, where our troops had not yet penetrated and where no military post was within reach, planters endeavored and partially succeeded in maintaining between themselves and the negroes the relation of master and slave, partly by concealing from them the great changes that had taken place, and partly by terrorizing them into submission to their behests. But aside from these exceptions, the country found itself thrown into that confusion which is naturally inseparable from a change so great and so sudden. The white people were afraid of the negroes, and the negroes did not trust the white people; the military power of the national government stood there, and was looked up to, as the protector of both.

Upon this power devolved the task to bring order into that chaos. But the order to be introduced was a new order, of which neither the late masters nor the late slaves had an adequate conception. All the elements of society being afloat, the difficulties were immense. The military officers and agents of the Freedmen's Bureau, to whom the negroes applied for advice and guidance, either procured them such employment as could be found, or persuaded them to return to their plantations and to continue in the cultivation of the crops, promising them that their liberty, rights, and interests should be protected. Upon the planters they urged the necessity of making fair and equitable contracts with the freedmen, admonishing them to treat their laborers as free men ought to be treated. These efforts met with such success as the difficulties surrounding the problem permitted to expect. Large numbers of negroes went back to the fields, according to the advice they had received, but considerable accumulations still remained in and around the towns and along the seaboard, where there was no adequate amount of profitable employment for them. The making and approving of contracts progressed as rapidly as the small number of officers engaged in that line of duty made it possible, but not rapidly in proportion to the vast amount of work to be accomplished. The business experience of many of the officers was but limited; here and there experiments were tried which had to be given up. In numerous cases contracts were made and then broken, either by the employers or the laborers, and the officers in charge were overwhelmed with complaints from both sides. While many planters wanted to have the laborers who had left them back on their plantations, others drove those that had remained away, and thus increased the number of the unemployed. Moreover, the great change had burst upon the country in the midst of the agricultural labor season when the crops that were in the ground required steady work to make them produce a satisfactory yield, and the interruption of labor, which could not but be very extensive, caused considerable damage. In one word, the efforts made could not prevent or remedy, in so short a time, the serious disorders which are always connected with a period of precipitous transition, and which, although natural, are exceedingly embarrassing to those who have to deal with them.

The solution of the social problem in the south, if left to the free action of the southern people, will depend upon two things: 1, upon the ideas entertained by the whites, the "ruling class," of the problem, and the manner in which they act upon their ideas; and 2, upon the capacity and conduct of the colored people.

OPTIONS OF THE WHITES.

That the result of the free labor experiment made under circumstances so extremely unfavorable should at once be a perfect success, no reasonable person would expect. Nevertheless, a large majority of the southern men with whom I came into contact announced their opinions with so positive an assurance as to produce the impression that their minds were fully made up. In at least nineteen cases of twenty the reply I received to my inquiry about their views on the new system was uniformly this: "You cannot make the negro work, without physical compulsion." I heard this hundreds of times, heard it wherever I went, heard it in nearly the same words from so many different persons, that at last I came to the conclusion that this is the prevailing sentiment among the southern people. There are exceptions to this rule, but, as far as my information extends, far from enough to affect the rule. In the accompanying documents you will find an abundance of proof in support of this statement. There is hardly a paper relative to the negro question annexed to this report which does not, in some direct or indirect way, corroborate it.

Unfortunately the disorders necessarily growing out of the transition state continually furnished food for argument. I found but few people who were willing to make due allowance for the adverse influence of exceptional circumstances. By a large majority of those I came in contact with, and they mostly belonged to the more intelligent class, every irregularity that occurred was directly charged against the system of free labor. If negroes walked away from the plantations, it was conclusive proof of the incorrigible instability of the negro, and the impracticability of free negro labor. If some individual negroes violated the terms of their contract, it proved unanswerably that no negro had, or ever would have, a just conception of the binding force of a contract, and that this system of free negro labor was bound to be a failure. If some negroes shirked, or did not perform their task with sufficient alacrity, it was produced as irrefutable evidence to show that physical compulsion was actually indispensable to make the negro work. If negroes, idlers or refugees crawling about the towns, applied to the authorities for subsistence, it was quoted as incontestably establishing the point that the negro was too improvident to take care of himself, and must necessarily be consigned to the care of a master. I heard a Georgia planter argue most seriously that one of his negroes had shown himself certainly unfit for freedom because he impudently refused to submit to a whipping. I frequently went into an argument with those putting forth such general assertions, quoting instances in which negro laborers were working faithfully, and to the entire satisfaction of their employers, as the employers themselves had informed me. In a majority of cases the reply was that we northern people did not understand the negro, but that they (the southerners) did; that as to the particular instances I quoted I was probably mistaken; that I had not closely investigated the cases, or had been deceived by my informants; that they *knew* the negro would not work without compulsion, and that nobody could make them believe he would. Arguments like these naturally finished such discussions. It frequently struck me that persons who conversed about every other subject calmly and sensibly would lose their temper as soon as the negro question was touched.

EFFECTS OF SUCH OPINIONS, AND GENERAL TREATMENT OF THE NEGRO.

A belief, conviction, or prejudice, or whatever you may call it, so widely spread and apparently so deeply rooted as this, that the negro will not work without physical compulsion, is certainly calculated to have a very serious influence upon the conduct of the people entertaining it. It naturally produced a desire to preserve slavery in its original form as much and as long as possible—and you may, perhaps, remember the admission made by one of the provisional governors, over two months after the close of the war, that the people of his State still indulged in a lingering hope slavery might yet be preserved—or to introduce into the new system that element of physical compulsion which would make the negro work. Efforts were, indeed, made to hold the negro in his old state of subjection, especially in such localities where our military forces had not yet penetrated, or where the country was not garrisoned in detail. Here and there planters succeeded for a limited period to keep their former slaves in ignorance, or at least doubt, about their new rights; but the main agency employed for that purpose was force and intimidation. In many instances negroes who walked away from the plantations, or were found upon the roads, were shot or otherwise severely punished, which was calculated to produce the impression among those remaining with their masters that an attempt to escape from slavery would result in certain destruction. A large proportion of the many acts of violence committed is undoubtedly attributable to this motive. The documents attached to this report abound in testimony to this effect. For the sake of illustration I will give some instances:

Brigadier General Fessenden reported to Major General Gillmore from Winnsboro, South Carolina, July 19, as follows: "The spirit of the people, especially in those districts not subject to the salutary influence of General Sherman's army, is that of concealed and, in some instances, of open hostility, though there are some who strive with honorable good faith to promote a thorough reconciliation between the government and their people. A spirit of bitterness and persecution manifests itself towards the negroes. They are shot and abused outside the immediate protection of our forces *by men who announce their determination to take the law into their own hands, in defiance of our authority*. To protect the negro and punish these still rebellious individuals it will be necessary to have this country pretty thickly settled with soldiers." I received similar verbal reports from other parts of South Carolina. To show the hopes still indulged in by some, I may mention that one of the sub-district commanders, as he himself informed me, knew planters within the limits of his command who had made contracts with their former slaves *avowedly* for the object of keeping them together on their plantations, so that they might have them near at hand, and thus more easily reduce them to their former condition, when, after the restoration of the civil power, the "unconstitutional emancipation proclamation" would be set aside.

Cases in which negroes were kept on the plantations, either by ruse or violence, were frequent enough in South Carolina and Georgia to call forth from General Saxton a circular threatening planters who persisted in this practice with loss of their property, and from Major General Steedman, commander of the department of Georgia, an order bearing upon the same subject. At Atlanta, Georgia, I had an opportunity to examine some cases of the nature above described myself. While I was there, 9th and 10th of August, several negroes came into town with bullet and buckshot wounds in their bodies. From their statements, which, however, were only corroborating information previously received, it appeared that the reckless and restless characters of that region had combined to keep the negroes where they belonged. Several freedmen were shot in the attempt to escape, others succeeded in eluding the vigilance of their persecutors; large numbers, terrified by what they saw and heard, quietly remained under the restraint imposed upon them, waiting for better opportunities. The commander of the sub-district and post informed me that bands of guerillas were prowling about within a few miles of the city, making it dangerous for soldiers and freedmen to show themselves outside of the immediate reach of the garrison, and that but a few days previous to my arrival a small squad of men he had sent out to serve an order upon a planter, concerning the treatment of freedmen, had been driven back by an armed band of over twenty men, headed by an individual in the uniform of a rebel officer.

As our troops in Georgia were at that time mostly concentrated at a number of central points, and not scattered over the State in small detachments, but little information was obtained of what was going on in the interior of the country. A similar system was followed in Alabama, but enough has become known to indicate the condition of things in localities not immediately under the eye of the military. In that State the efforts made to hold the negro in a state of subjection appear to have been of a particularly atrocious nature. Rumors to that effect which reached me at Montgomery induced me to make inquiries at the post hospital. The records of that institution showed a number of rather startling cases which had occurred immediately after the close of the war, and some of a more recent date; all of which proved that negroes leaving the plantations, and found on the roads, were exposed to the savagest treatment. An extract from the records of the hospital is appended, (accompanying document No. 20;) also a statement signed by the provost marshal at Selma, Alabama, Major J.P. Houston, (accompanying document No. 21.) He says: "There have come to my notice officially twelve cases, in which I am morally certain the trials have not been had yet, that negroes were killed by whites. In a majority of cases the provocation consisted in the negroes' trying to come to town or to return to the plantation after having been sent away. The cases above enumerated, I am convinced, are but a small part of those that have actually been perpetrated." In a report to General Swayne, assistant commissioner of the Freedmen's Bureau, in Alabama, communicated to me by the general, Captain Poillon, agent of the bureau at Mobile, says of the condition of things in the southwestern part of the State, July 29: "There are regular patrols posted on the rivers, who board some of the boats; after the boats leave they hang, shoot, or drown the victims they may find on them, and all those found on the roads or coming down the rivers are almost invariably murdered. The bewildered and terrified freedmen know not what to do—to leave is death; to remain is to suffer the increased burden imposed upon them by the cruel taskmaster, whose only interest is their labor, wrung from them by every device an inhuman ingenuity can devise; hence the lash and murder is resorted to to intimidate those whom fear of an awful death alone cause to remain, while patrols, negro dogs and spies, disguised as Yankees, keep constant guard over these unfortunate people." In a letter addressed to myself, September 9, Captain Poillon says: "Organized patrols, with negro hounds, keep guard over the thoroughfares; bands of lawless robbers traverse the country, and the unfortunate who attempts to escape, or he who returns for his wife or child, is waylaid or pursued with hounds, and shot or hung." (Accompanying document No. 22.)

In Mississippi I received information of a similar character. I would respectfully invite your attention to two letters—one by Colonel Hayne, 1st Texas cavalry, and one by Colonel Brinkerhoff—giving interesting descriptions of the condition of the freedmen, and the spirit of the whites shortly after the close of the war. (Accompanying documents Nos. 23 and 24.) Lieutenant Colonel P.J. Yorke, post commander at port Gibson, Mississippi, reported to General Davidson, on August 26, that a "county patrol" had been organized by citizens of his sub-district, which, for reasons given, he had been obliged to disband; one of these reasons was, in his own language, that: "The company was formed out of what they called picked men, *i.e.*, those only who had been actually engaged in the war, and were known as strong disunionists. The negroes in the sections of country these men controlled were kept in the most abject slavery, and treated in every way contrary to the requirements of General Orders No. 129, from the War Department." (Accompanying document No. 25.) As late as September 29, Captain J.H. Weber, agent of the Freedmen's Bureau, reported to Colonel Thomas, assistant commissioner of the bureau, in the State of Mississippi, as follows: "In many cases negroes who left their homes during the war, and have been within our military lines, and having provided homes here for their families, going back to get their wives and children, have been driven off, and told that they could not have them. In several cases guards have been sent to aid people in getting their families; in many others it has been impracticable, as the distance was too great. In portions of the northern part of this district the colored people are kept in slavery still. The white people tell them that they were free during the war, but the war is now over, and they must go to work again as before. The reports from sub-commissioners nearest that locality show that the blacks are in a much worse state than ever before, the able-bodied being kept at work under the lash, and the young and infirm driven off to care for themselves. As to protection from the civil authorities, there is no such thing outside of this city." (Accompanying document No. 26.)

The conviction, however, that slavery in the old form cannot be maintained has forced itself upon the minds of many of those who ardently desired its preservation. But while the necessity of a new system was recognized as far as the right of property in the individual negro is concerned, many attempts were made to introduce into that new system the element of physical compulsion, which, as above stated, is so generally considered indispensable. This was done by simply adhering, as to the treatment of the laborers, as much as possible to the traditions of the old system, even where the relations between employers and laborers had been fixed by contract. The practice of corporal punishment was still continued to a great extent, although, perhaps, not in so regular a manner as it was practiced in times gone by. It is hardly necessary to quote any documentary evidence on this point; the papers appended to this report are full of testimony corroborating the statement. The habit is so inveterate with a great many persons as to render, on the least provocation, the impulse to whip a negro almost irresistible. It will continue to be so until the southern people will have learned, so as never to forget it, that a black man has rights which a white man is bound to respect.

Here I will insert some remarks on the general treatment of the blacks as a class, from the whites as a class. It is not on the plantations and at the hands of the planters themselves that the negroes have to suffer the greatest hardships. Not only the former slaveholders, but the non-slaveholding whites, who, even previous to the war, seemed to be more ardent in their pro-slavery feelings than the planters themselves, are possessed by a singularly bitter and vindictive feeling against the colored race since the negro has ceased to be property. The pecuniary value which the individual negro formerly represented having disappeared, the maiming and killing of colored men seems to be looked upon by many as one of those venial offences which must be forgiven to the outraged feelings of a wronged and robbed people. Besides, the services rendered by the negro to the national cause during the war, which make him an object of special interest to the loyal people, make him an object of particular vindictiveness to those whose hearts were set upon the success of the rebellion. The number of murders and assaults perpetrated upon negroes is very great; we can form only an approximative estimate of what is going on in those parts of the south which are not closely garrisoned, and from which no regular reports are received, by what occurs under the very eyes of our military authorities. As to my personal experience, I will only mention that during my two days sojourn at Atlanta, one negro was stabbed with fatal effect on the street, and three were poisoned, one of whom died. While I was at Montgomery, one negro was cut across the throat evidently with intent to kill, and another was shot, but both escaped with their lives. Several papers attached to this report give an account of the number of capital cases that occurred at certain places during a certain period of time. It is a sad fact that the perpetration of those acts is not confined to that class of people which might be called the rabble. Several "gentlemen of standing" have been tried before military commissions for such offences.

These statements are naturally not intended to apply to all the individuals composing the southern people. There are certainly many planters who, before the rebellion, treated their slaves with kindness, and who now continue to treat them as free laborers in the same manner. There are now undoubtedly many plantations in the south on which the relations between employers and employees are based upon mutual good will. There are certainly many people there who entertain the best wishes for the welfare of the negro race, and who not only never participated in any acts of violence, but who heartily disapprove them. I have no doubt, a large majority can, *as to actual participation*—not, however, as to the bitter spirit—I offer a good plea of not guilty. But however large or small a number of people may be guilty of complicity in such acts of persecution, those who are opposed to them have certainly not shown themselves strong enough to restrain those who perpetrate or favor them. So far, the *spirit of persecution* has shown itself so strong as to make the protection of the freedman by the military arm of the government in many localities necessary—in almost all, desirable. It must not be forgotten that in a community a majority of whose members is peaceably disposed, but not willing or not able to enforce peace and order, a comparatively small number of bold and lawless men can determine the character of the whole. The rebellion itself, in some of the southern States, furnished a striking illustration of this truth.

GENERAL IDEAS AND SCHEMES OF WHITES CONCERNING THE FREEDMEN.

Some of the planters with whom I had occasion to converse expressed their determination to adopt the course which best accords with the spirit of free labor, to make the negro work by offering him fair inducements, to stimulate his ambition, and to extend to him those means of intellectual and moral improvement which are best calculated to make him an intelligent, reliable and efficient free laborer and a good and useful citizen. Those who expressed such ideas were almost invariably professed Union men, and far above the average in point of mental ability and culture. I found a very few instances of original secessionists also manifesting a willingness to give the free-labor experiment a fair trial. I can represent the sentiments of this small class in no better way than by quoting the language used by an Alabama judge in a conversation with me. "I am one of the most thoroughly whipped men in the south," said he; "I am a genuine old secessionist, and I believe now, as I always did, we had the constitutional right to secede. But the war has settled that matter, and it is all over now. As to this thing of free negro labor, I do not believe in it, but I will give it a fair trial. I have a plantation and am going to make contracts with my hands, and then I want a real Yankee to run the machine for me; not one of your New Yorkers or Pennsylvanians, but the genuine article from Massachusetts or Vermont—one who can not only farm, but sing psalms and pray, and teach school—a real abolitionist, who believes in the thing just as I don't believe in it. If he does not succeed, I shall consider it proof conclusive that you are wrong and I am right."

I regret to say that views and intentions so reasonable I found confined to a small minority. Aside from the assumption that the negro will not work without physical compulsion, there appears to be another popular notion prevalent in the south, which stands as no less serious an obstacle in the way of a successful solution of the problem. It is that the negro exists for the special object of raising cotton, rice and sugar *for the whites*, and that it is illegitimate for him to indulge, like other people, in the pursuit of his own happiness in his own way. Although it is admitted that he has ceased to be the property of a master, it is not admitted that he has a right to become his own master. As Colonel Thomas, assistant commissioner of the Freedmen's Bureau in Mississippi, in a letter addressed to me, very pungently expresses it: "The whites esteem the blacks their property by natural right, and, however much they may admit that the relations of masters and slaves have been destroyed by the war and by the President's emancipation proclamation, they still have an ingrained feeling that the blacks at large belong to the whites at large, and whenever opportunity serves, they treat the colored people just as their profit, caprice or passion may dictate." (Accompanying document No. 27.) An ingrained feeling like this is apt to bring forth that sort of class legislation which produces laws to govern one class with no other view than to benefit another. This tendency can be distinctly traced in the various schemes for regulating labor which here and there see the light.

Immediately after the emancipation of the slaves, when the general confusion was most perplexing, the prevalent desire among the whites seemed to be, if they could not retain their negroes as slaves, to get rid of them entirely. Wild speculations were indulged in, how to remove the colored population at once and to import white laborers to fill its place; how to obtain a sufficient supply of coolies, &c., &c. Even at the present moment the removal of the freedmen is strongly advocated by those who have the traditional horror of a free negro, and in some sections, especially where the soil is more adapted to the cultivation of cereals than the raising of the staples, planters appear to be inclined to drive the negroes away, at least from their plantations. I was informed by a prominent South Carolinian in July, that the planters in certain localities in the northwestern part of his State had been on the point of doing so, but better counsel had been made to prevail upon them; and Colonel Robinson, 97th United States Colored Infantry, who had been sent out to several counties in southern Alabama to administer the amnesty oath, reported a general disposition among the planters of that region to "set the colored people who had cultivated their crops during the summer, adrift as soon as the crops would be secured, and not to permit the negro to remain upon any footing of equality with the white man in that country." (Accompanying document No. 28.) The disposition to drive away all the negroes from the plantations was undoubtedly confined to a few districts; and as far as the scheme of wholesale deportation is concerned, practical men became aware, that if they wanted to have any labor done, it would have been bad policy to move away the laborers they now have before others were there to fill their places. All these devices promising at best only distant relief, and free negro labor being the only thing in immediate prospect, many ingenious heads set about to solve the problem, how to make free labor compulsory by permanent regulations.

Shortly after the close of the war some South Carolina planters tried to solve this problem by introducing into the contracts provisions leaving only a small share of the crops to the freedmen, subject to all sorts of constructive charges, and then binding them to work off the indebtedness they might incur. It being to a great extent in the power of the employer to keep the laborer in debt to him, the employer might thus obtain a permanent hold upon the person of the laborer. It was something like the system of peonage existing in Mexico. When these contracts were submitted to the military authorities for ratification, General Hatch, commanding at Charleston, at once issued an order prohibiting such arrangements. I had an opportunity to examine one of these contracts, and found it drawn up with much care, and evidently with a knowledge of the full bearings of the provisions so inserted.

Appended to this report is a memorandum of a conversation I had with Mr. W. King, of Georgia, a gentleman of good political sentiments and undoubtedly benevolent intentions. He recommends a kind of guardianship to be exercised by the employer over the freedman. He is a fair representative, not of the completely unprejudiced, but of the more liberal-minded class of planters, and his sayings show in what direction even those who are not actuated by any spirit of bitterness against the negro, seek a way out of their perplexities. (Accompanying document No. 29.)

I annex also two documents submitted to Mr. Benjamin F. Flanders, special treasury agent at New Orleans, who then had the management of freedmen's affairs in Louisiana, in November and December, 1864. They are not of a recent date, but may be taken as true representations of the ideas and sentiments entertained by large numbers to-day. The first (accompanying document No. 30) contains "suggestions on the wants of planters before embarking their capital in the cultivation of staple crops," and was submitted by a committee to a meeting of planters at New Orleans, November 21, 1864. It speaks for itself. The others (accompanying document No. 31) is a letter addressed to Mr. Flanders by Mr. T. Gibson, a Louisiana planter, who is well known in New Orleans as professing much affection for the negro. It commences with the assertion that he "has no prejudices to overcome, and would do the black all the good in his power," and winds up with a postscript strongly insisting upon the necessity of corporal punishment, the "great desideratum in obtaining labor from free blacks being *its enforcement*."

MUNICIPAL REGULATIONS.

The motives and spirit bringing forth such ideas found a still clearer expression in some attempted municipal regulations. In no State within the range of my observation had, at the time of my visit, so much progress been made in the reorganization of local government as in Louisiana. In most of the parishes the parish authorities had exercised their functions for some time; in others the organization was less complete. Governor Wells informed me that he had filled the parish offices with men recommended to him by the people of the parishes, and it is fair to assume that in most cases the appointees represented the views and sentiments of the ruling class. Some of the local authorities so appointed furnished us an indication of the principles upon which they thought it best to regulate free labor within their jurisdiction.

Mr. W.B. Stickney, agent of the Freedmen's Bureau at Shreveport, Louisiana, reported to the assistant commissioner of the bureau in Louisiana as follows: "August 1.—The following is a literal copy of a document brought to this office by a colored man, which is conclusive evidence that there are those who still claim the negro as their property:

"'This boy Calvin has permit to hire to whom he pleases, but I shall hold him as my property until set free by Congress. July 7, 1865. (Signed.) E.V. TULLY.'"

The spirit of the above also made its appearance in another form, in the action of the police board of the parish of Bossier, which was an attempt to revive at once the old slave laws, and to prevent the freedmen from obtaining employment (away) from their former masters. The gist of the enactment alluded to is contained in the paragraph directing the officers on patrol duty "to arrest and take up all idle and vagrant persons running at large without employment and carry them before the proper authorities, to be dealt with as the law directs." A regulation like this certainly would make it difficult for freedmen to leave their former masters for the purpose of seeking employment elsewhere. The matter was submitted to Brevet Major General Hawkins, commanding western district of Louisiana, who issued an order prohibiting the parish police forces from arresting freedmen unless for positive offence against the law.

Clearer and more significant was the ordnance passed by the police board of the town of Opelousas, Louisiana. (Accompanying document No. 34.) It deserves careful perusal. Among a number of regulations applying exclusively to the negro, and depriving him of all liberty of locomotion, the following striking provisions are found:

Section 3. No negro or freedman shall be permitted to rent or keep a house within the limits of the town *under any circumstances*, and any one thus offending shall be ejected and *compelled to find an employer* or leave the town within twenty-four hours. The lessor or furnisher of the house leased or kept as above shall pay a fine of ten dollars for each offence.

Section 4. No negro or freedman shall reside within the limits of the town of Opelousas *who is not in the regular service of some white person or former owner*.

Section 8. No freedman shall sell, barter or exchange, any articles of merchandise or traffic within the limits of Opelousas without permission in writing from his employer, or the mayor, or president of the board.

This ordinance was at first approved by a lieutenant colonel of the United States forces having local command there, and it is worthy of note that thereupon the infection spread at once, and similar ordinances were entertained by the police boards of the town of Franklin and of the parish of St. Landry. (Accompanying document No. 35). The parish ordinance of St. Landry differs from the town ordinances of Opelousas and Franklin in several points, and wherever there is any difference, it is in the direction of greater severity. It imposes heavier fines and penalties throughout, and provides, in addition, for a system of corporal punishment. It is also ordained "that the aforesaid penalties shall be *summarily enforced*, and that it shall be the duty of the *captain or chief of patrol* to see that the aforesaid ordinances are promptly executed." While the town ordinances provide that a negro who does not find an employer shall be compelled to leave the town, the parish or county ordinance knows nothing of letting the negro go, but simply *compels* him to find an employer. Finally, it is ordained "that it shall be the duty of every *citizen* to act as a police officer for the detection of offences and the apprehension of offenders, who shall be immediately handed over to the proper captain or chief of patrol."

It is true, an "organization of free labor" upon this plan would not be exactly the re-establishment of slavery in its old form, but as for the practical working of the system with regard to the welfare of the freedman, the difference would only be for the worse. The negro is not only not permitted to be idle, but he is positively prohibited from working or carrying on a business for himself; he is *compelled* to be in the "regular service" of a white man, and if he has no employer he is *compelled* to find one. It requires only a simple understanding among the employers, and the negro is just as much bound to his employer "for better and for worse" as he was when slavery existed in the old form. If he should attempt to leave his employer on account of non-payment of wages or bad treatment he is *compelled* to find another one; and if no other will take him he will be *compelled* to return to him from whom he wanted to escape. The employers, under such circumstances, are naturally at liberty to arrange the matter of compensation according to their tastes, for the negro will be compelled to be in the regular service of an employer, whether he receives wages or not. The negro may be permitted by his employer "to hire his own time," for in the spirit and intent of the ordinance his time never properly belongs to him. But even the old system of slavery was more liberal in this respect, for such "permission to hire his own time" "shall never extend over seven days at any one time." (Sec. 4.) The sections providing for the "*summary*" enforcement of the penalties and placing their infliction into the hands of the "chief of patrol"—which, by the way, throws some light upon the objects for which the militia is to be reorganized—place the freedmen under a sort of permanent martial law, while the provision investing every white man with the power and authority of a police officer as against every black man subjects them to the control even of those individuals who in other communities are thought hardly fit to control themselves. On the whole, this piece of legislation is a striking embodiment of the idea that although the former owner has lost his individual right of property in the former slave, "the blacks at large belong to the whites at large."

Such was the "organization of free labor" ordained by officials appointed by Governor Wells, and these ordinances were passed while both the emancipation proclamation and a provision in the new constitution of Louisiana abolishing slavery in that State forever were recognized as being in full force. It is needless to say that as soon as these proceedings came to the knowledge of the Freedmen's Bureau and the department commander they were promptly overruled. But Governor Wells did not remove the police boards that had thus attempted to revive slavery in a new form.

The opposition to the negro's controlling his own labor, carrying on business independently on his own account—in one word, working for his own benefit—showed itself in a variety of ways. Here and there municipal regulations were gotten up heavily taxing or otherwise impeding those trades and employments in which colored people are most likely to engage. As an illustration, I annex an ordinance passed by the common council of Vicksburg, (accompanying document No. 36,) together with a letter from Colonel Thomas, in which he says:

"You will see by the city ordinance that a drayman, or hackman, must file a bond of five hundred dollars, in addition to paying for his license. The mayor requires that the bondsmen must be freeholders. The laws of this State do not, and never did, allow a negro to own land or hold property; the white citizens refuse to sign any bonds for the freedmen. The white citizens and authorities say that it is for their interest to drive out all independent negro labor; that the freedmen must hire to white men if they want to do this kind of work." I found several instances of a similar character in the course of my observations, of which I neglected to procure the documentary evidence.

It may be said that these are mere isolated cases; and so they are. But they are the local outcroppings of a spirit which I found to prevail everywhere. If there is any difference, it is in the degree of its intensity and the impatience or boldness with which it manifests itself. Of the agencies which so far restrained it from venturing more general demonstrations I shall speak in another part of this report.

EDUCATION OF THE FREEDMEN.

It would seem that all those who sincerely desire to make the freedman a freeman in the true sense of the word, must also be in favor of so educating him as to make him clearly understand and appreciate the position he is to occupy in life, with all its rights and corresponding duties, and to impart to him all the knowledge necessary for enabling him to become an intelligent co-operator in the general movements of society. As popular education is the true ground upon which the efficiency and the successes of free-labor society grow, no man who rejects the former can be accounted a consistent friend of the latter. It is also evident that the education of the negro, to become general and effective after the full restoration of local government in the south, must be protected and promoted as an integral part of the educational systems of the States.

I made it a special point in most of the conversations I had with southern men to inquire into their views with regard to this subject. I found, indeed, some gentlemen of thought and liberal ideas who readily acknowledged the necessity of providing for the education of the colored people, and who declared themselves willing to co-operate to that end to the extent of their influence. Some planters thought of establishing schools on their estates, and others would have been glad to see measures taken to that effect by the people of the neighborhoods in which they lived. But whenever I asked the question whether it might be hoped that the legislatures of their States or their county authorities would make provisions for negro education, I never received an affirmative, and only in two or three instances feebly encouraging answers. At last I was forced to the conclusion that, aside from a small number of honorable exceptions, the popular prejudice is almost as bitterly set against the negro's having the advantage of education as it was when the negro was a slave. There may be an improvement in that respect, but it would prove only how universal the prejudice was in former days. Hundreds of times I heard the old assertion repeated, that "learning will spoil the nigger for work," and that "negro education will be the ruin of the south." Another most singular notion still holds a potent sway over the minds of the masses—it is, that the elevation of the blacks will be the degradation of the whites. They do not understand yet that the continual contact with an ignorant and degraded population must necessarily lower the mental and moral tone of the other classes of society. This they might have learned from actual experience, as we in the north have been taught, also by actual experience, that the education of the lower orders is the only reliable basis of the civilization as well as of the prosperity of a people.

The consequence of the prejudice prevailing in the southern States is that colored schools can be established and carried on with safety only under the protection of our military forces, and that where the latter are withdrawn the former have to go with them. There may be a few localities forming exceptions, but their number is certainly very small. I annex a few papers bearing upon this subject. One is a letter addressed to me by Chaplain Joseph Warren, superintendent of education under the Freedmen's Bureau in Mississippi. (Accompanying document No. 37.) The long and extensive experience of the writer gives the views he expresses more than ordinary weight. After describing the general spirit of opposition to the education of the negroes exhibited in Mississippi, and enumerating the reasons assigned for it, he says: "In view of these things I have no doubt but that, if our protection be withdrawn, negro education will be hindered in every possible way, including obstructions by fraud and violence. I have not the smallest expectation that, with the State authorities in full power, a northern citizen would be protected in the exercise of his constitutional right to teach and preach to the colored people, and shall look for a renewal of the fearful scenes in which northerners were whipped, tarred and feathered, warned off, and murdered, before the war." The letter gives many details in support of this conclusion, and is in every respect worth perusing.

In the letter of General Kirby Smith (Accompanying document No. 9) occurs the following statement referring to the condition of things in Mobile, Alabama: "Threats were made to destroy all school-houses in which colored children were taught, and in two instances they were fired. The same threats were made against all churches in which colored people assembled to worship, and one of them burned. Continued threats of assassination were made against the colored preachers, and one of them is now under special guard by order of Major General Woods."

While I was in Louisiana General Canby received a petition, signed by a number of prominent citizens of New Orleans, praying him "to annul Order No. 38, which authorizes a board of officers to levy a tax on the taxpayers of the parish of Orleans to defray the expense of educating the freedmen." The reasons given for making this request are as follows: "Most of those who have lost their slaves by the rebellion, and whose lands are in the course of confiscation, being thus deprived of the means of raising corn for their hungry children, have not anything left wherewith to pay such a tax. The order in question, they consider, violates that sacred principle which requires taxation to be equal throughout the United States. *If the freedmen are to be educated at public expense, let it be done from the treasury of the United States.*" (Accompanying document No. 38.) Many of the signers of this petition, who wanted to be relieved of the school tax on the ground of poverty, were counted among the wealthy men of New Orleans, and they forgot to state that the free colored element of Louisiana, which represents a capital of at least thirteen millions and pays a not inconsiderable proportion of the taxes, contributes at the same time for the support of the schools for whites, from which their children are excluded. I would also invite attention to some statements concerning this matter contained in the memorandum of my conversation with Mr. King, of Georgia. (Accompanying document No. 29.)

While travelling in the south I found in the newspapers an account of an interview between General Howard and some gentlemen from Mississippi, in which a Dr. Murdoch, from Columbus, Mississippi, figured somewhat conspicuously. He was reported to have described public sentiment in Mississippi as quite loyal, and especially in favor of giving the colored race a good education. I inquired at the Freedmen's Bureau whether anything was known there of a feeling so favorable to negro education among Dr. Murdoch's neighbors. The information I received is contained in a letter from the assistant commissioner, Colonel Thomas. (Accompanying document No. 39.) It appears that the feeling of Dr. Murdoch's neighbors at Columbus was not only not in favor of negro education, but that, according to the report of the agent of the Freedmen's Bureau at that place, "the citizens of the town are so prejudiced against the negroes that they are opposed to all efforts being made for their education or elevation;" that "the people will not give rooms or allow the children of their hired freedmen to attend the schools," and that the citizens of the place have written a letter to the officers, saying "that they would respectfully ask that no freedmen's schools be established under the auspices of the bureau, as it would tend to disturb the present labor system, and take from the fields labor that is so necessary to restore the wealth of the State." It seems Dr. Murdoch's neighbors do not form an exception to the general rule. In this connexion I may add that several instances have come to my notice of statements about the condition of things in the late rebel States, being set afloat by southerners visiting the north, which would not bear close investigation. The reason, probably,is that gentlemen are attributing their own good intentions to the rest of their people with too great a liberality.

Having thus given my experience and impressions with regard to the spirit actuating the southern people concerning the freedman and the free-labor problem, and before inquiring into their prospective action, I beg leave to submit a few remarks on the conduct of the negro.

THE FREEDMAN.

The first southern men with whom I came into contact after my arrival at Charleston designated the general conduct of the emancipated slaves as surprisingly good. Some went even so far as to call it admirable. The connexion in which they used these laudatory terms was this: A great many colored people while in slavery had undoubtedly suffered much hardship and submitted to great wrongs, partly inseparably connected with the condition of servitude, and partly aggravated by the individual wilfulness and cruelty of their masters and overseers. They were suddenly set free; and not only that: their masters but a short time ago almost omnipotent on their domains, found themselves, after their defeat in the war, all at once face to face with their former slaves as a conquered and powerless class. Never was the temptation to indulge in acts of vengeance for wrongs suffered more strongly presented than to the colored people of the south; but no instance of such individual revenge was then on record, nor have I since heard of any case of violence that could be traced to such motives. The transition of the southern negro from slavery to freedom was untarnished by any deeds of blood, and the apprehension so extensively entertained and so pathetically declaimed upon by many, that the sudden and general emancipation of the slaves would at once result in "all the horrors of St. Domingo," proved utterly groundless. This was the first impression I received after my arrival in the south, and I received it from the mouths of late slaveholders. Nor do I think the praise was unjustly bestowed. In this respect the emancipated slaves of the south can challenge comparison with any race long held in servitude and suddenly set free. As to the dangers of the future, I shall speak of them in another connexion.

But at that point the unqualified praise stopped and the complaints began: the negroes would not work; they left their plantations and went wandering from place to place, stealing by the way; they preferred a life of idleness and vagrancy to that of honest and industrious labor; they either did not show any willingness to enter into contracts, or, if they did, showed a stronger disposition to break them than to keep them; they were becoming insubordinate and insolent to their former owners; they indulged in extravagant ideas about their rights and relied upon the government to support them without work; in one word, they had no conception of the rights freedom gave, and of the obligations freedom imposed upon them. These complaints I heard repeated with endless variations wherever I went. Nor were they made without some show of reason. I will review them one after another.

Unwillingness to work.—That there are among the negroes a good many constitutionally lazy individuals is certainly true. The propensity to idleness seems to be rather strongly developed in the south generally, without being confined to any particular race. It is also true that the alacrity negroes put into their work depends in a majority of cases upon certain combinations of circumstances. It is asserted that the negroes have a prejudice against working in the cultivation of cotton, rice, and sugar. Although this prejudice, probably arising from the fact that the cotton, rice, and sugar fields remind the former slave of the worst experiences of his past life, exists to some extent, it has not made the freedmen now on the plantations unwilling to cultivate such crops as the planters may have seen fit to raise. A few cases of refusal may have occurred. But there is another fact of which I have become satisfied in the course of my observations, and which is of great significance: while most of the old slaveholders complain of the laziness and instability of their negro laborers, the northern men engaged in planting, with whom I have come into contact, almost uniformly speak of their negro laborers with satisfaction, and these northern men almost exclusively devote themselves to the cultivation of cotton. A good many southern planters, in view of the fact, expressed to me their intention to engage northern men for the management of their plantations. This circumstance would seem to prove that under certain conditions the negro may be expected to work well. There are two reasons by which it may be explained: first, that a northern man knows from actual experience what free labor is, and understands its management, which the late slaveholder, still clinging to the traditions of the old system, does not; and then, that the negro has more confidence in a northern man than in his former master. When a northern man discovers among his laboring force an individual that does not do his duty, his first impulse is to discharge him, and he acts accordingly. When a late slaveholder discovers such an individual among his laborers, his first impulse is to whip him, and he is very apt to suit the act to the impulse. Ill treatment is a doubtful encouragement for free laborers, and it proves more apt to drive those that are still at work away than to make the plantation attractive to others. But if the reasons above stated are sufficient to explain why the negroes work better for northern than for southern men, it will follow that a general improvement will take place as soon as the latter fulfil the same conditions—that is, as soon as southern men learn what free labor is and how to manage it in accordance with its principles, and as soon as they succeed in gaining the confidence of the colored people.

In the reports of officers of the Freedmen's Bureau, among the documents annexed to this, you will find frequent repetitions of the statement that the negro generally works well where he is decently treated and well compensated. Nor do the officers of the Freedmen's Bureau alone think and say so. Southern men, who were experimenting in the right direction, expressed to me their opinion to the same effect. Some of them told me that the negroes on their plantations worked "as well as ever," or even "far better than they had expected." It is true the number of planters who made that admission was small, but it nearly corresponded with the number of those who, according to their own statements, gave free negro labor a perfectly fair trial, while all those who prefaced everything they said with the assertion that "the negro will not work without physical compulsion," could find no end to their complaints. There are undoubtedly negroes who will not do well under the best circumstances, just as there are others who will do well under the worst.

In another part of this report I have already set forth the exceptional difficulties weighing upon the free-labor experiment in the south during this period of transition. The sudden leap from slavery to freedom is an exciting event in a man's life, and somewhat calculated to disturb his equanimity for a moment. People are on such occasions disposed to indulge themselves a little. It would have shown much more wisdom in the negroes if all of them had quietly gone to work again the next day. But it is not reasonable to expect the negroes to possess more wisdom than other races would exhibit under the same circumstances. Besides, the willingness to work depends, with whites as well as blacks, somewhat upon the nature of the inducements held out, and the unsatisfactory regulation of the matter of wages has certainly something to do with the instability of negro labor which is complained of. Northern men engaged in planting almost uniformly pay wages in money, while southern planters, almost uniformly, have contracted with their laborers for a share in the crop. In many instances the shares are allotted between employers and laborers with great fairness; but in others the share promised to the laborers is so small as to leave them in the end very little or nothing. Moreover, the crops in the south looked generally very unpromising from the beginning, which naturally reduced the value falling to the lot of the laborer. I have heard a good many freedmen complain that, taking all things into consideration, they really did not know what they were working for except food, which in many instances was bad and scanty; and such complaints were frequently well founded. In a large number of cases the planters were not to blame for this; they had no available pecuniary means, and in many localities found it difficult to procure provisions. But these unfavorable circumstances, combined with the want of confidence in northern men, were well calculated to have an influence upon the conduct of the negro as a laborer.

I have heard it said that money is no inducement which will make a negro work. It is certain that many of them, immediately after emancipation, had but a crude conception of the value of money and the uses it can be put to. It may, however, be stated as the general rule, that whenever they are at liberty to choose between wages in money and a share in the crop, they will choose the former and work better. Many cases of negroes engaged in little industrial pursuits came to my notice, in which they showed considerable aptness not only for gaining money, but also for saving and judiciously employing it. Some were even surprisingly successful. I visited some of the plantations divided up among freedmen and cultivated by them independently without the supervision of white men. In some instances I found very good crops and indications of general thrift and good management; in others the corn and cotton crops were in a neglected and unpromising state. The excuse made was in most cases that they had obtained possession of the ground too late in the season, and that, until the regular crops could be harvested, they were obliged to devote much of their time to the raising and sale of vegetables, watermelons, &c., for the purpose of making a living in the meantime.

On the whole I feel warranted in making the following statement: Many freedmen—not single individuals, but whole "plantation gangs"—are working well; others do not. The difference in their efficiency coincides in a great measure with a certain difference in the conditions under which they live. The conclusion lies near, that if the conditions under which they work well become general, their efficiency as free laborers will become general also, aside from individual exceptions. Certain it is, that by far the larger portion of the work done in the south is done by freedmen.

Vagrancy.—Large numbers of colored people left the plantations as soon as they became aware that they could do so with impunity. That they could so leave their former masters was for them the first test of the reality of their freedom. A great many flocked to the military posts and towns to obtain from the "Yankees" reliable information as to their new rights. Others were afraid lest by staying on the plantations where they had been held as slaves they might again endanger their freedom. Still others went to the cities, thinking that there the sweets of liberty could best be enjoyed. In some places they crowded together in large numbers, causing serious inconvenience. But a great many, probably a very large majority, remained on the plantations and made contracts with their former masters. The military authorities, and especially the agents of the Freedmen's Bureau, succeeded by continued exertions in returning most of those who were adrift to the plantations, or in finding other employment for them. After the first rush was over the number of vagrants grew visibly less.

It may be said that where the Freedmen's Bureau is best organized there is least vagrancy among the negroes. Here and there they show considerable restlessness, partly owing to local, partly to general causes. Among the former, bad treatment is probably the most prominent; among the latter, a feeling of distrust, uneasiness, anxiety about their future, which arises from their present unsettled condition. It is true, some are going from place to place because they are fond of it. The statistics of the Freedmen's Bureau show that the whole number of colored people supported by the government since the close of the war was remarkably small and continually decreasing. This seems to show that the southern negro, when thrown out of his accustomed employment, possesses considerable ability to support himself. It is possible, however, that in consequence of short crops, the destitution of the country, and other disturbing influences, there may be more restlessness among the negroes next winter than there is at present. Where the results of this year's labor were very unsatisfactory, there will be a floating about of the population when the contracts of this year expire. It is to be expected, however, that the Freedmen's Bureau will be able to remedy evils of that kind. Other emancipatory movements, for instance the abolition of serfdom in Russia, have resulted in little or no vagrancy; but it must not be forgotten that the emancipated serfs were speedily endowed with the ownership of land, which gave them a permanent moral and material interest in the soil upon which they lived. A similar measure would do more to stop negro vagrancy in the south than the severest penal laws. In every country the number of vagrants stands in proportion to the number of people who have no permanent local interests, unless augmented by exceptional cases, such as war or famine.

Contracts.—Freedmen frequently show great disinclination to make contracts with their former masters. They are afraid lest in signing a paper they sign away their freedom, and in this respect they are distrustful of most southern men. It generally requires personal assurances from a United States officer to make them feel safe. But the advice of such an officer is almost uniformly followed. In this manner an immense number of contracts has been made, and it is daily increasing. A northern man has no difficulty in making contracts, and but little in enforcing them. The complaints of southern men that the contracts are not well observed by the freedmen are in many instances well founded. The same can be said of the complaints of freedmen with regard to the planters. The negro, fresh from slavery, has naturally but a crude idea of the binding force of a written agreement, and it is galling to many of the planters to stand in such relations as a contract establishes to those who formerly were their slaves. I was, however, informed by officers of the Freedmen's Bureau, and by planters also, that things were improving in that respect. Contracts will be more readily entered into and more strictly kept as soon as the intimate relations between labor and compensation are better understood and appreciated on both sides.

Insolence and insubordination.—The new spirit which emancipation has awakened in the colored people has undoubtedly developed itself in some individuals, especially young men, to an offensive degree. Hence cases of insolence on the part of freedmen occur. But such occurrences are comparatively rare. On the whole, the conduct of the colored people is far more submissive than anybody had a right to expect. The acts of violence perpetrated by freedmen against white persons do not stand in any proportion to those committed by whites against negroes. Every such occurrence is sure to be noticed in the southern papers and we have heard of but very few.

When Southern people speak of the insolence of the negro, they generally mean something which persons who never lived under the system of slavery are not apt to appreciate. It is but very rarely what would be called insolence among equals. But, as an old planter said to me, "our people cannot realize yet that the negro is free." A negro is called insolent whenever his conduct varies in any manner from what a southern man was accustomed to when slavery existed.

The complaints made about the insubordination of the negro laborers on plantations have to be taken with the same allowance. There have been, no doubt, many cases in which freedmen showed a refractory spirit, where orders were disobeyed, and instructions disregarded. There have been some instances of positive resistance. But when inquiring into particulars, I found not unfrequently that the employer had adhered too strictly to his old way of doing things. I hardly heard any such complaints from Northern men. I have heard planters complain very earnestly of the insubordinate spirit of their colored laborers because they remonstrated against the practice of corporeal punishment. This was looked upon as a symptom of an impending insurrection. A great many things are regarded in the old slave States as acts of insubordination on the part of the laborer which, in the free States, would be taken as perfectly natural and harmless. The fact is, a good many planters are at present more nervously jealous of their authority than before, while the freedmen are not always inclined to forget that they are free men.

Extravagant notions.—In many localities I found an impression prevailing among the negroes that some great change was going to take place about Christmas. Feeling uneasy in their present condition, they indulged in the expectation that government intended to make some further provision for their future welfare, especially by ordering distributions of land among them. To counteract this expectation, which had a tendency to interfere seriously with the making of contracts for the next season, it was considered necessary to send military officers, and especially agents of the Freedmen's Bureau, among them, who, by administering sound advice and spreading correct information, would induce them to suit their conduct to their actual circumstances. While in the south I heard of many instances in which this measure had the desired effect, and it is to be expected that the effect was uniformly good wherever judicious officers were so employed.

Impressions like the above are very apt to spread among the negroes, for the reason that they ardently desire to become freeholders. In the independent possession of landed property they see the consummation of their deliverance. However mistaken their notions may be in other respects, it must be admitted that this instinct is correct.

Relations between the two races.—There are whites in the south who profess great kindness for the negro. Many of them are, no doubt, sincere in what they say. But as to the feelings of the masses, it is hardly necessary to add anything to what I have already stated. I have heard it asserted that the negroes also cherish feelings of hostility to the whites. Taking this as a general assertion, I am satisfied that it is incorrect. The negroes do not trust their late masters because they do not feel their freedom sufficiently assured. Many of them may harbor feelings of resentment towards those who now ill-treat and persecute them, but as they practiced no revenge after their emancipation for wrongs suffered while in slavery, so their present resentments are likely to cease as soon as the persecution ceases. If the persecution and the denial of their rights as freemen continue, the resentments growing out of them will continue and spread. The negro is constitutionally docile and eminently good-natured. Instances of the most touching attachment of freedmen to their old masters and mistresses have come to my notice. To a white man whom they believe to be sincerely their friend they cling with greater affection even than to one of their own race. By some northern speculators their confidence has been sadly abused. Nevertheless, the trust they place in persons coming from the north, or in any way connected with the government, is most childlike and unbounded. There may be individual exceptions, but I am sure they are not numerous. Those who enjoy their confidence enjoy also their affection. Centuries of slavery have not been sufficient to make them the enemies of the white race. If in the future a feeling of mutual hostility should develop itself between the races, it will probably not be the fault of those who have shown such an inexhaustible patience under the most adverse and trying circumstances.

In some places that I visited I found apprehensions entertained by whites of impending negro insurrections. Whenever our military commanders found it expedient to subject the statements made to that effect by whites to close investigation, they uniformly found them unwarranted by fact. In many instances there were just reasons for supposing that such apprehensions were industriously spread for the purpose of serving as an excuse for further persecution. In the papers annexed to this report you will find testimony supporting this statement. The negro is easily led; he is always inclined to follow the advice of those he trusts. I do, therefore, not consider a negro insurrection probable as long as the freedmen are under the direct protection of the government, and may hope to see their grievances redressed without resorting to the extreme means of self-protection. There would, perhaps, be danger of insurrections if the government should withdraw its protection from them, and if, against an attempt on the part of the whites to reduce them to something like their former condition, they should find themselves thrown back upon their own resources. Of this contingency I shall speak below.

Education.—That the negroes should have come out of slavery as an ignorant class is not surprising when we consider that it was a penal offence to teach them while they were in slavery; but their eager desire to learn, and the alacrity and success with which they avail themselves of every facility offered to them in that respect, has become a matter of notoriety. The statistics of the Freedmen's Bureau show to what extent such facilities have been offered and what results have been attained. As far as my information goes, these results are most encouraging for the future.

PROSPECTIVE—THE REACTIONARY TENDENCY.

I stated above that, in my opinion, the solution of the social problem in the south did not depend upon the capacity and conduct of the negro alone, but in the same measure upon the ideas and feelings entertained and acted upon by the whites. What their ideas and feelings were while under my observation, and how they affected the contact of the two races, I have already set forth. The question arises, what policy will be adopted by the "ruling class" when all restraint imposed upon them by the military power of the national government is withdrawn, and they are left free to regulate matters according to their own tastes? It would be presumptuous to speak of the future with absolute certainty; but it may safely be assumed that the same causes will always tend to produce the same effects. As long as a majority of the southern people believe that "the negro will not work without physical compulsion," and that "the blacks at large belong to the whites at large," that belief will tend to produce a system of coercion, the enforcement of which will be aided by the hostile feeling against the negro now prevailing among the whites, and by the general spirit of violence which in the south was fostered by the influence slavery exercised upon the popular character. It is, indeed, not probable that a general attempt will be made to restore slavery in its old form, on account of the barriers which such an attempt would find in its way; but there are systems intermediate between slavery as it formerly existed in the south, and free labor as it exists in the north, but more nearly related to the former than to the latter, *the introduction of which will be attempted*. I have already noticed some movements in that direction, which were made under the very eyes of our military authorities, and of which the Opelousas and St. Landry ordinances were the most significant. Other things of more recent date, such as the new negro code submitted by a committee to the legislature of South Carolina, are before the country. They have all the same tendency, because they all spring from the same cause.

It may be objected that evidence has been given of a contrary spirit by the State conventions which passed ordinances abolishing slavery in their States, and making it obligatory upon the legislatures to enact laws for the protection of the freedmen. While acknowledging the fact, I deem it dangerous to be led by it into any delusions. As to the motives upon which they acted when abolishing slavery, and their understanding of the bearings of such an act, we may safely accept the standard they have set up for themselves. When speaking of popular demonstrations in the south in favor of submission to the government, I stated that the principal and almost the only argument used was, that they found themselves in a situation in which "they could do no better." It was the same thing with regard to the abolition of slavery; wherever abolition was publicly advocated, whether in popular meetings or in State conventions, it was on the ground of necessity—not unfrequently with the significant addition that, as soon as they had once more control of their own State affairs, they could settle the labor question to suit themselves, whatever they might have to submit to for the present. Not only did I find this to be the common talk among the people, but the same sentiment was openly avowed by public men in speech and print. Some declarations of that kind, made by men of great prominence, have passed into the newspapers and are undoubtedly known to you. I append to this report a specimen, (accompanying document, No. 40,) not as something particularly remarkable, but in order to represent the current sentiment as expressed in the language of a candidate for a seat in the State convention of Mississippi. It is a card addressed to the voters of Wilkinson county, Mississippi, by General W.L. Brandon. The general complains of having been called "an unconditional, immediate emancipationist—an abolitionist." He indignantly repels the charge and avows himself a good pro-slavery man. "But, fellow-citizens," says he, "what I may in common with you have to submit to, is a very different thing. Slavery has been taken from us; the power that has already practically abolished it threatens totally and forever to abolish it. *But does it follow that I am in favor of this thing? By no means.* My honest conviction is, we must accept the situation as it is,*until we can get control once more of our own State affairs. We cannot do otherwise and get our place again in the Union, and occupy a position, exert an influence that will protect us against greater evils which threaten us.* I must, as any other man who votes or holds an office, submit*for the time* to evils I cannot remedy."

General Brandon was elected on that platform, and in the convention voted for the ordinance abolishing slavery, and imposing upon the legislature the duty to pass laws for the protection of the freedmen. And General Brandon is certainly looked upon in Mississippi as an honorable man, and an honest politician. What he will vote for when his people have got once more control of their own State affairs, and his State has regained its position and influence in the Union, it is needless to ask. I repeat, his case is not an isolated one. He has only put in print what, as my observations lead me to believe, a majority of the people say even in more emphatic language; and the deliberations of several legislatures in that part of the country show what it means. I deem it unnecessary to go into further particulars.

It is worthy of note that the convention of Mississippi—and the conventions of other States have followed its example—imposed upon subsequent legislatures the obligation not only to pass laws for the protection of the freedmen in person and property, but also *to guard against the dangers arising from sudden emancipation*. This language is not without significance; not the blessings of a full development of free labor, but only the dangers of emancipation are spoken of. It will be observed that this clause is so vaguely worded as to authorize the legislatures to place any restriction they may see fit upon the emancipated negro, in perfect consistency with the amended State constitutions; for it rests with them to define what the dangers of sudden emancipation consist in, and what measures may be required to guard against them. It is true, the clause does not authorize the legislatures to re-establish slavery in the old form; but they may pass whatever laws they see fit, stopping short only one step of what may strictly be defined as "slavery." Peonage of the Mexican pattern, or serfdom of some European pattern, may under that clause be considered admissible; and looking at the legislative attempts already made, especially the labor code now under consideration in the legislature of South Carolina, it appears not only possible, but eminently probable, that the laws which will be passed to guard against the dangers arising from emancipation will be directed against the spirit of emancipation itself.

A more tangible evidence of good intentions would seem to have been furnished by the admission of negro testimony in the courts of justice, which has been conceded in some of the southern States, at least in point of form. This being a matter of vital interest to the colored man, I inquired into the feelings of people concerning it with particular care. At first I found hardly any southern man that favored it. Even persons of some liberality of mind saw seemingly insurmountable objections. The appearance of a general order issued by General Swayne in Alabama, which made it optional for the civil authorities either to admit negro testimony in the State courts or to have all cases in which colored people were concerned tried by officers of the bureau or military commissions, seemed to be the signal for a change of position on the part of the politicians. A great many of them, seeing a chance for getting rid of the jurisdiction of the Freedmen's Bureau, dropped their opposition somewhat suddenly and endeavored to make the admission of negro testimony in the State courts palatable to the masses by assuring them that at all events it would rest with the judges and juries to determine in each case before them whether the testimony of negro witnesses was worth anything or not. One of the speeches delivered at Vicksburg, already referred to in another connexion, and a card published by a candidate for office, (accompanying document No. 14,) furnish specimens of that line of argument.

In my despatch from Montgomery, Alabama, I suggested to you that instructions be issued making it part of the duty of agents of the Freedmen's Bureau to appear in the State courts as the freedmen's next friend, and to forward reports of the proceedings had in the principal cases to the headquarters of the bureau. In this manner it would have been possible to ascertain to what extent the admission of negro testimony secured to the colored man justice in the State courts. As the plan does not seem to have been adopted, we must form our conclusions from evidence less complete. Among the annexed documents there are several statements concerning its results, made by gentlemen whose business it was to observe. I would invite your attention to the letters of Captain Paillon, agent of the Freedmen's Bureau at Mobile; Major Reynolds, assistant commissioner of the bureau at Natchez; and Colonel Thomas, assistant commissioner for the State of Mississippi. (Accompanying documents Nos. 41 and 27.) The opinions expressed in these papers are uniformly unfavorable. It is to be hoped that at other places better results have been attained. But I may state that even by prominent southern men, who were anxious to have the jurisdiction of the State courts extended over the freedmen, the admission was made to me that the testimony of a negro would have but little weight with a southern jury. I frequently asked the question, "Do you think a jury of your people would be apt to find a planter who has whipped one of his negro laborers guilty of assault and battery?" The answer almost invariably was, "You must make some allowance for the prejudices of our people."

It is probable that the laws excluding negro testimony from the courts will be repealed in all the States lately in rebellion if it is believed that a satisfactory arrangement of this matter may in any way facilitate the "readmission" of the States, but I apprehend such arrangements will hardly be sufficient to secure to the colored man impartial justice as long as the feelings of the whites are against him and they think that his rights are less entitled to respect than their own. More potent certainly than the laws of a country are the opinions of right and wrong entertained by its people. When the spirit of a law is in conflict with such opinions, there is but little prospect of its being faithfully put in execution, especially where those who hold such opinions are the same who have to administer the laws.

The facility with which southern politicians acquiesce in the admission of negro testimony is not surprising when we consider that the practical management of the matter will rest with their own people. I found them less accommodating with regard to "constitutional amendment." Nine-tenths of the intelligent men with whom I had any conversation upon that subject expressed their willingness to ratify the first section, abolishing slavery throughout the United States, but not the second section, empowering Congress "to enforce the foregoing by appropriate legislation." I feel warranted in saying that, while I was in the south, this was the prevailing sentiment. Nevertheless, I deem it probable that the "constitutional amendment" will be ratified by every State legislature, provided the government insists upon such ratification as a *conditio sine qua non* of readmission. It is instructive to observe how powerful and immediate an effect the announcement of such a condition by the government produces in southern conventions and legislatures. It would be idle to assume, however, that a telegraphic despatch, while it may beat down all parliamentary opposition to this or that measure, will at the same time obliterate the prejudices of the people; nor will it prevent those prejudices from making themselves seriously felt in the future. It will require measures of a more practical character to prevent the dangers which, as everybody that reads the signs of the times must see, are now impending.

THE MILITIA.

I do not mean to say that the southern people intend to retrace the steps they have made as soon as they have resumed control of their State affairs. Although they regret the abolition of slavery, they certainly do not intend to re-establish it in its old form. Although they are at heart opposed to the admission of negro testimony in the courts of justice, they probably will not re-enact the laws excluding it. But while accepting the "abolition of slavery," they think that some species of serfdom, peonage, or some other form of compulsory labor is not slavery, and may be introduced without a violation of their pledge. Although formally admitting negro testimony, they think that negro testimony will be taken practically for what they themselves consider it "worth." What particular shape the reactionary movement will assume it is at present unnecessary to inquire. There are a hundred ways of framing apprenticeship, vagrancy, or contract laws, which will serve the purpose. Even the mere reorganization of the militia upon the old footing will go far towards accomplishing the object. To this point I beg leave to invite your special attention.

The people of the southern States show great anxiety to have their militia reorganized, and in some instances permission has been given. In the case of Mississippi I gave you my reasons for opposing the measure under existing circumstances. They were, first, that county patrols had already been in existence, and had to be disbanded on account of their open hostility to Union people and freedmen. (See Colonel Yorke's report, accompanying document No. 25.) Second, that the governor proposed to arm the people upon the ground that the inhabitants refused to assist the military authorities in the suppression of crime, and that the call was addressed, not to the loyal citizens of the United States, but expressly to the "young men who had so distinguished themselves for gallantry" in the rebel service. (See correspondence between Governor Sharkey and General Osterhaus, accompanying document No. 42.) And third, because the State was still under martial law, and the existence of organized and armed bodies not under the control of the military commander was inconsistent with that state of things.

But there are other more general points of view from which this question must be looked at in order to be appreciated in its most important bearings. I may state, without fear of contradiction, that, in every case, where permission was asked for reorganizing the militia, the privilege or duty of serving in that armed organization was intended to be confined to the whites. In the conversations I had with southern men about this matter, the idea of admitting colored people to the privilege of bearing arms as a part of the militia was uniformly treated by them as a thing not to be thought of. The militia, whenever organized, will thus be composed of men belonging to one class, to the total exclusion of another. This concentration of organized physical power in the hands of one class will necessarily tend, and is undoubtedly designed, to give that class absolute physical control of the other. The specific purpose for which the militia is to be reorganized appears clearly from the uses it was put to whenever a local organization was effected. It is the restoration of the old patrol system which was one of the characteristic features of the regime of slavery. The services which such patrols are expected to perform consist in maintaining what southern people understand to be the order of society. Indications are given in several of the accompanying documents. Among others, the St. Landry and Bossier ordinances define with some precision what the authority and duties of the "chief patrols" are to be. The militia, organized for the distinct purpose of enforcing the authority of the whites over the blacks, is in itself practically sufficient to establish and enforce a system of compulsory labor without there being any explicit laws for it; and, being sustained and encouraged by public opinion, the chief and members of "county patrols" are not likely to be over-nice in the construction of their orders. This is not a mere supposition, but an opinion based upon experience already gathered. As I stated above, the reorganization of the county patrol system upon the basis here described will result in the establishment of a sort of permanent martial law over the negro.

It is, therefore, not even necessary that the reaction against that result of the war, which consists in emancipation, should manifest itself by very obnoxious legislative enactments, just as in some of the slave States slavery did not exist by virtue of the State constitution. It may be practically accomplished, and is, in fact, practically accomplished whenever the freed man is not protected by the federal authorities, without displaying its character and aims upon the statute book.

NEGRO INSURRECTIONS AND ANARCHY.

That in times like ours, and in a country like this, a reaction in favor of compulsory labor cannot be ultimately successful, is as certain as it was that slavery could not last forever. But a movement in that direction can prevent much good that might be accomplished, and produce much evil that might be avoided. Not only will such a movement seriously interfere with all efforts to organize an efficient system of free labor, and thus very materially retard the return of prosperity in the south, but it may bring on a crisis as dangerous and destructive as the war of the rebellion itself.

I stated above that I did not deem a negro insurrection probable as long as the freedmen were assured of the direct protection of the national government. Whenever they are in trouble, they raise their eyes up to that power, and although they may suffer, yet, as long as that power is visibly present, they continue to hope. But when State authority in the south is fully restored, the federal forces withdrawn, and the Freedmen's Bureau abolished, the colored man will find himself turned over to the mercies of those whom he does not trust. If then an attempt, is made to strip him again of those rights which he justly thought he possessed, he will be apt to feel that he can hope for no redress unless he procure it himself. If ever the negro is capable of rising, he will rise then. Men who never struck a blow for the purpose of gaining their liberty, when they were slaves, are apt to strike when, their liberty once gained, they see it again in danger. However great the patience and submissiveness of the colored race may be, it cannot be presumed that its active participation in a war against the very men with whom it again stands face to face, has remained entirely without influence upon its spirit.

What a general insurrection of the negroes would result in, whether it would be easy or difficult to suppress it, whether the struggle would be long or short, what race would suffer most, are questions which will not be asked by those who understand the problem to be, not how to suppress a negro insurrection, but how to prevent it. Certain it is, it would inflict terrible calamities upon both whites and blacks, and present to the world the spectacle of atrocities which ought to be foreign to civilized nations. The negro, in his ordinary state, is docile and good-natured; but when once engaged in a bloody business, it is difficult to say how far his hot impulses would carry him; and as to the southern whites, the barbarous scenes the country has witnessed since the close of the rebellion, indicate the temper with which they would fight the negro as an insurgent. It would be a war of extermination, revolting in its incidents, and with ruin and desolation in its train. There may be different means by which it can be prevented, but there is only one certain of effect: it is, that the provocations be avoided which may call it forth.

But even if it be prevented by other means, it is not the only danger which a reactionary movement will bring upon the south. Nothing renders society more restless than a social revolution but half accomplished. It naturally tends to develop its logical consequences, but is hindered by adverse agencies which work in another direction; nor can it return to the point from which it started. There are, then, continual vibrations and fluctuations between two opposites which keep society in the nervous uneasiness and excitement growing from the lingering strife between the antagonistic tendencies. All classes of society are intensely dissatisfied with things as they are. General explosions may be prevented, but they are always imminent. This state of uncertainty impedes all successful working of the social forces; people, instead of devoting themselves with confidence and steadiness to solid pursuits, are apt to live from hand to mouth, or to indulge in fitful experiments; capital ventures out but with great timity; the lawless elements of the community take advantage of the general confusion and dissatisfaction, and society drifts into anarchy. There is probably at the present moment no country in the civilized world which contains such an accumulation of anarchical elements as the south. The strife of the antagonistic tendencies here described is aggravated by the passions inflamed and the general impoverishment brought about by a long and exhaustive war, and the south will have to suffer the evils of anarchical disorder until means are found to effect a final settlement of the labor question in accordance with the logic of the great revolution.

THE TRUE PROBLEM.—DIFFICULTIES AND REMEDIES.

In seeking remedies for such disorders, we ought to keep in view, above all, the nature of the problem which is to be solved. As to what is commonly termed "reconstruction," it is not only the political machinery of the States and their constitutional relations to the general government, but the whole organism of southern society that must be reconstructed, or rather constructed anew, so as to bring it in harmony with the rest of American society. The difficulties of this task are not to be considered overcome when the people of the south take the oath of allegiance and elect governors and legislatures and members of Congress, and militia captains. That this would be done had become Certain as soon as the surrenders of the southern armies had made further resistance impossible, and nothing in the world was left, even to the most uncompromising rebel, but to submit or to emigrate. It was also natural that they should avail themselves of every chance offered them to resume control of their home affairs and to regain their influence in the Union. But this can hardly be called the first step towards the solution of the true problem, and it is a fair question to ask, whether the hasty gratification of their desire to resume such control would not create new embarrassments.

The true nature of the difficulties of the situation is this: The general government of the republic has, by proclaiming the emancipation of the slaves, commenced a great social revolution in the south, but has, as yet, not completed it. Only the negative part of it is accomplished.

The slaves are emancipated in point of form, but free labor has not yet been put in the place of slavery in point of fact. And now, in the midst of this critical period of transition, the power which originated the revolution is expected to turn over its whole future development to another power which from the beginning was hostile to it and has never yet entered into its spirit, leaving the class in whose favor it was made completely without power to protect itself and to take an influential part in that development. The history of the world will be searched in vain for a proceeding similar to this which did not lead either to a rapid and violent reaction, or to the most serious trouble and civil disorder. It cannot be said that the conduct of the southern people since the close of the war has exhibited such extraordinary wisdom and self-abnegation as to make them an exception to the rule.

In my despatches from the south I repeatedly expressed the opinion that the people were not yet in a frame of mind to legislate calmly and understandingly upon the subject of free negro labor. And this I reported to be the opinion of some of our most prominent military commanders and other observing men. It is, indeed, difficult to imagine circumstances more unfavorable for the development of a calm and unprejudiced public opinion than those under which the southern people are at present laboring. The war has not only defeated their political aspirations, but it has broken up their whole social organization. When the rebellion was put down they found themselves not only conquered in a political and military sense, but economically ruined. The planters, who represented the wealth of the southern country, are partly laboring under the severest embarrassments, partly reduced to absolute poverty. Many who are stripped of all available means, and have nothing but their land, cross their arms in gloomy despondency, incapable of rising to a manly resolution. Others, who still possess means, are at a loss how to use them, as their old way of doing things is, by the abolition of slavery, rendered impracticable, at least where the military arm of the government has enforced emancipation. Others are still trying to go on in the old way, and that old way is in fact the only one they understand, and in which they have any confidence. Only a minority is trying to adopt the new order of things. A large number of the plantations, probably a considerable majority of the more valuable estates, is under heavy mortgages, and the owners know that, unless they retrieve their fortunes in a comparatively short space of time, their property will pass out of their hands. Almost all are, to some extent, embarrassed. The nervous anxiety which such a state of things produces extends also to those classes of society which, although not composed of planters, were always in close business connexion with the planting interest, and there was hardly a branch of commerce or industry in the south which was not directly or indirectly so connected. Besides, the southern soldiers, when returning from the war, did not, like the northern soldiers, find a prosperous community which merely waited for their arrival to give them remunerative employment. They found, many of them, their homesteads destroyed, their farms devastated, their families in distress; and those that were less unfortunate found, at all events, an impoverished and exhausted community which had but little to offer them. Thus a great many have been thrown upon the world to shift as best they can. They must do something honest or dishonest, and must do it soon, to make a living, and their prospects are, at present, not very bright. Thus that nervous anxiety to hastily repair broken fortunes, and to prevent still greater ruin and distress, embraces nearly all classes, and imprints upon all the movements of the social body a morbid character.

In which direction will these people be most apt to turn their eyes? Leaving the prejudice of race out of the question, from early youth they have been acquainted with but one system of labor, and with that one system they have been in the habit of identifying all their interests. They know of no way to help themselves but the one they are accustomed to. Another system of labor is presented to them, which, however, owing to circumstances which they do not appreciate, appears at first in an unpromising light. To try it they consider an experiment which they cannot afford to make while their wants are urgent. They have not reasoned calmly enough to convince themselves that the trial must be made. It is, indeed, not wonderful that, under such circumstances, they should study, not how to introduce and develop free labor, but how to avoid its introduction, and how to return as much and as quickly as possible to something like the old order of things. Nor is it wonderful that such studies should find an expression in their attempts at legislation. But the circumstance that this tendency is natural does not render it less dangerous and objectionable. The practical question presents itself: Is the immediate restoration of the late rebel States to absolute self-control so necessary that it must be done even at the risk of endangering one of the great results of the war, and of bringing on in those States insurrection or anarchy, or would it not be better to postpone that restoration until such dangers are passed? If, as long as the change from slavery to free labor is known to the southern people only by its destructive results, these people must be expected to throw obstacles in its way, would it not seem necessary that the movement of social "reconstruction" be kept in the right channel by the hand of the power which originated the change, until that change can have disclosed some of its beneficial effects?

It is certain that every success of free negro labor will augment the number of its friends, and disarm some of the prejudices and assumptions of its opponents. I am convinced one good harvest made by unadulterated free labor in the south would have a far better effect than all the oaths that have been taken, and all the ordinances that have as yet been passed by southern conventions. But how can such a result be attained? The facts enumerated in this report, as well as the news we receive from the south from day to day, must make it evident to every unbiased observer that unadulterated free labor cannot be had at present, unless the national government holds its protective and controlling hand over it. It appears, also, that the more efficient this protection of free labor against all disturbing and reactionary influences, the sooner may such a satisfactory result be looked for. One reason why the southern people are so slow in accommodating themselves to the new order of things is, that they confidently expect soon to be permitted to regulate matters according to their own notions. Every concession made to them by the government has been taken as an encouragement to persevere in this hope, and, unfortunately for them, this hope is nourished by influences from other parts of the country. Hence their anxiety to have their State governments restored *at once*, to have the troops withdrawn, and the Freedmen's Bureau abolished, although a good many discerning men know well that, in view of the lawless spirit still prevailing, it would be far better for them to have the general order of society firmly maintained by the federal power until things have arrived at a final settlement. Had, from the beginning, the conviction been forced upon them that the adulteration of the new order of things by the admixture of elements belonging to the system of slavery would under no circumstances be permitted, a much larger number would have launched their energies into the new channel, and, seeing that they could do "no better," faithfully co-operated with the government. It is hope which fixes them in their perverse notions. That hope nourished or fully gratified, they will persevere in the same direction. That hope destroyed, a great many will, by the force of necessity, at once accommodate themselves to the logic of the change. If, therefore, the national government firmly and unequivocally announces its policy not to give up the control of the free-labor reform until it is finally accomplished, the progress of that reform will undoubtedly be far more rapid and far less difficult than it will be if the attitude of the government is such as to permit contrary hopes to be indulged in.

The machinery by which the government has so far exercised its protection of the negro and of free labor in the south—the Freedmen's Bureau—is very unpopular in that part of the country, as every institution placed there as a barrier to reactionary aspirations would be. That abuses were committed with the management of freedmen's affairs; that some of the officers of the bureau were men of more enthusiasm than discretion, and in many cases went beyond their authority: all this is certainly true. But, while the southern people are always ready to expatiate upon the shortcomings of the Freedmen's Bureau, they are not so ready to recognize the services it has rendered. I feel warranted in saying that not half of the labor that has been done in the south this year, or will be done there next year, would have been or would be done but for the exertions of the Freedmen's Bureau. The confusion and disorder of the transition period would have been infinitely greater had not an agency interfered which possessed the confidence of the emancipated slaves; which could disabuse them of any extravagant notions and expectations and be trusted; which could administer to them good advice and be voluntarily obeyed. No other agency, except one placed there by the national government, could have wielded that moral power whose interposition was so necessary to prevent southern society from falling at once into the chaos of a general collision between its different elements. That the success achieved by the Freedmen's Bureau is as yet very incomplete cannot be disputed. A more perfect organization and a more carefully selected personnel may be desirable; but it is doubtful whether a more suitable machinery can be devised to secure to free labor in the south that protection against disturbing influences which the nature of the situation still imperatively demands.

IMMIGRATION.

A temporary continuation of national control in the southern States would also have a most beneficial effect as regards the immigration of northern people and Europeans into that country; and such immigration would, in its turn, contribute much to the solution of the labor problem. Nothing is more desirable for the south than the importation of new men and new ideas. One of the greatest drawbacks under which the southern people are laboring is, that for fifty years they have been in no sympathetic communion with the progressive ideas of the times. While professing to be in favor of free trade, they adopted and enforced a system of prohibition, as far as those ideas were concerned, which was in conflict with their cherished institution of slavery; and, as almost all the progressive ideas of our days were in conflict with slavery, the prohibition was sweeping. It had one peculiar effect, which we also notice with some Asiatic nations which follow a similar course. The southern people honestly maintained and believed, not only that as a people they were highly civilized, but that their civilization was the highest that could be attained, and ought to serve as a model to other nations the world over. The more enlightened individuals among them felt sometimes a vague impression of the barrenness of their mental life, and the barbarous peculiarities of their social organization; but very few ever dared to investigate and to expose the true cause of these evils. Thus the people were so wrapt up in self-admiration as to be inaccessible to the voice even of the best-intentioned criticism. Hence the delusion they indulged in as to the absolute superiority of their race—a delusion which, in spite of the severe test it has lately undergone, is not yet given up; and will, as every traveller in the south can testify from experience, sometimes express itself in singular manifestations. This spirit, which for so long a time has kept the southern people back while the world besides was moving, is even at this moment still standing as a serious obstacle in the way of progress.

Nothing can, therefore, be more desirable than that the contact between the southern people and the outside world should be as strong and intimate as possible; and in no better way can this end be subserved than by immigration in mass. Of the economical benefits which such immigration would confer upon the owners of the soil it is hardly necessary to speak.

Immigration wants encouragement. As far as this encouragement consists in the promise of material advantage, it is already given. There are large districts in the south in which an industrious and enterprising man, with some capital, and acting upon correct principles, cannot fail to accumulate large gains in a comparatively short time, as long as the prices of the staples do not fall below what they may reasonably be expected to be for some time to come. A northern man has, besides, the advantage of being served by the laboring population of that region with greater willingness.

But among the principal requisites for the success of the immigrant are personal security and a settled condition of things. Personal security is honestly promised by the thinking men of the south; but another question is, whether the promise and good intentions of the thinking men will be sufficient to restrain and control the populace, whose animosity against "Yankee interlopers" is only second to their hostile feeling against the negro. If the military forces of the government should be soon and completely withdrawn, I see reasons to fear that in many localities immigrants would enjoy the necessary security only when settling down together in numbers strong enough to provide for their own protection. On the whole, no better encouragement can be given to immigration, as far as individual security is concerned, than the assurance that the national government will be near to protect them until such protection is no longer needed.

The south needs capital. But capital is notoriously timid and averse to risk itself, not only where there actually is trouble, but where there is serious and continual danger of trouble. Capitalists will be apt to consider—and they are by no means wrong in doing so—that no safe investments can be made in the south as long as southern society is liable to be convulsed by anarchical disorders. No greater encouragement can, therefore, be given to capital to transfer itself to the south than the assurance that the government will continue to control the development of the new social system in the late rebel States until such dangers are averted by a final settlement of things upon a thorough free-labor basis.

How long the national government should continue that control depends upon contingencies. It ought to cease as soon as its objects are attained; and its objects will be attained sooner and with less difficulty if nobody is permitted to indulge in the delusion that it will cease *before* they are attained. This is one of the cases in which a determined policy can accomplish much, while a half-way policy is liable to spoil things already accomplished. The continuance of the national control in the south, although it may be for a short period only, will cause some inconvenience and expense; but if thereby destructive collisions and anarchical disorders can be prevented, justice secured to all men, and the return of peace and prosperity to all parts of this country hastened, it will be a paying investment. For the future of the republic, it is far less important that this business of reconstruction be done quickly than that it be well done. The matter well taken in hand, there is reason for hope that it will be well done, and quickly too. In days like these great changes are apt to operate themselves rapidly. At present the southern people assume that free negro labor will not work, and therefore they are not inclined to give it a fair trial. As soon as they find out that they must give it a fair trial, and that their whole future power and prosperity depend upon its success, they will also find out that it will work, at least far better than they have anticipated. Then their hostility to it will gradually disappear. This great result accomplished, posterity will not find fault with this administration for having delayed complete "reconstruction" one, two, or more years.

Although I am not called upon to discuss in this report the constitutional aspects of this question, I may be pardoned for one remark. The interference of the national government in the local concerns of the States lately in rebellion is argued against by many as inconsistent with the spirit of our federal institutions. Nothing is more foreign to my ways of thinking in political matters than a fondness for centralization or military government. Nobody can value the blessings of local self-government more highly than I do. But we are living under exceptional circumstances which require us, above all, to look at things from a practical point of view; and I believe it will prove far more dangerous for the integrity of local self-government if the national control in the south be discontinued—while by discontinuing it too soon, it may be rendered necessary again in the future—than if it be continued, when by continuing it but a limited time all such future necessity may be obviated. At present these acts of interference are but a part of that exceptional policy brought forth by the necessities into which the rebellion has plunged us. Although there will be some modifications in the relations between the States and the national government, yet these acts of direct interference in the details of State concerns will pass away with the exceptional circumstances which called them forth. But if the social revolution in the south be now abandoned in an unfinished state, and at some future period produce events provoking new and repeated acts of direct practical interference—and the contingency would by no means be unlikely to arise—such new and repeated acts would not pass over without most seriously affecting the political organism of the republic.

NEGRO SUFFRAGE.

It would seem that the interference of the national authority in the home concerns of the southern States would be rendered less necessary, and the whole problem of political and social reconstruction be much simplified, if, while the masses lately arrayed against the government are permitted to vote, the large majority of those who were always loyal, and are naturally anxious to see the free labor problem successfully solved, were not excluded from all influence upon legislation. In all questions concerning the Union, the national debt, and the future social organization of the south, the feelings of the colored man are naturally in sympathy with the views and aims of the national government. While the southern white fought against the Union, the negro did all he could to aid it; while the southern white sees in the national government his conqueror, the negro sees in it his protector; while the white owes to the national debt his defeat, the negro owes to it his deliverance; while the white considers himself robbed and ruined by the emancipation of the slaves, the negro finds in it the assurance of future prosperity and happiness. In all the important issues the negro would be led by natural impulse to forward the ends of the government, and by making his influence, as part of the voting body, tell upon the legislation of the States, render the interference of the national authority less necessary.

As the most difficult of the pending questions are intimately connected with the status of the negro in southern society, it is obvious that a correct solution can be more easily obtained if he has a voice in the matter. In the right to vote he would find the best permanent protection against oppressive class-legislation, as well as against individual persecution. The relations between the white and black races, even if improved by the gradual wearing off of the present animosities, are likely to remain long under the troubling influence of prejudice. It is a notorious fact that the rights of a man of some political power are far less exposed to violation than those of one who is, in matters of public interest, completely subject to the will of others. A voter is a man of influence; small as that influence may be in the single individual, it becomes larger when that individual belongs to a numerous class of voters who are ready to make common cause with him for the protection of his rights. Such an individual is an object of interest to the political parties that desire to have the benefit of his ballot. It is true, the bringing face to face at the ballot-box of the white and black races may here and there lead to an outbreak of feeling, and the first trials ought certainly to be made while the national power is still there to prevent or repress disturbances; but the practice once successfully inaugurated under the protection of that power, it would probably be more apt than anything else to obliterate old antagonisms, especially if the colored people—which is probable, as soon as their own rights are sufficiently secured—divide their votes between the different political parties.

The effect of the extension of the franchise to the colored people upon the development of free labor and upon the security of human rights in the south being the principal object in view, the objections raised on the ground of the ignorance of the freedmen become unimportant. Practical liberty is a good school, and, besides, if any qualification can be found, applicable to both races, which does not interfere with the attainment of the main object, such qualification would in that respect be unobjectionable. But it is idle to say that it will be time to speak of negro suffrage when the whole colored race will be educated, for the ballot may be necessary to him to secure his education. It is also idle to say that ignorance is the principal ground upon which southern men object to negro suffrage, for if it were, that numerous class of colored people in Louisiana who are as highly educated, as intelligent, and as wealthy as any corresponding class of whites, would have been enfranchised long ago.

It has been asserted that the negro would be but a voting machine in the hand of his employer. On this point opinions seem to differ. I have heard it said in the south that the freedmen are more likely to be influenced by their schoolmasters and preachers. But even if we suppose the employer to control to a certain extent the negro laborer's vote, two things are to be taken into consideration: 1. The class of employers, of landed proprietors, will in a few years be very different from what it was heretofore in consequence of the general breaking up, a great many of the old slaveholders will be obliged to give up their lands and new men will step into their places; and 2. The employer will hardly control the vote of the negro laborer so far as to make him vote against his own liberty. The beneficial effect of an extension of suffrage does not always depend upon the intelligence with which the newly admitted voters exercise their right, but sometimes upon the circumstances in which they are placed; and the circumstances in which the freedmen of the south are placed are such that, when they only vote for their own liberty and rights, they vote for the rights of free labor, for the success of an immediate important reform, for the prosperity of the country, and for the general interests of mankind. If, therefore, in order to control the colored vote, the employer, or whoever he may be, is first obliged to concede to the freedman the great point of his own rights as a man and a free laborer, the great social reform is completed, the most difficult problem is solved, and all other questions it will be comparatively easy to settle.

In discussing the matter of negro suffrage I deemed it my duty to confine myself strictly to the practical aspects of the subject. I have, therefore, not touched its moral merits nor discussed the question whether the national government is competent to enlarge the elective franchise in the States lately in rebellion by its own act; I deem it proper, however, to offer a few remarks on the assertion frequently put forth, that the franchise is likely to be extended to the colored man by the voluntary action of the southern whites themselves. My observation leads me to a contrary opinion. Aside from a very few enlightened men, I found but one class of people in favor of the enfranchisement of the blacks: it was the class of Unionists who found themselves politically ostracised and looked upon the enfranchisement of the loyal negroes as the salvation of the whole loyal element. But their numbers and influence are sadly insufficient to secure such a result. The masses are strongly opposed to colored suffrage; anybody that dares to advocate it is stigmatized as a dangerous fanatic; nor do I deem it probable that in the ordinary course of things prejudices will wear off to such an extent as to make it a popular measure. Outside of Louisiana only one gentleman who occupied a prominent political position in the south expressed to me an opinion favorable to it. He declared himself ready to vote for an amendment to the constitution of his State bestowing the right of suffrage upon all male citizens without distinction of color who could furnish evidence of their ability to read and write, without, however, disfranchising those who are now voters and are not able to fulfil that condition. This gentleman is now a member of one of the State conventions, but I presume he will not risk his political standing in the south by moving such an amendment in that body.

The only manner in which, in my opinion, the southern people can be induced to grant to the freedman some measure of self-protecting power in the form of suffrage, is to make it a condition precedent to "readmission."

DEPORTATION OF THE FREEDMEN.

I have to notice one pretended remedy for the disorders now agitating the south, which seems to have become the favorite plan of some prominent public men. It is that the whole colored population of the south should be transported to some place where they could live completely separated from the whites. It is hardly necessary to discuss, not only the question of right and justice, but the difficulties and expense necessarily attending the deportation of nearly four millions of people. But it may be asked, what would become of the industry of the south for many years, if the bulk of its laboring population were taken away? The south stands in need of an increase and not of a diminution of its laboring force to repair the losses and disasters of the last four years. Much is said of importing European laborers and northern men; this is the favorite idea of many planters who want such immigrants to work on their plantations. But they forget that European and northern men will not come to the south to serve as hired hands on the plantations, but to acquire property for themselves, and that even if the whole European immigration at the rate of 200,000 a year were turned into the south, leaving not a single man for the north and west, it would require between fifteen and twenty years to fill the vacuum caused by the deportation of the freedmen. Aside from this, the influx of northern men or Europeans will not diminish the demand for hired negro labor; it will, on the contrary, increase it. As Europeans and northern people come in, not only vast quantities of land will pass from the hands of their former owners into those of the immigrants, but a large area of new land will be brought under cultivation; and as the area of cultivation expands, hired labor, such as furnished by the colored people, will be demanded in large quantities. The deportation of the labor so demanded would, therefore, be a very serious injury to the economical interests of the south, and if an attempt were made, this effect would soon be felt.

It is, however, a question worthy of consideration whether it would not be wise to offer attractive inducements and facilities for the voluntary migration of freedmen to some suitable district on the line of the Pacific railroad. It would answer a double object: 1. It would aid in the construction of that road, and 2. If this migration be effected on a large scale it would cause a drain upon the laboring force of the south; it would make the people affected by that drain feel the value of the freedmen's labor, and show them the necessity of keeping that labor at home by treating the laborer well, and by offering him inducements as fair as can be offered elsewhere.

But whatever the efficiency of such expedients may be, the true problem remains, not how to remove the colored man from his present field of labor, but how to make him, where he is, a true freeman and an intelligent and useful citizen. The means are simple: protection by the government until his political and social status enables him to protect himself, offering to his legitimate ambition the stimulant of a perfectly fair chance in life, and granting to him the rights which in every just organization of society are coupled with corresponding duties.

CONCLUSION.

I may sum up all I have said in a few words. If nothing were necessary but to restore the machinery of government in the States lately in rebellion in point of form, the movements made to that end by the people of the south might be considered satisfactory. But if it is required that the southern people should also accommodate themselves to the results of the war in point of spirit, those movements fall far short of what must be insisted upon.

The loyalty of the masses and most of the leaders of the southern people, consists in submission to necessity. There is, except in individual instances, an entire absence of that national spirit which forms the basis of true loyalty and patriotism.

The emancipation of the slaves is submitted to only in so far as chattel slavery in the old form could not be kept up. But although the freedman is no longer considered the property of the individual master, he is considered the slave of society, and all independent State legislation will share the tendency to make him such. The ordinances abolishing slavery passed by the conventions under the pressure of circumstances, will not be looked upon as barring the establishment of a new form of servitude.

Practical attempts on the part of the southern people to deprive the negro of his rights as a freeman may result in bloody collisions, and will certainly plunge southern society into restless fluctuations and anarchical confusion. Such evils can be prevented only by continuing the control of the national government in the States lately in rebellion until free labor is fully developed and firmly established, and the advantages and blessings of the new order of things have disclosed themselves. This desirable result will be hastened by a firm declaration on the part of the government, that national control in the south will not cease until such results are secured. Only in this way can that security be established in the south which will render numerous immigration possible, and such immigration would materially aid a favorable development of things.

The solution of the problem would be very much facilitated by enabling all the loyal and free-labor elements in the south to exercise a healthy influence upon legislation. It will hardly be possible to secure the freedman against oppressive class legislation and private persecution, unless he be endowed with a certain measure of political power.

As to the future peace and harmony of the Union, it is of the highest importance that the people lately in rebellion be not permitted to build up another "peculiar institution" whose spirit is in conflict with the fundamental principles of our political system; for as long as they cherish interests peculiar to them in preference to those they have in common with the rest of the American people, their loyalty to the Union will always be uncertain.

I desire not to be understood as saying that there are no well-meaning men among those who were compromised in the rebellion. There are many, but neither their number nor their influence is strong enough to control the manifest tendency of the popular spirit. There are great reasons for hope that a determined policy on the part of the national government will produce innumerable and valuable conversions. This consideration counsels lenity as to persons, such as is demanded by the humane and enlightened spirit of our times, and vigor and firmness in the carrying out of principles, such as is demanded by the national sense of justice and the exigencies of our situation.

In submitting this report I desire to say that I have conscientiously endeavored to see things as they were, and to represent them as I saw them: I have been careful not to use stronger language than was warranted by the thoughts I intended to express. A comparison of the tenor of the annexed documents with that of my report, will convince you that I have studiously avoided overstatements. Certain legislative attempts at present made in the south, and especially in South Carolina, seem to be more than justifying the apprehensions I have expressed.

Conscious though I am of having used my best endeavors to draw, from what I saw and learned, correct general conclusions, yet I am far from placing too great a trust in my own judgment, when interests of such magnitude are at stake. I know that this report is incomplete, although as complete as an observation of a few months could enable me to make it. Additional facts might be elicited, calculated to throw new light upon the subject. Although I see no reason for believing that things have changed for the better since I left for the south, yet such may be the case. Admitting all these possibilities, I would entreat you to take no irretraceable step towards relieving the States lately in rebellion from all national control, until such favorable changes are clearly and unmistakably ascertained.

To that end, and by virtue of the permission you honored me with when sending me out to communicate to you freely and unreservedly my views as to measures of policy proper to be adopted, I would now respectfully suggest that you advise Congress to send one or more "investigating committees" into the southern States, to inquire for themselves into the actual condition of things, before final action is taken upon the readmission of such States to their representation in the legislative branch of the government, and the withdrawal of the national control from that section of the country.

I am, sir, very respectfully, your obedient servant,

CARL SCHURZ.

His Excellency ANDREW JOHNSON,*President of the United States.*

DOCUMENTS ACCOMPANYING THE REPORT OF MAJOR GENERAL CARL SCHURZ.

No. 1.

HEADQUARTERS DEPARTMENT OF SOUTH CAROLINA,

Hilton Head, S.C., July 27, 1865.

Dear Sir: I have received your letter of the 17th instant, from Charleston, propounding to me three questions, as follows:

1st. Do you think that there are a number of *bona fide* loyal persons in this State large enough to warrant the early establishment of civil government?

2d. Do you think that the white population of South Carolina, if restored to the possession of political power in this State, would carry out the spirit of the emancipation proclamation, and go to work in a *bona fide* manner to organize free labor?

3d. What measures do you think necessary to insure such a result in this State?

The first of these questions I am forced to answer in the negative, provided that white persons only are referred to in the expression "*bona fide loyal persons*," and provided that "the early establishment of civil government" means the early withdrawal of the general control of affairs from the United States authorities.

To the second question, I answer that I do not think that the white inhabitants of South Carolina, if left to themselves, are yet prepared to carry out the spirit of the emancipation proclamation; neither do I think that they would organize free labor upon any plan that would be of advantage to both whites and blacks until the mutual distrust and prejudice now existing between the races are in a measure removed.

To the third question I answer, that, in order to secure the carrying out of the "spirit of the emancipation proclamation," and the organization of really free labor in good faith, it appears to me necessary that the military, or some other authority derived from the national government, should retain a supervisory control over the civil affairs in this State until the next season's crops are harvested and secured.

The reasons which have dictated my replies I shall notice quite briefly.

Loyalty in South Carolina—such loyalty as is secured by the taking of the amnesty oath and by the reception of Executive clemency—does not approach the standard of loyalty in the north. It is not the golden fruit of conviction, but the stern and unpromising result of necessity, arising from unsuccessful insurrection. The white population of the State accept the condition which has been imposed upon them, simply because there is no alternative.

They entered upon the war in the spring of 1861 and arrayed themselves on the side of treason with a unanimity of purpose and a malignity of feeling not equalled by that displayed in any other State.

The individual exceptions to this rule were too few in numbers and were possessed of too little power to be taken into account at all. Although the overt treason then inaugurated has been overcome by superior force, few will claim that it has been transformed into loyalty toward the national government. I am clearly of the opinion that it has not, and that time and experience will be necessary to effect such a change.

All intelligent whites admit that the "abolition of slavery" and the "impracticability of secession" are the plain and unmistakable verdicts of the war. Their convictions as yet go no further. Their preference for the "divine institution," and their intellectual belief in the right of a State to secede, are as much articles of faith in their creed at the present moment as they were on the day when the ordinance of secession was unanimously adopted. When the rebel armies ceased to exist, and there was no longer any force that could be invoked for waging war against the nation, the insurgents accepted that fact simply as proof of the impossibility of their establishing an independent government. This sentiment was almost immediately followed by a general desire to save as much property as possible from the general wreck. To this state of the public mind, which succeeded the surrender of the rebel armies with noteworthy rapidity, I am forced to attribute the prevailing willingness and desire of the people to "return" to their allegiance, and resume the avocations of peace.

I do not regard this condition of things as at all discouraging. It is, indeed, better than I expected to see or dared to hope for in so short a time. One good result of it is, that guerilla warfare, which was so very generally apprehended, has never been resorted to in this State. There was a sudden and general change from a state of war to a state of peace, and, with the exception of frequent individual conflicts, mostly between the whites and blacks, and often, it is true, resulting in loss of life, that peace has rarely been disturbed.

It is, however, a peace resulting from a cool and dispassionate appeal to reason, and not from any convictions of right or wrong; it has its origin in the head, and not in the heart. Impotency and policy gave it birth, and impotency, policy and hope keep it alive. It is not inspired by any higher motives than these, and higher motives could hardly be expected to follow immediately in the footsteps of armed insurrection. The hopes of the people are fixed, as a matter of course, upon the President. The whites hope and expect to recover the preponderating influence which they have lost by the war, and which has been temporarily replaced by the military authority throughout the State, and they receive with general satisfaction the appointment of Mr. Perry as provisional governor of the State, and regard it as a step toward their restoration to civil and political power. Even those men who have taken the lead during the war, not only in the heartiness and liberality of their support of the rebel cause, but also in the bitterness of their denunciation of the national government and the loyal people of the northern States, express themselves as entirely satisfied with the shape which events are taking.

The colored population, on the contrary, or that portion of it which moulds the feelings and directs the passions of the mass, look with growing suspicion upon this state of affairs, and entertain the most lively apprehensions with regard to their future welfare. They have no fears of being returned to slavery, having the most implicit faith in our assurance of its abolition for all time to come, but they think they see the power which has held the lash over them through many generations again being restored to their former masters, and they are impressed with a greater or less degree of alarm.

Thus the "irrepressible conflict," the antagonism of interest, thought, and sentiment between the races is perpetuated. The immediate resumption by the whites of the civil and political power of the State would have a tendency to augment this evil. At the present time all differences between the whites and blacks, but more especially those growing out of agreements for compensated labor, are promptly and willingly referred to the nearest military authority for adjustment; the whites well knowing that simple justice will be administered, and the blacks inspired by the belief that we are their friends. This plan works smoothly and satisfactorily. Many of the labor contracts upon the largest plantations have been made with special reference to the planting and harvesting of the next year's crops; others expire with the present year. The immediate restoration of the civil power by removing military restraint from those planters who are not entirely sincere in their allegiance, and have not made their pledges andespecially their labor contracts in good faith, and by withdrawing from the blacks that source of protection to which alone they look for justice with any degree of confidence, would, by engendering new suspicions, and new prejudices between the races, work disadvantageously to both in a pecuniary sense, while the successful solution of the important question of free black labor would be embarrassed, deferred, and possibly defeated, inasmuch as it would be placed thereby in the hands of men who are avowedly suspicious of the negro, and have no confidence in his fitness for freedom, or his willingness to work; who regard the abolition of slavery as a great sectional calamity, and who, under the semblance and even the protection of the law, and without violating the letter of the emancipation proclamation, would have it in their power to impose burdens upon the negro race scarcely less irksome than those from which it has theoretically escaped. Indeed, the ordinary vagrancy and apprenticeship laws now in force in some of the New England States (slightly modified perhaps) could be so administered and enforced upon the blacks in South Carolina as to keep them in practical slavery. They could, while bearing the name of freeman, be legally subjected to all the oppressive features of serfdom, peonage, and feudalism combined, without possessing the right to claim, much less the power to exact, any of the prerogatives and amenities belonging to either of those systems of human bondage. All this could be done without violating the letter of the emancipation proclamation; no argument is necessary to prove that it would be a total submission of its spirit. Even upon the presumption that the whites, when again clothed with civil authority, would be influenced by a sincere desire to enforce the emancipation proclamation, and organize free labor upon a wise and just basis, it would seem injudicious to intrust them with unlimited power, which might be wielded to the injury of both races until the prejudices and animosities which generated the rebellion and gave it life and vigor have had time to subside. Few men have any clear conception of what the general good at the present time requires in the way of State legislation. A thousand vague theories are floating upon the public mind.

The evils which we would have to fear from an immediate re-establishment of civil government would be not only hasty and ignorant but excessive legislation. While there may be wide differences of opinion as to which is the greater of these two evils *per se*, I am free to express my belief that one or the other of them would be very likely to follow the immediate restoration of civil government, and that it would be not only injudicious in itself but productive of prospective harm, to whites as well as blacks, to place the former in a position where a community of feeling, the promptings of traditional teachings, and the instincts of self-interest and self-preservation, would so strongly tempt them to make a choice. I believe that a respectable majority of the most intelligent whites would cordially aid any policy calculated, in their opinion, to secure the greatest good of the greatest number, blacks included, but I do not regard them as yet in a condition to exercise an unbiassed judgment in this matter.

Inasmuch as very few of them are yet ready to admit the practicability of ameliorating the condition of the black race to any considerable extent, they would not be likely at the present time to devise a wise system of free black labor. Neither would they be zealous and hopeful co-laborers in such a system if desired by others.

I have spoken of the contract system which has been inaugurated by the military authorities throughout the State as working smoothly and satisfactorily. This statement should, of course, be taken with some limitation. It was inaugurated as an expedient under the pressure of stringent necessity at a time when labor was in a greatly disorganized state, and there was manifest danger that the crops, already planted, would be lost for want of cultivation. Many of the negroes, but more especially the able-bodied ones and those possessing no strong family ties, had, under the novel impulses of freedom, left the plantation where they had been laboring through the planting season, and flocked to the nearest military post, becoming a useless and expensive burden upon our hands. Very many plantations, under extensive cultivation, were entirely abandoned. At places remote from military posts, and that had never been visited by our troops, this exodus did not take place so extensively or to a degree threatening a very general loss of crops. The negroes were retained partly through ignorance or uncertainty of their rights and partly through fear of their former masters and the severe discipline unlawfully enforced by them.

Under the assurance that they were free, that they would be protected in the enjoyment of their freedom and the fruits of their labor, but would not be supported in idleness by the government so long as labor could be procured, the flow of negroes into the towns and military posts was stopped, and most of them already accumulated there were induced to return to the plantations and resume work under contracts to be approved and enforced by the military authorities. Both planters and negroes very generally, and apparently quite willingly, fell into this plan as the best that could be improvised. Although there have been many instances of violation of contracts, (more frequently, I think, by the black than by the white,) and although the plan possesses many defects, and is not calculated to develop all the advantages and benefits of a wise free-labor system. I am not prepared to recommend any material modification of it, or anything to replace it, at least for several months to come.

For reasons already suggested I believe that the restoration of civil power that would take the control of this question out of the hands of the United States authorities (whether exercised through the military authorities or through the Freedmen's Bureau) would, instead of removing existing evils, be almost certain to augment them.

Very respectfully, your obedient servant,

Q.A. GILLMORE,*Major General.*

General CARL SCHURZ, *Charleston, S.C.*

No. 4.

Charleston, South Carolina, *July* 25, 1865.

General: Since handing you my letter of yesterday I have read a speech reported to have been delivered in Greenville, South Carolina, on the 3d instant.

I have judged of Mr. Perry by reports of others, but as I now have an opportunity from his own lips of knowing his opinions, I must request that you will cross out that portion of my letter referring to him.

Very respectfully, your obedient servant,

JOHN P. HATCH,*Brevet Major General, Commanding.*

Major General CARL SCHURZ.

HEADQUARTERS MILITARY DISTRICT OF CHARLESTON,

Charleston, South Carolina, July 24, 1865.

General: In answer to your question as to the disposition of the people being such as to justify their speedy return to the control of political power, I would say no.

Many portions of the State have not yet been visited by our troops, and in other parts not long enough occupied to encourage the formation of a new party, disposed to throw off the old party rulers, who, after thirty years preaching sedition, succeeded in carrying their point and forcing the people into rebellion.

Were elections to be held now, the old leaders already organized would carry everything by the force of their organization. I would say delay action, pardon only such as the governor can recommend, and let him only recommend such as he feels confident will support the views of the government. Men who supported nullification in thirty-two, and have upheld the doctrine of States' rights since, should not be pardoned; they cannot learn new ways. I have read with care the published proceedings of every public meeting held in this State, and have observed that not one single resolution has yet been passed in which the absolute freedom of the colored man was recognized, or the doctrine of the right of secession disavowed. Why is this? Because the old leaders have managed the meetings, and they cannot see that a new order of things exists. They still hope to obtain control of the State, and then to pass laws with reference to the colored people which shall virtually re-establish slavery; and although they look upon secession as at present hopeless, a future war may enable them to again raise the standard.

You ask what signs do they show of a disposition to educate the blacks for the new position they are to occupy? This is a question that has so far been but little discussed. No education, except as to their religious duties, was formerly allowed, and this only to make them contented in their position of servitude. Whilst thoroughly instructed in the injunction, "servants obey your masters," adultery was not only winked at, but, unfortunately, in too many cases practically recommended. A few gentlemen have said to me that they were willing to have the blacks taught to read and write, but little interest appears to be felt on the subject.

With reference to the benefit to be derived by the general government by delaying the formation for the present of a State government, I will be brief. It will discourage the old leaders who are anxious to seize immediately the reins of power. It will, by allowing time for discussion, give the people an opportunity to become acquainted with subjects they have heretofore trusted to their leaders. Wherever our troops go, discussion follows, and it would be best that the people should not commit themselves to a line of policy, they have not had time to examine and decide upon coolly. It will give the young men ambitious of rising opportunity for organizing on a new platform a party which, assisted by the government, can quiet forever the questions which have made the State of South Carolina a thorn in the side of the Union. These young men, many of whom have served in the army, take a practical view of their present condition that the old stay-at-homes cannot be brought to understand. Give them time and support and they will do the work required of them. Their long absence has made it necessary to become acquainted with the people; but they will be listened to as men who have honestly fought in a cause which has failed, and will be respected for as honestly coming out in support of the now only reasonable chance of a peaceful government for the future.

Where our troops have been the longest time stationed we have the most friends; and were the people thoroughly convinced that the government (until they have shown a disposition to unite heartily in its support) is determined not to give them a State government, the change would go on much more rapidly.

The selection of Governor Perry was most fortunate. I know of no other man in South Carolina who could have filled the position.

I remain, general, very respectfully, your obedient servant,

JNO. P. HATCH,*Brevet Major General Commanding*.

General CARL SCHURZ.

No. 5.

Charleston, S.C., *July* 24, 1865.

General: In compliance with your verbal request, made at our interview this a.m., to express to you my opinions and impressions regarding the status of the people of South Carolina, and of such others of the insurrectionary States with whom I have come in contact, respecting a return to their allegiance to the federal government, and a willingness on their part to sustain and support the same in its efforts to restore and accomplish the actual union of the States, and also their probable adhesion to the several acts and proclamations which have been enacted and promulgated by the legislative and executive branches of the government, I beg to reply, that, as an officer of one of the departments, I have been enabled by constant intercourse with large numbers of this people to form an approximate estimate of the nature of their loyalty, and also to gain a knowledge of the prejudices which remain with them towards the forces, military and political, which have prevailed against them after the struggle of the last four years, and established the integrity and power of the republic.

Whatever may be said upon the abstract question of voluntary or forcible State secession, the defeat of the insurrectionary forces has been so perfect and complete, that the most defiant have already avowed their allegiance to the national government. The first experience of the insurgents is a complete submission, followed by a promise to abstain from all further acts of rebellion—in fact, the nucleus of their loyalty is necessity, while perhaps some with still a sentiment of loyalty in their hearts for the old flag turn back, like the prodigal, with tearful eyes, wasted means, and exhausted energies.

At the present time there can be but few loyal men in the State of South Carolina who, through evil and good report, have withstood the wiles of secession. South Carolina has been sown broadcast for the last thirty years with every conceivable form of literature which taught her children the divine right of State sovereignty, carrying with it all its accompanying evils. The sovereign State of South Carolina in her imperial majesty looked down upon the republic itself, and only through a grand condescension, remained to supervise and balance the power which, when not controlling, she had sworn to destroy. The works of Calhoun were the necessary companion of every man of culture and education. They were by no means confined to the libraries of the economist and politician. When the national troops pillaged the houses and deserted buildings of Charleston, the streets were strewn with the pamphlets, sermons and essays of politicians, clergymen, and belles-lettres scholars, all promulgating, according to the ability and tastes of their several authors, the rights of the sovereign State. No public occasion passed by which did not witness an assertion of these rights, and the gauntlet of defiance was ever upon the ground.

It is the loyalty of such a people that we have to consider. As a people the South Carolinians are brave and generous in certain directions. In their cities there is great culture, and many of the citizens are persons of refinement, education and taste. The educated classes are well versed in the history of our country, and many have an intimate knowledge of the varied story of political parties. But from the lowest to the highest classes of the white population there is an instinctive dread of the negro and an utter abhorrence of any doctrine which argues an ultimate improvement of his condition beyond that of the merest chattel laborer.

The first proposition made by the southerner on all occasions of discussion is, that the emancipation proclamation of the President was a grievous error from every point of view; that in the settlement of the various questions arising from the insurrection, the national government assumes a responsibility which belongs to the several States, and now that the supremacy of the general government is established, and the prospect of a resuscitation, rehabilitation, reconstruction, or simple assertion of the legislative and executive powers of the separate States, a lingering hope yet remains with many, that although African slavery is abolished, the States may yet so legislate as to place the negro in a state of actual peonage and submission to the will of the employer. Therefore, we have combined with a forced and tardy loyalty a lingering hope that such State legislation can be resorted to as will restore the former slave to, as nearly as possible, the condition of involuntary servitude. And the question naturally arises, how long must we wait for a higher and purer expression of fealty to the Union, and for a more intelligent and just appreciation of the question of free colored, labor which the results of the contest have forced upon us?

I am satisfied, that while no efforts must be spared to instil into the minds of the freedmen the necessity of patient labor and endeavor, and a practical knowledge of the responsibilities of their new condition, by a judicious system of education, the white southerner is really the most interesting pupil, and we must all feel a solicitude for his enlightenment.

The principles of liberty have been working for a number of years in our republic, and have secured various great political results. Latterly they have worked with wonderful and rapid effect, and it has ever been by aid of all the forces of education and enlightened commerce between man and man that the progress of true freedom has been hastened and made secure. When the southern planter sees it demonstrated beyond a doubt that the free labor of the black man, properly remunerated, conduces to his pecuniary interests, at that moment he will accept the situation, and not before, unless it is forced upon him; therefore, it is the white southerner that must be educated into a realization of his responsibility in the settlement of these questions, and by a systematic and judicious education of the freedman a citizen will gradually be developed; and the two classes, finding their interests mutual, will soon settle the now vexed question of suffrage. I am firmly of opinion that the government cannot afford to relax its hold upon these States until a loyal press, representing the views of the government, shall disseminate its sentiments broadcast all over this southern land; and when all the avenues and channels of communication shall have been opened, and the policy of the government shall be more easily ascertained and promulgated, and the States, or the citizens thereof in sufficient numbers, shall have avowed by word and act their acceptance of the new order of things, we may then safely consider the expediency of surrendering to each State legislature the duty of framing its necessary constitution and code, and all other adjuncts of civil government. If the form of our government were monarchical, we might be more sanguine of the success of any proposed measure of amnesty, because of the immediate power of the government to suppress summarily any disorder arising from too great leniency; but to delegate to the States themselves the quelling of the tumult which they have themselves raised, is, to say the least, a doubtful experiment. Many thinking Carolinians have said that they preferred that the government should first itself demonstrate the system of free labor, to such an extent that the planter would gladly avail himself of the system and carry it on to its completion.

The presence of a strong military force is still needed in the State of South Carolina to maintain order, and to see that the national laws are respected, as well as to enforce such municipal regulations as the occasion demands. For such service, officers of sound, practical sense should be chosen—men whose appreciation of strict justice both to employer and employee would compensate even for a lack of mere skilful military knowledge; men without the mean prejudices which are the bane of some who wear the insignia of the national service.

I believe that affairs in South Carolina are yet in a very crude state; that outrages are being practiced upon the negro which the military arm should prevent. Doubtless many stories are fabricated or exaggerated, but a calm and candid citizen of Charleston has said: "Is it wonderful that this should be so; that men whose slaves have come at their call, but now demur, hesitate, and perhaps refuse labor or demand certain wages therefor—that such men, smarting under their losses and defeats, should vent their spite upon a race slipping from their power and asserting their newly acquired rights? Is abuse not a natural result?" But time, enlightenment, and the strenuous efforts of the government can prevent much of this.

I am, therefore, convinced that the education of the white and black must go hand in hand together until the system of free labor is so absolutely demonstrated that the interest of the employer will be found in the intelligence, the well-being, and the comfort of the employed. I believe that the great sources of benevolence at the north should still flood this southern land with its bounty—that the national government should encourage each State to receive all the implements of labor, education and comfort which a generous people can bestow, not merely for the benefit of the black freedman, but for the disenthralled white who has grovelled in the darkness of a past age, and who has been, perhaps, the innocent oppressor of a people he may yet serve, and with them enter into the enjoyment of a more glorious freedom than either have ever conceived.

With sentiments of respect and esteem, I beg to remain, general, your obedient servant,

JOHN H. PILSBURY,*Deputy Supervising and Assistant Special Agent Treasury Department.*

Major General CARL SCHURZ, &c., &c., &c.

No. 6.

VIEWS EXPRESSED BY MAJOR GENERAL STEEDMAN IN CONVERSATION WITH CARL SCHURZ.

Augusta, Georgia, *August* 7, 1864.

I have been in command of this department only a month, and can, therefore, not pretend to have as perfect a knowledge of the condition of affairs, and the sentiments of the people of Georgia, as I may have after longer experience. But observations so far made lead me to the following conclusions:

The people of this State, with only a few individual exceptions, are submissive but not loyal.

If intrusted with political power at this time they will in all probability use it as much as possible to escape from the legitimate results of the war. Their political principles, as well as their views on the slavery question, are the same as before the war, and all that can be expected of them is that they will submit to actual necessities from which there is no escape.

The State is quiet, in so far as there is no organised guerilla warfare. Conflicts between whites and blacks are not unfrequent, and in many instances result in bloodshed.

As to the labor question, I believe that the planters of this region have absolutely no conception of what free labor is. I consider them entirely incapable of legislating understandingly upon the subject at the present time.

The organization of labor in this State, especially in the interior, has so far, in most cases, been left to the planters and freedmen themselves, the organization of the Freedmen's Bureau being as yet quite imperfect. A great many contracts have been made between planters and freedmen, some of which were approved by the military authorities and some were not.

General Wilde, the principal agent of the Freedmen's Bureau in this State, is, in my opinion, entirely unfit for the discharge of the duties incumbent upon him. He displays much vigor where it is not wanted, and shows but very little judgment where it is wanted. Until the Freedmen's Bureau will be sufficiently organized in this State I deem it necessary to temporarily intrust the provost marshals, now being stationed all over the State, one to every four counties, with the discharge of its functions, especially as concerns the making of contracts and the adjustment of difficulties between whites and blacks.

I deem it impracticable to refer such difficulties for adjustment to such civil courts as can at present be organized in this State. It would be like leaving each party to decide the case for itself, and would undoubtedly at once result in a free fight. It will be so until the people of this State have a more accurate idea of the rights of the freedmen. The military power is, in my opinion, the only tribunal which, under existing circumstances, can decide difficulties between whites and blacks to the satisfaction of both parties and can make its decisions respected.

As for the restoration of civil power in this State, I apprehend it cannot be done without leading to the necessity of frequent interference on the part of the military until the sentiments of the people of Georgia have undergone a very great change.

This memorandum was read to General Steedman by me and he authorized me to submit it in this form to the President.

C. SCHURZ.

No. 7.

HEADQUARTERS DISTRICT OF COLUMBUS,

Macon, Georgia, August 14, 1885.

General: There are no loyal people in Georgia, except the negroes; nor are there any considerable number who would under any circumstances offer armed resistance to the national authority. An officer, without arms or escort, could arrest any man in the State. But, while their submission is thus complete and universal, it is not a matter of choice, but a stern necessity which they deplore.

If allowed they will readily reorganize their State government and administer it upon correct principles, except in matters pertaining to their former slaves. On this subject they admit the abolition of the institution, and will so frame their constitution, hoping thereby to procure their recognition as a State government, when they will at once, by legislation, reduce the freedmen to a condition worse than slavery. Yet while they will not recognize the rights of their former slaves themselves, they will submit to its full recognition by the national government, which can do just as it pleases and no resistance will be offered. My own clear opinion is, it will have to do everything that may be necessary to secure real practical freedom to the former slaves.

The disturbances at present are chiefly due, I think, to the swarm of vagrants thrown upon society by the disbanding of the rebel armies and the emancipation of the slaves at a season of the year when it is difficult for those who seek to find employment.

After the 1st of January I apprehend no trouble, as the culture of the next crop will absorb all the labor of the country. In the interim a great deal of care and diligence will be required. Hence I recommend the importance of sending men of energy and business capacity to manage the affairs of the Freedmen's Bureau.

I am, general, very respectfully, your obedient servant,

JOHN T. CROXTON,*Brigadier General United States.*

General CARL SCHURZ.

No. 8.

HEADQUARTERS DEPARTMENT OF THE GULF,

New Orleans, June 20, 1865.

Sir: I have the honor to transmit for your consideration a copy of the correspondence between the governor of Louisiana and myself touching the relations between the State and the military authorities in this department.

The instructions upon this subject are, and probably designedly, indefinite. They indicate, however, the acceptance by the President of the constitution of the State, adopted in September, 1864, as the means of re-establishing civil government in the State and the recognition of the governor as his agent in accomplishing this work. The same principle gives validity to such of the State laws as are not in conflict with this constitution, or repealed by congressional legislation, or abrogated by the President's proclamation or orders issued during the rebellion.

This leaves many questions undetermined, except so far as they are settled by the law of nations and the laws of war, so far as my authority extends. I will turn over all such questions to the State government; and in cases that do not come within the legitimate authority of a military commander, will report them for such action as his excellency the President, or the War Department, may think proper to adopt.

I have had a very free conference with the governor upon this subject, and I believe that he concurs with me that the course I have indicated in the correspondence with him is not only the legal but the only course that will avoid the appeals to the local courts by interested or designing men, which are now dividing those who profess to be working for the same object—the re-establishment of civil authority throughout the State.

Then, in addition, many questions, in which the interests of the government are directly involved, or in which the relations of the general government to the States, as affected by the rebellion, are left unsettled by any adequate legislation. I do not think it will be wise to commit any of these questions, either directly or indirectly, to the jurisdiction of the State or other local courts, and will not so commit them unless instructed to do so.

It is very possible that in the varied and complicated questions that will come up there may be differences of opinion between the governor and myself, but there shall be no discord of action, and I will give to his efforts the fullest support in my power.

I have the honor to be, very respectfully, sir,

E.R.S. CANBY,*Major General Commanding*.

The SECRETARY OF WAR, *Washington, D.C.*

Official copy:

R. DES ANGES,*Major, A.A.G.*

STATE OF LOUISIANA, EXECUTIVE DEPARTMENT,

New Orleans, June 10, 1865.

General: There is a class of officers holding and exercising the duties of civil officers in this State who claim to hold their right to the same by virtue of deriving their appointment from military authority exercised either by General Shepley as military governor, or Michael Hahn, and in some cases by Major General Banks, commander of the department of the Gulf. These men resist my power to remove on the ground that I am not clothed with military power, although the offices they fill are strictly civil offices, and the power of appointing to the same to fill vacancies (which constructively exist until the office is filled according to law) is one of my prerogatives as civil governor. To dispossess these men by legal process involves delay and trouble. Many of the persons so holding office are obnoxious to the charges of official misconduct and of obstructing my efforts to re-establish civil government.

For the purpose, therefore, of settling the question, and relieving the civil government of the State from the obstructions to its progress caused by the opposition of these men, I would respectfully suggest to you, general, the expediency of your issuing an order revoking all appointments made by military or semi-military authority to civil offices in this State prior to the 4th of March, 1865, the date on which I assumed the duties of governor. I fix that date because it is only since that period the governor has been confined to strictly civil powers, and what military power has been exercised since in appointments to office has been from necessity and was unavoidable.

I throw out these suggestions, general, for your consideration. On my recent visit to the capital I had full and free conversation with President Johnson on the subject of reorganizing civil government in Louisiana, and while deprecating the interference of military power in civil government beyond the point of actual necessity, yet he fully appreciated the difficulties of my position, and assured me that I should be sustained by him in all necessary and legal measures to organize and uphold civil government.

I have the honor to be, very respectfully, &c.,

J. MADISON WELLS,*Governor of Louisiana.*

Major General E.R.S. CANBY, *Commanding Department of the Gulf.*

Official copy:

R. DES ANGES,*Major, A.A.G.*

HEADQUARTERS DEPARTMENT OF THE GULF,

New Orleans, June 19, 1865.

Sir: I have the honor to acknowledge the receipt of your communication of the 10th instant, asking me to revoke all appointments made by military or semi-military authority to civil offices in the State prior to the 4th of March, 1865.

I have given this subject the attention and serious consideration which its importance demands, and I find it complicated not only with the private and public interests of the people and State of Louisiana, but also with the direct interests of the government of the United States, or with the obligations imposed upon the government by the condition of the country or by the antecedent exercise of lawful military authority. To the extent that these considerations obtain they are controlling considerations, and I cannot find that I have any authority to delegate the duties devolved upon me by my official position, or to evade the responsibilities which it imposes. I venture the suggestion, also, that the evils complained of, and which are so apparent and painful to all who are interested in the restoration of civil authority, will scarcely be obtained by the course you recommend, but will, in my judgment, give rise to complications that will embarrass not only the State but the general government.

All officers who hold their offices by the tenure of military appointment are subject to military authority and control, and will not be permitted to interfere in any manner whatever with the exercise of functions that have been committed to you as governor of Louisiana. If they are obnoxious to the charge of misconduct in office, or of obstructing you in your efforts to re-establish civil government, they will, upon your recommendation, be removed. If, under the constitution and laws of the State, the power of appointment resides in the governor, my duty will be ended by vacating the appointment. If the office is elective, the military appointment will be cancelled so soon as the successor is elected and qualified. In the alternative cases the removal will be made, and successors recommended by you, and against whom there are no disqualifying charges, will be appointed.

This, in my judgment, is the only course which will remove all legal objections, or even legal quibbles.

I desire to divest myself as soon as possible of all questions of civil administration, and will separate, as soon and as far as I can, all such questions from those that are purely military in their character, and commit them to the care of the proper officers of the civil government.

Some of these questions are complicated in their character, and involve not only private and public interests, but the faith of the national government; originating in the legal exercise of military authority, they can only be determined by the same authority.

There is another consideration, not directly but incidentally involved in the subject of your communication, to which I have the honor to invite your attention. The results of the past four years have worked many changes both as to institutions and individuals within the insurrectionary States, giving to some of the interests involved an absolutely national character, and in others leaving the relations between the general government and the States undetermined. So far as Congress has legislated upon these subjects, it has placed them under the direct control of the general government, and under the laws of nations and laws of war the same principle applies to the other subject. Until Congress has legislated upon this subject, or until Executive authority sanctions it, no questions of this character will be committed to the jurisdiction of the local courts.

I make these suggestions to you for the reason that I have already found a strong disposition in some sections of the country to forestall the action of the general government by bringing these subjects more or less directly under the control of the local courts; and I have neither the authority nor the disposition to establish precedents that may possibly embarrass the future action of the government.

I take this occasion to assure your excellency of my hearty co-operation in your efforts to re-establish civil government, and in any measures that may be undertaken for the benefit of the State or people of Louisiana.

I shall be happy at all times to confer with you upon any of these subjects, and to give you, whenever necessary, any assistance that you may require.

I have the honor to be, very respectfully, your obedient servant,

E.R.S. CANBY,*Major General, Commanding*.

His Excellency the GOVERNOR OF LOUISIANA, *New Orleans, La*.

Official copy:

R. DES ANGES,*Major, A.A.G.*

STATE OF LOUISIANA, EXECUTIVE DEPARTMENT,

New Orleans, June 23, 1865.

General: I have the honor to acknowledge the receipt of your communication of the 16th instant, in answer to mine of the 13th, relating to the expediency of your revoking the appointment of all civil officers in the State made by military or semi-military authority. I desire to state that your views and suggestions, as regards your duty and proper course of action in the premises, are entirely satisfactory to me. For the care you have bestowed on the subject, and the earnest disposition you evince to do all in your power to promote the interests of civil government in this unfortunate State, by co-operating with and sustaining me in all legitimate measures to that end, I beg to return you, not only my own thanks, but I feel authorized to speak for the great mass of our fellow-citizens, and to include them in the same category.

With high respect, I subscribe myself, your obedient servant,

J. MADISON WELLS,*Governor of Louisiana*.

Major General E.R.S. CANBY,*Commanding Department of the Gulf*.

Official copy:

R. DES ANGES,*Major, A.A.G.*

HEADQUARTERS DEPARTMENT OF LOUISIANA,

New Orleans, September 8, 1865.

Sir: In compliance with your request, I have the honor to submit some remarks upon the civil government of Louisiana, and its relation to the military administration of this department. These relations are more anomalous and complicated, probably, than in any other insurrectionary State, and it will be useful in considering these questions to bear in mind the changes that have occurred since the occupation of this city by the Union forces. These are, briefly—

1. The military administration of the commander of the department of the Gulf, Major General Butler.

2. The military government, of which Brigadier General Shepley was the executive, by appointment of the President.

3. The provisional government, of which the Hon. M. Hahn was the executive, by appointment of the President, upon nomination by the people at an election held under military authority.

4. The constitutional government, organized under the constitution adopted by the convention in July, 1864, and ratified by the people at an election held in September of that year. Of this government the Hon. J.M. Wells is the present executive.

This government has not yet been recognized by Congress, and its relation to the military authority of the department has never been clearly defined. Being restrained by constitutional limitations, its powers are necessarily imperfect, and it is frequently necessary to supplant them by military authority. Many of the civil officers still hold their positions by the tenure of military appointments holding over until elections can be held under the constitution. These appointments may be vacated by the commander of the department, and, if under the constitution the power of appointment reside in the governor, be filled by him: if it does not, the appointment must be filled by the military commander. Very few removals and no appointments have been made by me during my command of the department; but the governor has been advised that all persons holding office by the tenure of military appointment were subject to military supervision and control, and would not be permitted to interfere in the duties committed to him by the President of restoring "civil authority in the State of Louisiana;" that upon his recommendation, and for *cause*, such officers would be removed; and if the power of appointment was not under the constitution vested in him, the appointment would be made by the department commander, if, upon his recommendation, there was no disqualifying exception.

The instructions to the military commanders, in relation to the previous governments, were general, and I believe explicit; but, as their application passed away with the existence of these governments, it is not necessary to refer to them here. Those that relate to the constitutional government are very brief, so far, at least, as they have reached me. In a confidential communication from his excellency to the late President, in which he deprecated, in strong terms, any military interferences, and expressed very freely his own views and wishes, he concluded by saying that "the military must be judge and master so long as the necessity for the military remains;" and, in my instructions from the War Department, of May 28, 1865, the Secretary of War says: "The President directs me to express his wish that the military authorities render all proper assistance to the civil authorities in control in the State of Louisiana, and not to interfere with its action further than it may be necessary for the peace and security of the department."

These directions and wishes have been conclusive, and I have given to the civil authorities whatever support and assistance they required, and have abstained from any interference with questions of civil or local State administration, except when it was necessary to protect the freedmen in their newly acquired rights, and to prevent the local courts from assuming jurisdiction in cases where, of law and of right, the jurisdiction belongs inclusively to the United States courts or United States authorities. With the appointments made by the governor I have no right to interfere unless the appointees are disqualified by coming under some one of the exceptions made by the President in his proclamation of May 29, 1865, or, (as in one or two instances that have occurred,) in the case of double appointments to the same office, when a conflict might endanger the peace and security of the department.

My personal and official intercourse with the governor has been of the most cordial character. I have had no reason to distrust his wish and intention to carry out the views of the President. I do distrust both the loyalty and the honesty (political) of some of his advisers, and I look with apprehension upon many of the appointments made under these influences during the past two months. The feeling and temper of that part of the population of Louisiana which was actively engaged in or sympathized with the rebellion have also materially changed within that period.

The political and commercial combinations against the north are gaining in strength and confidence every day. Political, sectional, and local questions, that I had hoped were buried with the dead of the past four years, are revived. Independent sovereignty, State rights, and nullification, where the power to nullify is revoked, are openly discussed. It may be that these are only ordinary political discussions, and that I attach undue importance to them from the fact that I have never before been so intimately in contact with them; but, to my judgment, they indicate very clearly that it will not be wise or prudent to commit any question involving the paramount supremacy of the government of the United States to the States that have been in insurrection until the whole subject of restoration has been definitively and satisfactorily adjusted.

Before leaving this subject I think it proper to invite your attention to the position of a part of the colored population of this State. By the President's proclamation of January 1, 1863, certain parishes in this State (thirteen in number) were excepted from its provisions—the condition of the negroes as to slavery remaining unchanged until they were emancipated by the constitution of 1864. If this constitution should be rejected (the State of Louisiana not admitted under it) the legal condition of these people will be that of slavery until this defect can be cured by future action.

The government of the city of New Orleans, although administered by citizens, derives its authority from military orders, and its offices have always been under the supervision and control of the commander of the department, or of the military governor of the State. The present mayor was appointed by Major General Hurlbut, removed by Major General Banks, and reinstated by myself. Under the constitution and laws of the State the principal city offices are elective, but the time has not yet been reached when an election for these offices should be held. Although standing in very different relations from the State government, I have thought it proper to apply the same rule, and have not interfered with its administration except so far as might be necessary to protect the interests of the government, or to prevent the appointment to offices of persons excepted by the President's proclamation.

Very respectfully, your obedient servant,

ED. R.S. CANBY,*Major General, Commanding*.

Major General CARL SCHURZ*United States Volunteers, New Orleans*.

No. 9.

STATEMENT OF GENERAL THOMAS KILBY SMITH.

New Orleans, *September* 14, 1865.

I have been in command of the southern district of Alabama since the commencement of General Canby's expedition against Mobile, and have been in command of the district and post of Mobile, with headquarters at Mobile, from June until the 25th of August, and relinquished command of the post on September 4. During my sojourn

I have become familiar with the character and temper of the people of all of southern Alabama.

It is my opinion that with the exception of a small minority, the people of Mobile and southern Alabama are disloyal in their sentiments and hostile to what they call the United States, and that a great many of them are still inspired with a hope that at some future time the "confederacy,"as they style it, will be restored to independence.

In corroboration of this assertion, I might state that in conversation with me Bishop Wilmer, of the diocese of Alabama, (Episcopal), stated that to be his belief; that when I urged upon him the propriety of restoring to the litany of his church that prayer which includes the prayer for the President of the United States, the whole of which he had ordered his rectors to expunge, he refused, first, upon the ground that he could not pray for a continuance of martial law; and secondly, that he would stultify himself in the event of Alabama and the southern confederacy regaining their independence. This was on the 17th of June. This man exercises a widespread influence in the State, and his sentiments are those of a large proportion of what is called the better class of people, and particularly the women. Hence the representatives of the United States flag are barely tolerated. They are not welcome among the people in any classes of society. There is always a smothered hatred of the uniform and the flag. Nor is this confined to the military, but extends to all classes who, representing northern interests, seek advancement in trade, commerce, and the liberal professions, or who, coming from the North, propose to locate in the South.

The men who compose the convention do, in my opinion, not represent the people of Alabama, because the people had no voice in their election. I speak with assurance on this subject, because I have witnessed the proceedings in my district. I do not desire to reflect upon the personnel of the delegation from Mobile, which is composed of clever and honorable men, but whatever may be their political course, they will not act as the true representatives of the sentiments and feelings of the people.

I desire in this connexion to refer to the statements of Captain Poillon, which you have submitted to me, and to indorse the entire truthfulness thereof. I have known Captain Poillon intimately, and have been intimately acquainted with the proceedings of the Freedmen's Bureau. Many of the facts stated by Captain Poillon I know of my own personal knowledge, and all I have examined into and believe.

On the 4th of July I permitted in Mobile a procession of the freedmen, the only class of people in Mobile who craved of me the privilege of celebrating the anniversary of the Declaration of Independence. Six thousand well-dressed and orderly colored people, escorted by two regiments of colored troops, paraded the streets, assembled in the public squares, and were addressed in patriotic speeches by orators of their own race and color. These orators counselled them to labor and to wait. This procession and these orations were the signal for a storm of abuse upon the military and the freedmen and their friends, fulminated from the street corners by the then mayor of the city and his common council and in the daily newspapers, and was the signal for the hirelings of the former slave power to hound down, persecute, and destroy the industrious and inoffensive negro. These men were found for the most part in the police of the city, acting under the direction of the mayor, R.H. Hough, since removed. The enormities committed by these policemen were fearful. Within my own knowledge colored girls seized upon the streets had to take their choice between submitting to outrage on the part of the policemen or incarceration in the guard-house. These men, having mostly been negro drivers and professional negro whippers, were fitting tools for the work in hand. Threats of and attempts at assassination were made against myself. Threats were made to destroy all school-houses in which colored children were taught, and in two instances they were fired. The same threats were made against all churches in which colored people assembled to worship, and one of them burned. Continued threats of assassination were made against the colored preachers, and one of them is now under special guard by order of Major General Wood. When Mayor Hough was appealed to by this man for protection, he was heard to say that no one connected with the procession of the 4th of July need to come into his court, and that their complaints would not be considered. Although Mayor Hough has been removed, a large majority of these policemen are still in office. Mayor Forsyth has promised to reform this matter. It is proper to state that he was put in office by order of Governor Parsons, having twice been beaten at popular elections for the mayoralty by Mr. Hough. This gives an indication of what will result when the office will again be filled by a popular election.

The freedmen and colored people of Mobile are, as a general thing, orderly, quiet, industrious, and well dressed, with an earnest desire to learn and to fit themselves for their new status. My last report from the school commissioners of the colored schools of Mobile, made on the 28th of July, showed 986 pupils in daily attendance. They give no cause for the wholesale charges made against them of insurrection, lawlessness, and hostility against their former masters or the whites generally. On the contrary, they are perfectly docile and amenable to the laws, and their leaders and popular teachers of their own color continually counsel them to industry and effort to secure their living in an honorable way. They had collected from themselves up to the 1st of August upwards of $5,000 for their own eleemosynary institutions, and I know of many noble instances where the former slave has devoted the proceeds of his own industry to the maintenance of his former master or mistress in distress. Yet, in the face of these facts, one of the most intelligent and high-bred ladies of Mobile, having had silver plate stolen from her more than two years ago, and having, upon affidavit, secured the incarceration of two of her former slaves whom she suspected of the theft, came to me in my official capacity, and asked my order to have them whipped and tortured into a confession of the crime charged and the participants in it. This lady was surprised when I informed her that the days of the rack and the thumbscrew were passed, and, though pious, well bred, and a member of the church, thought it a hardship that a negro might not be whipped or tortured till he would confess what he *might* know about a robbery, although not even a *prima facie* case existed against him, or that sort of evidence that would induce a grand jury to indict. I offer this as an instance of the feeling that exists in all classes against the negro, and their inability to realize that he is a free man and entitled to the rights of citizenship.

With regard to municipal law in the State of Alabama, its administration is a farce. The ministers of the law themselves are too often desperadoes and engaged in the perpetration of the very crime they are sent forth to prohibit or to punish. Without the aid of the bayonets of the United States Alabama is an anarchy. The best men of Alabama have either shed their blood in the late war, emigrated, or become wholly incapacitated by their former action from now taking part in the government of the State. The more sensible portion of the people tremble at the idea of the military force being eliminated, for, whatever may be their hatred of the United States soldier, in him they find their safety.

It has not been my lot to command to any great extent colored troops. I have had ample opportunity, however, of observing them in Tennessee, Mississippi, Louisiana, and Alabama, and, comparing them with white troops, I unhesitatingly say that they make as good soldiers. The two colored regiments under my command in Mobile were noted for their discipline and perfection of drill, and between those troops and the citizens of Mobile no trouble arose until after the proclamation of the provisional governor, when it became necessary to arm them going to and from their fatigue duty, because they were hustled from the sidewalk by infuriated citizens, who, carrying out the principles enunciated by Mayor Hough and the common council and the newspapers heretofore alluded to, sought to incite mob. I have said that a great deal of the trouble alluded to in the government of the State has arisen since the appointment and proclamation of the provisional governor. The people of Alabama then believed they were relieved from coercion of the United States and restored to State government, and that having rid themselves of the bayonets, they might assume the reins, which they attempted to do in the manner above described. When I speak of the people I mean the masses, those that we call the populace. There are thinking, intelligent men in Alabama, as elsewhere, who understand and appreciate the true condition of affairs. But these men, for the most part, are timid and retiring, unwilling to take the lead, and even when subjected to outrage, robbery, and pillage by their fellow-citizens, refrain from testifying, and prefer to put up with the indignity rather than incur an unpopularity that may cost their lives. Hence there is danger of the mob spirit running riot and rampant through the land, only kept under by our forces.

That there are organized bands throughout the country who, as guerillas or banditti, now still keep up their organization, with a view to further troubles in a larger arena, I have no doubt, though, of course, I have no positive testimony. But this I know, that agents in Mobile have been employed to transmit ammunition in large packages to the interior. One man by the name of Dieterich is now incarcerated in the military prison at Mobile charged with this offence. A detective was sent to purchase powder of him, who represented himself to be a guerilla, and that he proposed to take it out to his band. He bought $25 worth the first, and $25 worth the second day, and made a contract for larger quantities. Deputations of citizens waited upon me from time to time to advise me that these bands were in being, and that they were in imminent peril upon their avowing their intentions to take the oath of allegiance, or evincing in any other way their loyalty to the government; and yet these men, while they claimed the protection of the military, were unwilling to reveal the names of the conspirators. I have seen General Wood's statement, which is true in all particulars so far as my own observation goes, and I have had even far better opportunities than General Wood of knowing the character of the people he now protects, and while protecting, is ignored socially and damned politically; for it is a noticeable fact that, after a sojourn in Mobile of upwards of six weeks in command of the State, during part of which time he was ill and suffering, he received but one call socially out of a community heretofore considered one of the most opulent, refined, and hospitable of all the maritime cities of the South, the favorite home of the officers of the army and the navy in by-gone days; and that one call from General Longstreet, who was simply in transitu.

THOMAS KILBY SMITH,*Brigadier General United States Volunteers.*

No. 10.

HEADQUARTERS NORTHERN DISTRICT OF MISSISSIPPI,

Jackson, Mississippi, August 27, 1865.

General: The northern district of Mississippi embraces that portion of the
State north of southern boundary lines of Clark, Jasper, Smith, Simpson,
and Hinds counties, except the six counties (Warren, Yazoo, Issaquena, Washington, Sunflower, and Bolivar) constituting the western district.

The entire railroad system of the State is within my district, and although these lines of communication were seriously injured during the war, steps are being taken everywhere to repair them as fast as means can be procured. The break of thirty-five miles on the Southern (Vicksburg Mendrain) railroad, between Big Black and Jackson, is, by authority of the department commander, being repaired by my troops, and will be ready for operation in a few days.

The thirty-six counties under my military control constitute the richest portion of the State, the soil being the most available for agricultural purposes, cotton (Upland) being the great staple, while in the eastern counties, in the valley of the upper Tombigbee, corn was grown very extensively, the largest proportion of the usual demand in the State for this cereal being supplied from that section.

The war and its consequences have laid waste nearly all the old fields, only a few acres were cultivated this year to raise sufficient corn for the immediate use of the respective families and the small amount of stock they succeeded in retaining after the many raids and campaigns which took place in the State of Mississippi. Even these attempts will only prove partially successful, for, although the final suppression of the rebellion was evident for the past two years, the collapse which followed the surrender of the rebel armies brought with it all the consequences of an unforeseen surprise. The people had in no way provided for this contingency, and of course became very restive, when all property which they had so long been accustomed to look upon as their own suddenly assumed a doubtful character. Their "slaves" began to wander off and left their masters, and those growing crops, which could only be matured and gathered by the labor of the former slaves. For the first time the people saw and appreciated the extreme poverty into which they were thrown by the consequences of the rebellion, and it will hardly surprise any one familiar with human nature, that people in good standing before the war should resort to all kinds of schemes, even disreputable ones, to retrieve their broken fortunes.

Theft and every species of crime became matters of every-day occurrence. The large amount of government cotton in all parts of the State proved a welcome objective point for every description of lawlessness. Absent owners of cotton were looked upon by these people as public enemies and became the victims of their (mostly illegal) speculations during the rebellion. This state of affairs continued for some time in all portions of the district not occupied by United States troops, and were in most instances accompanied by outrages and even murder perpetrated on the persons of the late "slaves."

As soon as a sufficient number of troops could be brought into the district, I placed garrisons at such points as would, as far as my means permitted, give me control of almost every county. By the adoption of this system I succeeded in preventing this wholesale system of thieving, and a portion of the stolen goods was recovered and returned to the owners, while the outrages on negroes and Union men sensibly diminished.

From the beginning of the occupation until a recent period only five (5) cases of murder or attempted murder occurred in my whole district, and I had no apprehension but what I would be able to stop the recurrence of such crimes effectually. The troops at my disposal were, however, sadly reduced by the recent muster-out of cavalry and infantry regiments.

Attala and Holmes counties were, on my arrival, the theatre of the greatest outrages; the interior of these counties was garrisoned by cavalry detachments, which communicated with the infantry posts along the railroad, and they (the cavalry) were most effective in preventing crime and arresting malefactors, thus affording the much needed protection to peaceable inhabitants. The cavalry garrisons, however, were withdrawn about two (2) weeks ago for muster-out, and since that time four (4) murders, two of white Union men and two of negroes, have been reported to me from Attala county. The infantry garrisons along the railroad are actively endeavoring to effect the arrest of the suspected parties, but the chances of success are exceedingly doubtful, as only mounted troops can be successfully used for that purpose.

There is no doubt whatever that the state of affairs would be intolerable for all Union men, all recent immigrants from the north; and all negroes, the moment the protection of the United States troops was withdrawn.

In support of this opinion permit me to make a few remarks about the citizens. Although the people, as a general thing, are very anxious for peace, and for the restoration of law and order, they hardly realize the great social change brought about by the war. They all know that slavery, in the form in which it existed before the war, and in which they idolized it, is at an end; but these former slave owners are very loth to realize the new relative positions of employer and employee, and all kinds of plans for "new systems of labor" are under constant discussion. The principal feature of all plans proposed is that the labor of the nominally freedmen should be secured to their old masters without risk of interruption or change. This desire is very natural in an agricultural community, which has been left for generations in the undisturbed enjoyment of all the comforts and independent luxuries induced by a system where the laborer and not the labor was a marketable commodity. It is, however, just as natural that those most interested should differ essentially with the slaveholder on that point. They naturally claim that they (the laborers) have by the war and its consequences gained the right to hire out their labor to whomsoever they please, and to change their relations so as to insure for themselves the best possible remuneration. The defenders and protectors of this last position are principally the agents of the Freedmen's Bureau and the co-operating military forces, and of course they are not liked. Their decisions and rules are looked upon by former slaveholders, and late rebels generally, as the commands of a usurper and a tyrant, and they will continue to be so regarded until a general resumption of agricultural pursuits shall have brought about a practical solution o this much vexed question, which, "in abstracts," is rather perplexing. I think that if each party is compelled to remain within the bounds of justice and equity by the presence of a neutral force, i.e.United States troops, one year's experience will assign to both employers and employees their respective relative positions.

As soon as this most desirable end is attained, and the labor of the southern States regenerated on a real free labor basis, and thus brought into harmony with the other portions of the Union, the exclusive and peculiar notions of the southern gentlemen, so much at variance with the views of the North, will have no longer any cause to exist, and the southern people will be glad to recognize the American nationality without reserve, and without the sectional limitation of geographical linos.

I desire to affirm that loyalty and patriotism have not as yet gained any solid foundation among the white population of the States, and such cannot be expected until the relations between employers and laborers have become a fixed and acknowledged fact; then, and not before, will a feeling of contentment and loyalty replace the now prevalent bitterness and recriminations.

The taking of the amnesty oath has not changed the late rebels (and there are hardly any white people here who have not been rebels) into loyal citizens. It was considered and looked upon as an act of expediency and necessity to enable them to build their shattered and broken fortunes up again.

The elevating feeling of true patriotism will return with the smile of prosperity, and it should be the duty of all men to co-operate together in securing that end. This can only be done by securing for the black race also a state of prosperity. This race, which at present furnishes the only labor in the State, must be prevented from becoming a wandering and restless people, and they must be taught to become steady citizens. This will best be accomplished by guaranteeing them the right to acquire property and to become freeholders, with protection in the undisturbed possession of their property. This and a general system of education will work a quicker and more satisfactory change than the most stringent police regulations could ever achieve.

At present the occupancy of the State by the United States troops is the only safeguard for the preservation of peace between the different classes.

I am, general, with great respect, your obedient servant,

P. JOS. OSTERHAUS,*Major General U.S. Vols*.

Major General CARL SCHURZ, *Present*.

No. 11.

STATEMENT OF MAJOR GENERAL CHARLES R. WOODS, COMMANDING DEPARTMENT OF ALABAMA.

Mobile, Ala., *September* 9, 1865.

I do not interfere with civil affairs at all, unless called upon by the governor of the State to assist the civil authorities. There are troops within reach of every county ready to respond to the call of the civil authorities, but there are some counties where the sheriffs and other officers of the law appear to be afraid to execute their warrants, even with the aid of my troops, because the protection the troops might give them is liable to be withdrawn as soon as the duties for which they are called upon are fulfilled, although the troops are continually ready to aid them at short notice.

In many of the counties, where there are no garrisons stationed, the civil authorities are unable or unwilling to carry out the laws. One case has come to my official notice where persons had been arrested on the complaint of citizens living in the country, for stealing, marauding, &c., but when called upon to come down to testify, the complainants declared that they did not know anything about the matter. There being no testimony, the accused parties had to be released. One of those who, by the offenders, was supposed to have made complaint, was, shortly after the release of the accused, found with his throat cut. It appears that in that locality the lawless element predominates, and keeps the rest of the community in fear of having their houses burnt, and of losing their lives. The case mentioned happened in Washington county, about forty miles from this city, up the Alabama river. There is a garrison of four companies at Mount Vernon arsenal, not far from that place, which at all times are ready to render aid to the civil authorities.

I have sent a detachment of troops with an officer of the Freedmen's Bureau into Clark, Washington, Choctaw, and Marengo counties to investigate the reports of harsh treatment of the negroes that had come into the Freedmen's Bureau.

Cotton-stealing is going on quite generally, and on a large scale, wherever there is any cotton, and the civil authorities have completely failed in stopping it. It has been reported to me by citizens that armed bands attack and drive away the watchmen, load the cotton upon wagons, and thus haul it away. No case has come to my knowledge in which such offenders have been brought to punishment. Horse, mule, and cattle stealing is likewise going on on a large scale.

In compliance with instructions from General Thomas, I have issued orders to arrest, and try by military commission, all citizens who are charged with stealing government horses, mules, or other property. No such cases had been taken cognizance of by civil authorities within my knowledge.

As to the treatment of negroes by whites, I would refer to the reports of the Freedmen's Bureau.

I sent out officers to every point in the State designated by the governor, on an average at least two officers to a county, for the purpose of administering the amnesty oath, but owing to a misapprehension on the part of the people, but few were taken before these officers until the governor's second proclamation came out, requiring them to do so, when the oath was administered to a great many.

I have found myself compelled to give one of the papers appearing in this city (the Mobile Daily News) a warning, on account of its publishing sensational articles about impending negro insurrections, believing that they are gotten up without any foundation at all, for the purpose of keeping up an excitement.

CHAS. R. WOODS,*Brevet Major General, Commanding Department of Alabama.*

No. 12.

[General Orders No. 22.]

HEADQUARTERS DEPARTMENT OF MISSISSIPPI,

Vicksburg, Miss., August 24, 1865.

The attention of district commanders is called to a proclamation of the provisional governor of the State of Mississippi, of the 19th instant, which provides for the organization of a military force in each county of the State.

While the general government deems it necessary to maintain its authority here by armed forces, it is important that the powers and duties of the officers commanding should be clearly defined.

The State of Mississippi was one of the first that engaged in the recent rebellion. For more than four years all her energies have been devoted to a war upon our government. At length, from exhaustion, she has been compelled to lay down her arms; but no orders have as yet been received by the military authorities on duty here, indicating that the State has been relieved from the hostile position which she voluntarily assumed towards the United States.

The general government, earnestly desiring to restore the State to its former position, has appointed a provisional governor, with power to call a convention for the accomplishment of that purpose. Upon the military forces devolve the duties of preserving order, and of executing the laws of Congress and the orders of the War Department. The orders defining the rights and privileges to be secured to freedmen meet with opposition in many parts of the State, and the duties devolving upon military officers, in the execution of these orders, are often of a delicate nature. It has certainly been the desire

Civil War Classic Library

of the department commander, and, so far as he has observed, of all officers on duty in the State, to execute these orders in a spirit of conciliation and forbearance, and, while obeying implicitly all instructions of the President and the War Department, to make military rule as little odious as possible to the people. While the military authorities have acted in this spirit, and have been as successful as could have been anticipated, the provisional governor has thought proper, without consultation with the department commander or with any other officer of the United States on duty here, to organize and arm a force in every county, urging the "young men of the State who have so distinguished themselves for gallantry" to respond promptly to his call, meaning, thereby, that class of men who have as yet scarcely laid down the arms with which they have been opposing our government. Such force, if organized as proposed, is to be independent of the military authority now present, and superior in strength to the United States forces on duty in the State. To permit the young men, who have so distinguished themselves, to be armed and organized independently of United States military officers on duty here, and to allow them to operate in counties now garrisoned by colored troops, filled, as many of these men are, not only with prejudice against those troops and against the execution of the orders relative to freedmen, but even against our government itself, would bring about a collision at once, and increase in a ten-fold degree the difficulties that now beset the people. It is to be hoped that the day will soon come when the young men called upon by Governor Sharkey and the colored men now serving the United States will zealously co-operate for the preservation of order and the promotion of the interests of the State and nation. It will be gratifying to the friends of the colored race to have the assurance in an official proclamation from the provisional governor, that the day has already arrived when the experiment can be safely attempted. But as the questions on which these two classes will be called to co-operate are those with regard to which there would undoubtedly be some difference of opinion, particularly as to the construction of certain laws relative to freedmen, the commanding general prefers to postpone the trial for the present. It is the earnest desire of all military officers, as it must be of every good citizen, to hasten the day when the troops can with safety be withdrawn from this State, and the people be left to execute their own laws, but this will not be hastened by arming at this time the young men of the State.

The proclamation of the provisional governor is based on the supposed necessity of increasing the military forces in the State to prevent the commission of crime by bad men. It is a remarkable fact that most of the outrages have been committed against northern men, government couriers, and colored people. Southern citizens have been halted by these outlaws, but at once released and informed that they had been stopped by mistake; and these citizens have refused to give information as to the parties by whom they were halted, although frankly acknowledging that they knew them.

Governor Sharkey, in a communication written after his call for the organization of militia forces was made, setting forth the necessity for such organization, states that the people are unwilling to give information to the United States military authorities which will lead to the detection of these outlaws, and suggests as a remedy for these evils the arming of the very people who refuse to give such information.

A better plan will be to disarm all such citizens, and make it for their interest to aid those who have been sent here to restore order and preserve peace.

It is therefore ordered, that district commanders give notice at once to all persons within their respective districts that no military organizations, except those under the control of the United States authorities, will be permitted within their respective commands, and that if any attempt is made to organize after such notice, those engaged in it will be arrested. Whenever any outrages are committed upon either citizens or soldiers, the commander of the post nearest the point at which the offence is committed will report the fact at once to the district commander, who will forthwith send as strong a force to the locality as can be spared. The officer in command of such force will at once disarm every citizen within ten miles of the place where the offence was committed. If any citizen, possessing information which would lead to the capture of the outlaws, refuses to impart the same, he will be arrested and held for trial. The troops will be quartered on his premises, and he be compelled to provide for the support of men and animals. These villains can be arrested, unless they receive encouragement from some portion of the community in which they operate; and such communities must be held responsible for their acts, and must be made to realize the inevitable consequences of countenancing such outrages.

By order of Major General SLOCUM:

J. WARREN MILLER,*Assistant Adjutant General.*

No. 14.

[Reported for the Vicksburg Journal.]

Speeches of Hon. Sylvanus Evans and Richard Cooper, candidates for Congress and attorney general, Vicksburg, September 19, 1865.

Pursuant to a call published in our yesterday's issue, a large number of citizens assembled at Apollo Hall last evening to listen to addresses from prominent candidates for office at the ensuing election.

Shortly after 8 o'clock Hon. A. Burwell introduced Hon. Richard Cooper to the meeting, who addressed them as follows:

SPEECH OF MR. COOPER.

Fellow-citizens: I present myself before you to-night as a candidate for the office of attorney general. I have not before spoken in public since announcing myself, relying wholly upon my friends and past record. I have resided in this State twenty-nine years, and have for twelve years been a prosecuting attorney.

Soon after announcing myself I found I had an opponent, and I concluded to accompany my friend, Judge Evans, to Vicksburg, merely to make myself known, not intending to make a speech.

I was born in Georgia. The first vote I ever cast was with the old-line Whig party. [Applause.] In 1850 I opposed an attempt to break up the United States government, and in, 1860 I did the same thing. I travelled in Alabama and Mississippi to oppose the measure. [Applause.] But after the State did secede I did all in my power to sustain it. [Heavy applause.] I never entered the army, having held a civil office, and was advised by my friends that I could do more good in that way than by entering the service. I believed in secession while it lasted, but am now as good a Union man as exists, and am in favor of breaking down old barriers, and making harmony and peace prevail.

I was a delegate to the State convention lately in session at Jackson, and hope the legislature will carry out the suggestions of the convention. I believe the negro is entitled to the claims of a freeman, now that he is made free, and I hope he will have them secured to him. I am thankful that Mississippi has the right of jurisdiction, and I hope she will always have it. The office I am a candidate for is not a political, but strictly a judicial office. If elected I shall use my utmost endeavors to promote the interests of the State and country.

Hon. Sylvanus Evans was then introduced to the audience by Mr. Cooper, who spoke substantially as follows:

SPEECH OF JUDGE EVANS.

FELLOW-CITIZENS OF WARREN COUNTY: I am grateful to meet you here this evening, although a stranger to most of you. Here you must judge of my standing, and I hope you will pardon me while I attempt to explain my position to you. I came to Mississippi in 1837, and moved to Lauderdale county in 1839; by profession, in early life, a blacksmith, latterly a lawyer, practicing in eastern Mississippi; to some extent a politician, always believing in the policy of the old-line Whigs, and always acting with them. In 1851 I was a delegate from Lauderdale county to the State convention, then, as in 1860, being opposed to the act of secession, and fought against it with all my powers. But after the State had seceded I went with it as a matter of duty, and I sustained it until the day of the surrender with all my body and heart and mind. [Great applause.] I believed that the majority of the people did not know what was to come, but, blending their interests with mine, I could not, with honor, keep from it.

We are now emerging; now daylight is dawning upon us. But whether peace and prosperity shall return in its fulness is now a question with the people. I am a candidate before you for the United States Congress. Let me say to you, as wise men, that unless the people and the legislature do their duty, it is useless to send me or any one else to Washington, as we cannot there obtain seats in Congress.

My opponent, Mr. West, was nominated at Jackson by a lot of unauthorized delegates, which nomination was, in my judgment, of no account. Were your delegates from this county authorized to nominate candidates for Congress? Ours were not. I am before the people at the urgent request of many friends; not by any nomination made at Jackson.

I heartily approve of the action of the convention. But this action will be useless unless the legislature you elect meet and build the structure upon the foundation laid by the convention. The convention did not abolish slavery. The result of four and a half years of struggle determined whether it was abolished by the bayonet or by legislation. It remains for you to show by your action whether this was done to rid the State of bayonets, or to obtain your representation in Washington. It is not enough to say the negro is free. The convention requires the legislature to adopt such laws as will protect the negro in his rights of person and property.

We are not willing that the negro shall testify in our courts. We all revolt at it, and it is natural that we should do so; but we must allow it as one of the requisites of our admission to our original standing in the Union. To-day the negro is as competent a witness in our State as the white man, made so by the action of the convention. The credibility of the witness is to be determined by the jurors and justices. If you refuse his testimony, as is being done, the result will be the military courts and Freedmen's Bureau will take it up, and jurisdiction is lost, and those who best know the negro will be denied the privilege of passing judgment upon it, and those who know him least are often more in favor of his testimony than yours. I am opposed to negro testimony, but by the constitution it is admitted. (The speaker was here interrupted by an inquiry by one of the audience: "Has this constitution been ratified by the people, and has the old constitution been abolished?" To which Mr. Evans replied: The people did not have an opportunity to ratify it. The convention did not see fit to submit it to them, and its action in the matter is final.)

Slavery was destroyed eternally before the convention met, by the last four years of struggle. The convention only indorsed it, because it could do nothing else. I consider that convention the most important ever held on this continent—the determination of the war pending upon its action, and its great influence upon our southern sister States. The unanimity of the convention was unparalleled: the result of which has met with universal approval.

The only objectors to its action is the radicalism of the north, which thinks it should have conferred universal suffrage on the freedmen.

It is useless to send any one to Washington to gain admission to the Congress of the United States unless the legislature carries out the dictations of the convention for the protection of the freedmen's rights and property, and let them have access to the courts of justice.

Do you not desire to get rid of the Freedmen's Bureau and the bayonets and meet the President half way in his policy of reconstruction? If you do, be careful and send men to the legislature who will carry out this point, and thereby enable your congressmen to obtain their seats, and not have to return.

The speaker was here again interrupted by Mr. John Vallandigham, who wished to inform the gentleman and all present that there were no secessionists now.

(The speaker requested not to be interrupted again.) [Great applause.] I am no demagogue. Supposing you fail to meet the President in his policy, what will be the result? The convention has done its duty. It remains for you to elect men to the next legislature who will secure to the freedman his right. There are large republican majorities in the United States Congress. The northern press, denouncing the President's policy, are assuming that Congress has the right to dictate to you who shall be your rulers. The result of the large majorities will be to give the right of suffrage to every man in the State, and the negroes will elect officers to govern you.

The President and the conservative element of the north are determinedthat the negro shall be placed where nature places him, in spite of the fanatics.

We can only make free labor profitable by giving the negro justice and a right at the courts.

It is hard to accept the fact that our slaves stand as freedmen, and that we have no more right to direct them. It is hard to realize, but let us look at it as it is, and act accordingly.

Your country is laid desolate, your farms have been ravished and impoverished by the war. Vicksburg, the city of hills, everywhere bears marks of war. The Mississippi valley is desolate. You have been deprived of your property in the negro, your houses burned and destroyed.

We can meet the President and the conservative element of the north by a simple act of legislation, and it becomes us as a country-loving people to look well to the candidates for the legislature. If they fail to take the necessary step, the result will be that the Freedmen's Bureau and bayonets will remain with us until they do.

Although somewhat ignorant of the proceeding of the federal Congress, if elected I shall try to promote the especial interests of this State. I shall urge that the United States government owe it as a duty to the State of Mississippi to repair her levees; her people are so impoverished by the war that they cannot stand the taxation necessary to rebuild them. I believe it to be the duty of the general government to appropriate money to assist the people to improve their railroads, rivers, and assist in like new enterprises.

Another important question, that of labor, I believe can only be settled by legislation. I believe it to be for the interests of the people of the south to have the vagrant freedmen removed, as they are the cause of continued strife and tumult.

I am sure we do not want the scenes of St. Domingo and Hayti repeated in our midst. I believe such will be the case if they are not removed. If elected, I shall urge upon the general government the duty of colonizing the negroes; it being the duty of the government to do this, as we are deprived of that amount of property, and the negroes should be removed where they can be distinct and by themselves. It is impossible for the two classes to exist equal together, for we would always be liable to outbreaks and bloodshed. We must either educate them or abolish them, for they know but little more now than to lie all day in the sun and think some one will look out for them. Though free, they cannot yet understand what freedom is, and in many cases it is an injury rather than a benefit. It would be better to have white labor than to try and retain the black.

Another important point—a great debt has been contracted by the federal government. The south cannot pay a proportion of that debt. I am opposed to repudiation, but am in favor of relieving the south of the internal revenue tax.

My opponent, Mr. West, contends that Mississippi must pay her taxes up to 1865. I do not think so; and this is the only issue between us. I deny that the government has a right to levy such a tax, and contend that the government cannot impose a tax upon a State unless that State participates in the accumulation of that debt. At the time this debt was contracted we were recognized as belligerents, and not liable to a share of the debt then contracted for. That back tax can only be collected by a special act of Congress, and, if elected, I shall oppose any such act.

Mr. West proposed an amendment in favor of secession into the State senate, while I was opposed to it. I always contended that slavery would die with secession, while Mr. West said it was the only remedy. But I do not consider this any time to talk of secession, but rather bury all such in oblivion, and talk of the best way to restore peace.

In many instances those who opposed secession the most were the first to enter the army and fight most valiantly. (Applause.) I believe it to be our duty to forget all this and attend to present issues.

It is time the war was over, and it is time that the results of the war were settled, and those are to be settled by the actions of the people themselves.

Determine for yourselves whether or not the President does not offer terms that should suit any of us; is he not trying to stay the tide of fanaticism at the north that would overwhelm us? Has he not shown it in our own State in the appointment of our military governor? No man in the State could have been appointed to give more general satisfaction than W.L. Sharkey, an able, straightforward, just man.

The President, in his speech to the southern delegation, assures them that he is determined to stay the tremendous tide of the fanatics of the north, and that suffrage to the negro shall not be forced upon the people of the south.

If elected, I will heartily co-operate with the President in his policy of reconstruction, for I am bitterly opposed to conferring the right of suffrage upon the negro. I believe it to be the right of the States to settle that matter.

The radicals of the north now contend that they have a right to confer the right of suffrage on the negro, and we must at this hour support the President in approving that idea; if not, he will be overpowered, and that will be the result.

In conclusion, if honored with an election I pledge myself to exert every energy in my power in behalf of the State and district.

At the conclusion of the remarks of Judge Evans, loud and repeated calls for Colonel Patridge brought that gentleman to his feet. He was received with much applause, which was somewhat protracted, showing the favor in which he was held by the audience. Upon rising and attempting to speak from his place on the floor, loud and urgent calls demanded that he should take the stand. Colonel Patridge replied that he would not take the stand until he met his competitor there.

REMARKS OF COLONEL PATRIDGE.

He said that as a public journalist he had gone in and out before this people for many years. His views were as well known as those of any man who ever approached the people, asking their suffrage. He was a union man before the war, and a soldier in the war. He had performed his duty as a private and an officer, on the battle field and on the staff. At the close of the struggle, terminating as it had in our overthrow, he had used his entire exertions to speedily restore Mississippi to her former relations with the federal government. The convention had done this, in entire accordance with the views he had entertained, and if elected to the legislature, he should finish the work in the same spirit, and carry out fully the policy of the convention.

So far as the question of admitting the testimony of negroes into our courts was concerned, he expressed no opinion upon it, as a separate question. He had as many prejudices as other southern men. But in his public acts he had always endeavored to discard prejudice. He looked to the happiness and welfare of the people. But there was one phase of the negro testimony question which was settled. The negro was already regarded as a competent witness. He alluded to the cases which, by an act of Congress, came under the jurisdiction of the Freedmen's Bureau. The question was not whether their testimony should be received or not. It was already received. The question was whether, in receiving it, it shall be received before our own civil magistrates or juries, or before the provost marshals of the Freedmen's Bureau. He had no hesitation in expressing himself in favor of the former. He was opposed to all systems of repudiation, whether styled stay laws, bankrupt laws, or insolvent acts, and in general was in favor of placing Mississippi in the front rank of States. He desired to see our congressmen admitted at the next session, and to that end would do all in his power to promote the policy of President Johnson for the rehabilitation which it was understood was the ultimatum. His remarks, which were exceedingly well received, were continued for fifteen or twenty minutes, at the close of which he announced himself ready to meet his competitor, whom he spoke of in high terms, at any time to discuss the momentous issues devolving upon the next legislature.

No. 15.

To the voters of the sixth judicial district, composed of the counties of Lowndes, Oktibbeha, Noxubee, Neshoba, Kemper, and Winston:

Until the spring of 1861 I was a citizen of Kentucky, but my native State having elected to abide by the fortunes of the Union in the tremendous struggle that has lately terminated, while all my sympathies and instincts bound me to the southern people, I assumed new relations so far as citizenship was concerned, and for the last three years have been a resident of Mississippi. I entered the army as a private soldier, and until the end of the conflict sustained, what I knew in the beginning to be, a desperate and doubtful cause. I went down in battle, never to rise up again a sound man, upon the frontier of this broad abounding land of yours. I therefore cannot feel that I am an alien in your midst, and, with something of confidence as to the result, appeal to you for your suffrages for the office of district attorney. I am as fully identified with the interests of Mississippi as it is possible for any one to be, and in my humble way, will strive as earnestly as any one to restore her lost franchises and lost prosperity. In former years I held in Kentucky a position similar to the one I now seek at your hands, and I hope that I violate no rule of propriety in saying that I deem myself equal to its duties and responsibilities.

Respectfully, your obedient servant,

JNO. T. HOGAN.

P.S.—Owing to the fact that I have but little acquaintance with the people of the sixth district, outside of the county of Lowndes, I will address them at different points so soon as I can prepare and publish a list of appointments.

J.T.H.

Columbus, *Mississippi, August* 26, 1865.

No. 16.

HEADQUARTERS DEPARTMENT OF LOUISIANA, OFFICE OF PROVOST MARSHAL GENERAL,

New Orleans, La., September 12, 1865.

General: In the matter of the investigation ordered to be made in relation to the loyalty of certain members of the board of public schools of this city, I have the honor to report as follows:

Thomas Sloo, in his capacity as president of the "Sun Mutual Insurance Company," subscribed fifty thousand dollars towards the confederate loan.

John I. Adams, a prominent and influential merchant, left this city immediately on the arrival of the federal forces, and did not return until the final overthrow of the rebellion. He presented a piece of ordnance, manufactured at his own expense, to the "Washington Artillery," to be used against the government of the United States. He also was a subscriber to the rebel loan.

Glendy Burke and George Ruleff, the former at one time a prominent politician, the latter a wealthy merchant, sent their sons into the confederacy, while they remained at home, refusing to assist in any way in the reorganization of the State government, and showing their contempt for the United States government and its constituted authorities. Their conduct was far from being loyal and patriotic; associating only with the avowed enemies of the government.

Edwin L. Jewell, editor and proprietor of the "Star" newspaper, is not a citizen of New Orleans. Previous to the rebellion he was a resident of the parish of Point Coupee, where he edited a newspaper, noted only for its bitter and violent opposition to the government and the strong and ardent manner in which it enunciated the principles of secession. He has only lately arrived here, and has not resided in the city for a sufficient length of time to entitle him to the rights of citizenship.

David McCoard is classed with those whose conduct throughout the war has been intent only in misrepresenting the government and treating its representatives with contumely.

Dr. Alfred Perry has served four years in the confederate army. Comment is unnecessary.

Messrs. Keep, Viavant, Turpise, Toyes, Holliday, Bear, Walsh, Moore and Ducongel, all contributed more or less in money and influence towards establishing a government hostile and inimical to the United States.

Dr. Holliday was at one time acting as surgeon in a rebel camp. (Moore.)

Mr. Rodgers, the candidate for the position of superintendent of public schools, held the same office at the commencement of the war. His conduct at that time was imbued with extreme bitterness and hate towards the United States, and in his capacity as superintendent he introduced the "Bonnie Blue Flag" and other rebel songs into the exercises of the schools under his charge. In histories and other books, where the initials "U.S." occurred, he had the same erased and "C.S." substituted. He used all means in his power to imbue the minds of the youths intrusted to his care with hate and malignity towards the Union. He has just returned from the late confederacy, where he has resided during the war. At the time he left the city to join the rebel army he left his property in the care of one Finley, who claims to be a British subject, but held the position of sergeant in a confederate regiment of militia.

I am, general, very respectfully, your obedient servant,

CHAS. W. LOWELL,*Major 80th United States Colored Infantry and Provost Marshal General.*

Major General E.R.S. CANBY,*Commanding Department.*

No. 17.

[From the New Orleans Times, September 12, 1865.]

THE PUBLIC SCHOOLS.

To the citizens of New Orleans our public schools have long been a cherished and peculiar interest. They have been regarded with pride, fostered with peculiar care, and looked up to as a source of future greatness. In their first organization, Samuel J. Peters, and those who acted with him, had to contend against the popular prejudices of the day, for parental pride—sometimes stronger than common sense—was shocked at the thought of an educational establishment in which the children of all classes of citizens met on a common level, and the difference between free schools and charity schools was not very readily discerned. Those prejudices, however, wore gradually away, and the free schools increased in numbers and efficiency till they were regarded by rich and poor with equal interest. Pride withdrew its frown and put on a patronizing smile. The children of the cavalier sat beside those of the roundhead, and heterogeneous differences of race were extinguished by a homogeneous fellowship.

For years previous to the war our public schools occupied a high position. No political or sectarian dogmas were taught. In politics and religion children naturally incline to the opinions of their parents, and it is well that they do so; for if the reverse were the case, there would be many divided households, which, under existing arrangements, are harmonious and happy. The teachers taught those branches only which are set down in the educational programme, and the knowledge they imparted was necessary, not only for the appreciation but for the preservation of our free form of government. It is true that schoolmasters, like other people, have their own notions of right and wrong—their own political and religious opinions—but we speak what we know when we state that up to the time of the rebellion no attempt was made to give the minds of the pupils in the public schools of New Orleans either a political or religious bias. Some incline to the opinion that the duties of the educational trust would have been more effectively performed had patriotic politics been made a prominent branch of study; but to such a course innumerable objections would have arisen. Patriotism does not always wear the same mantle, or point in the same direction. It accommodates itself to the peculiarities of different countries and forms of government. Sometimes it is a holy principle—sometimes a mere party catchword with no more real meaning than can be attached to the echo of an echo.

After the city was redeemed from rebel rule an earnest effort was made to include loyalty among the branches of our popular education, and tests were applied with perhaps an unnecessary degree of rigor. For this the excited state of public opinion, arising from the civil strife which then prevailed, was the sole excuse. Some seeds of bitterness were unfortunately sown. The antagonism of parents were repeated and intensified in the children, and love of country proved weak when compared with hatred of the rebels. Such enthusiastic displays, such hoistings of flags, such singings of patriotic songs were never known before. This made the children very loyal, but exceedingly revengeful and unchildlike. The divine advice, "love your enemy," they would have pronounced the height of madness, if not wickedness. In short, they were introduced before their time into the arena of political perplexities. For all this the teacher was perhaps not very much to blame. He was swept on by a current which he could not resist even if he would. A "higher law," irresponsible at the time, and backed up by the persuasive bayonet, was an authority which brooked no resistance. He merely obeyed orders and earned his daily bread. Under these circumstances it is not to be wondered at that the public schools lost a portion of their previous popularity, and, notwithstanding the diminished financial resources of our citizens, private schools multiplied among them beyond all precedent.

An effort is now made to get the schools once more under popular control, and render them what they were originally intended to be—mere educational institutions. To this end a school board has been appointed, but as soon as it undertook to act it was met, as to certain members, by a question of loyalty, raised, in all probability, by some interested party, who, being without offence himself, thought proper to fling a few stones at his offending neighbors. If there be any disloyalty in the board we trust that it will be speedily purged thereof, but, knowing most of the members, we greatly doubt that any such bill of indictment can be sustained. At any rate, a week has elapsed since the charge was made, and we imagine it will be disposed of before the meeting takes place, which was appointed for to-morrow evening.

One of our contemporaries, in his edition of yesterday evening, states, on the strength of a positive assurance, "that his excellency J. Madison Wells has been appointed provisional governor of Louisiana;" that his commission is here awaiting his acceptance, and that he "will probably order an election for members of a constitutional convention" soon after he returns to the city. If this proves so, it will create quite a stir in the political world hereabout. At the bare mention of "constitutional convention" a shudder involuntary creeps over us, visions of bankrupt treasuries present themselves, new species of taxation to frighten our patient but impoverished people, and a general "brandy and cigar" saturnalia for our disinterested and immensely patriotic politicians. But of this we suppose we need have no fear. The funds are deficient.

No. 18.

HEADQUARTERS SUB-DISTRICT OF JACKSON,

Jackson, Mississippi, September 17, 1865.

Major: I would respectfully make the following report as to what I saw and learned by conversing with officers and citizens during my recent visit to the northwest part of this sub-district, particularly in Holmes county. The only garrison at present in the county is at Goodman, situated on the railroad, sixteen miles from Lexington, the county seat, which place I visited. Of the male population of the county I would estimate that not more than one-tenth of the whites and one-fourth the blacks seemed to have any employment or business of any kind; universal idleness seemed to be the rule, and work the exception, and but few of those at work seemed to be doing so with any spirit, as though they had any idea of accomplishing anything—-just putting the time in. One-half of the male population can be met upon the road any day, and the travelling at night is much more than would be expected. In a common country road, probably thirty persons passed in a night on horseback. As to the character of the persons met by day or night many of them would be called suspicious, being supplied with arms, which they often take pains to display, riding United States and Confederate States horses and mules, government saddles and bridles, which it is useless to try to take away, as they have no difficulty in proving them to be theirs by the evidence of some comrade with whom they reciprocate in kind. They boast of Jeff. Davis and President Johnson, try in every way to show their contempt for the Yankee, boast of the number they have killed; &c. They want it understood that they are not whipped—simply overpowered. They have no visible means of support, and the impression is that they are living off the proceeds of government cotton and stock, and quite frequently of private property—-generally cotton.

The negroes complain that these same "gallant young men" make a practice of robbing them of such trifles as knives, tobacco, combs, &c. If any resistance is made, death is pretty sure to be the result; or if the poor negro is so unfortunate as to appear to recognize his persecutors, he can then expect nothing less. Negroes are often shot, as it appears, just out of wanton cruelty, for no reason at all that any one can imagine. The older and more respected class of white men seem to deplore the condition of things; think, however, that there is no way to stop it, except to let it have its own course; say such occurrences, though not so frequent, were by no means uncommon before the war. In conversing with such as were the leaders in politics and society before the war, and the leaders in the rebellion, one is reminded of their often-repeated assertions that the negro cannot take care of himself; capital must own labor, &c., &c. They have preached it, talked it, spoken it so long, that free labor would be a failure in the south, (and especially negro labor,) that it seems they have made themselves believe it, and very many act as though they were bound to make it so, if it was not going to be the natural result. Some, now their crops are gathered, drive off all the hands they do not want, without any compensation for their summer's work except food and clothing.

In many cases the negroes act just like children, roving around the country, caring nothing for the future, not even knowing one day what they are to eat the next. They also seem to think that in their present condition as freemen their former masters and present employers should address them in a more respectful manner than formerly. This the whites refuse to accede to, but persist in still treating them as niggers, giving them orders in the same austere manner as of old. In one day's travel I passed by different places where five colored men had been murdered during the five days just passed, and as many wounded. In one place it appears that one man was taken out of bed and killed because, as the neighbors say, he was a preacher, though they none of them contend that he had ever taught any doctrine or said anything against the peace and welfare of the neighborhood; but nearly all approve the act. Three men were engaged in it, and finding some colored men were witnesses to the transaction, they killed two of them and left all three together. At another place a party of men, women, and children were collected together at a plantation, with the consent of the owner, and were having a dance, when a squad of about twelve rode up and, without any warning of any kind, commenced firing at them, killing one and wounding several. It is of course known by the white persons in the vicinity who these murderers are, but no effort is made to arrest them. The negroes say they have recognized a number of them, and say most all lived near by. I found no one that thought there was anything objectionable about this particular meeting, but nearly all objected to the practice of their gathering together; think it gives them extravagant ideas of liberty, has a tendency to make them insubordinate, &c. Another place a colored man was killed—supposed to have been shot for a small amount of money he happened to have with him; no clue to the murderers. Another place within one-fourth of a mile of Lexington, a colored man was shot through the head on the public road, (was not yet dead,) and his pockets rifled of the few cents he had; also his knife. Over in Attala county I learned that not long since two white men, (merchants,) while sitting in their store, were both instantly killed, as is supposed, because they were finding out too much about where their stolen cotton had gone to.

When returning, near Canton I was informed by the commanding officer of the post that recently, near by, a colored boy was met by a couple of these "honorable young men" of the south, and his hands tied, was shot, his throat cut, and his ears cut off. No one has been able to ascribe any reason for it, as he was a very quiet, inoffensive lad. Two persons have been arrested for the deed. When arraigned by the civil authorities they were acquitted, as no white witnesses were knowing to the murder, and colored witnesses were not permitted to testify; but they were again arrested by the captain commanding the post, add forwarded for trial by military commission. All, both black and white, are afraid to give evidence against any one. They say in some instances that they would like to see the rascals get their just deserts; but if they were instrumental in bringing it about they would have to move to a military post for safety, and when the troops are withdrawn they would have to go also. An insurrection among the colored people is quite a subject of conversation among the whites, and they appear to fear it will develop itself in a general uprising and massacre about the 1st of January next. I do not consider there are any grounds for their suspicions, and believe it arises from their troubled consciences, which are accusing them of the many cruel acts perpetrated against their former slaves, and these barbarities are continued by some for the purpose of still keeping them under subjection. In some places there will evidently be a scarcity of food the coming winter, and white and black, as the season for foraging has passed, will soon have to get assistance or starve, as they seem determined not to work. I did not find among those I talked with one person who was in favor of organizing militia as contemplated in the governor's proclamation. Some thought it might be of service if it was composed of the right kind of men, but they know it would be composed of just a lot of roving fellows, the very ones who now most need watching. Militia finds favor only with the politicians, who are much in want of a hobby to ride, bar-room loafers, who think it would give their present calling a little more respectability, and the rambling fellows who would like some show of authority to cover up their robberies, with probably a few men who honestly believe it would be composed of better material.

If it were not for the classes above described, a large majority would be in favor of the United States forces remaining in the State. I am of the opinion that a large amount of good might be done, if good speakers would travel around the country and explain to the freedmen what their rights are, what their duties are, and to the planters what the government expects of them and wishes them to do. A better understanding of this matter would be of advantage to all concerned. In conclusion I would respectfully state that I find myself unable in many instances to arrest parties accused of crime, for the reason no horses or mules can be obtained to mount soldiers sent in pursuit, and on account of the scarcity of officers in the command to take charge of squads.

I am, major, very respectfully, &c.,

CHARLES H. GILCHRIST,*Colonel 50th United States Colored Infantry, commanding.*

Major W.A. GORDON,*Assistant Adjutant General, Northern District Mississippi.*

Official: T. WAHREN MILLER,*Assistant Adjutant General.*

No. 19.

HEADQUARTERS DISTRICT OF NORTHERN ALABAMA,

Nashville, Tennessee, September 29, 1865.

General: About the middle of September last while I was in command of the district of Huntsville, formerly district of northern Alabama, several citizens of Jackson county called on me at Huntsville, complaining that the sheriff of the county, Colonel Snodgrass, late of the confederate army, had arrested fifteen citizens of that county on charges of murder, which they were accused of having committed while in the service of the United States, under orders from their superiors, in fights with guerrillas. The trial was to take place before the probate judge, of Jackson county, no regular courts being held at that time. I sent an order to the sheriff to release the prisoners. I also sent an order to the judge before whom the trial was to take place to suspend action in their cases. At the same time I reported the case to General Thomas, commander of the military division of the Tennessee, and asked for instructions. I received answer that my action was approved. A few days afterwards it was reported to me that the sheriff refused to obey the order, and had used the most disrespectful language against the military authorities of the United States. I ordered his arrest, but about the same time I received orders to muster out all white regiments in my district, and my own regiment being among them, I relinquished command of the district. I deem the lives of southern men that have served in the United States army unsafe when they return to their homes. As to the feeling of the people in that section of the country, the majority at this day are as bitter enemies of the United States government as they were during the war.

General, I have the honor to remain your obedient servant,

W. KRZYZANOWSKI,*Late Brevet Brigadier General, U.S.V.*

Major General C. SCHURZ.

No. 20.

List of colored people killed or maimed by white men and treated at post hospital, Montgomery.

1. Nancy, colored woman, ears cut off. She had followed Wilson's column towards Macon two or three days, and when returning camped near the road, and while asleep a white man by the name of Ferguson, or Foster, an overseer, came upon her and cut her ears off. This happened in April, about thirty miles east of Montgomery.

2. Mary Steel, one side of her head scalped; died. She was with Nancy.

3. Jacob Steel, both ears cut off; was with the same party.

4. Amanda Steel, ears cut off; was with the same party.

5. Washington Booth, shot in the back, near Montgomery, while returning from his work, May 1. He was shot by William Harris, of Pine Level, thirty miles from here, without any provocation.

6. Sutton Jones, beard and chin cut off. He belonged to Nancy's party, and was maimed by the same man.

7. About six colored people were treated at this hospital who were shot by persons in ambuscade during the months of June and July. Their names cannot be found in a hasty review of the record.

8. Robert, servant of Colonel Hough, was stabbed while at his house by a man wearing in part the garb of a confederate soldier; died on the 26th of June, in this hospital, about seven days after having been stabbed.

9. Ida, a young colored girl, was struck on the head with a club by an overseer, about thirty miles from here; died of her wound at this hospital June 20.

10. James Taylor, stabbed about half a mile from town; had seven stabs that entered his lungs, two in his arms, two pistol-shots grazed him, and one arm cut one-third off, on the 18th of June. Offender escaped.

11. James Monroe, cut across the throat while engaged in saddling a horse. The offender, a white man by the name of Metcalf, was arrested. No provocation. Case happened on August 19, in this city.

These cases came to my notice as surgeon in charge of the post hospital at Montgomery. I treated them myself, and certify that the above statements are correct.

Montgomery Hall, *August* 21, 1865.

J.M. PHIPPS,*Acting Staff Surgeon, in charge Post Hospital*.

List of colored people wounded and maimed by white people, and treated in Freedmen's hospital since July 22, 1865.

1. William Brown, shot in the hand; brought here July 22.

2. William Mathews, shot in the arm; brought here August 11. Shot on Mathews's plantation by a neighbor of Mr. Mathews, who was told by Mr. Mathews to shoot the negro.

3. Amos Whetstone, shot in the neck by John A. Howser, August 18, in this city. Howser halted the man, who was riding on a mule on the

road; had an altercation with Mr. Whetstone; Howser, Whetstone's son-in-law, shot him while he was going to town.

The above cases came to my notice as assistant surgeon at this hospital. Similar cases may have been treated here before I entered upon my duties, of which I can give no reliable account.

J.E. HARVEY, _Assistant Surgeon 58th Illinois.

Freedmen's Hospital,*Montgomery, Alabama, August* 21, 1865.

No. 21.

OFFICE PROVOST MARSHAL,

Post of Selma, Alabama, August 22, 1865.

I have the honor to report the following facts in regard to the treatment of colored persons by whites within the limits of my observation:

There have come under my notice, officially, twelve cases in which I am morally certain (the trials have not been had yet) that negroes were killed by whites. In a majority of cases the provocation consisted in the negroes trying to come to town, or to return to the plantation after having been sent away. These cases are in part as follows:

Wilson H. Gordon, convicted by military commission of having shot and drowned a negro, May 14, 1865.

Samuel Smiley, charged with having shot one negro and wounded another, acquitted on proof of an alibi. It is certain, however, that one negro was shot and another wounded, as stated. Trial occurred in June.

Three negroes were killed in the southern part of Dallas county; it is supposed by the Vaughn family. I tried twice to arrest them, but they escaped into the woods.

Mr. Alexander, Perry county, shot a negro for being around his quarters at a late hour. He went into his house with a gun and claimed to have shot the negro accidentally. The fact is, the negro is dead.

Mr. Dermott, Perry county, started with a negro to Selma, having a rope around the negro's neck. He was seen dragging him in that way, but returned home before he could have reached Selma. He did not report at Selma, and the negro has never since been heard of. The neighbors declare their belief that the negro was killed by him. This was about the 10th of July.

Mr. Higginbotham, and Threadgill, charged with killing a negro in Wilcox county, whose body was found in the woods, came to my notice the first week of August.

A negro was killed on Mr. Brown's place, about nine miles from Selma, on the 20th of August. Nothing further is known of it. Mr. Brown himself reported.

A negro was killed in the calaboose of the city of Selma, by being beaten with a heavy club; also, by being tied up by the thumbs, clear of the floor, for three hours, and by further gross abuse, lasting more than a week, until he died.

I can further state, that within the limits of my official observation crime is rampant; that life is insecure as well as property; that the country is filled with desperadoes and banditti who rob and plunder on every side, and that the county is emphatically in a condition of anarchy.

The cases of crime above enumerated, I am convinced, are but a small part of those that have actually been perpetrated.

I am, very respectfully, your obedient servant,

J.P. HOUSTON,*Major 5th Minnesota, and Provost Marshal U.S. forces at Selma, Alabama.*

Major General CARL SCHURZ.

No. 22.

FREEDMEN'S BUREAU,

Mobile, September 9, 1865.

Sir: In compliance with your request I have the honor to report the state of affairs as connected with the freedmen in this city and the counties of Washington, Monroe, Clark, Choctaw and Baldwin.

The civil authorities in this city have accepted General Swayne's order No. 7, (herewith enclosed,) but the spirit of the order is not complied with, and complaints of injustice and criminal partiality in the mayor's court have been frequently made at this office, and particularly when Mr. Morton presides there is no justice rendered to the freedmen. Little or no business is done before other magistrates, as the colored people are aware, from experience, that their oath is a mere farce and their testimony against a white man has no weight; consequently all complaints of the colored people come before this bureau.

I have by special order of General Swayne designated one of the justices of the peace, Mr. T. Starr, who adjudicates cases of debt, and in matters where both parties are of color he has so far given satisfaction, but the prejudice so universal against colored people here is already beginning to affect his decisions.

The civil police department of this city is decidedly hostile to color, and the daily acts of persecution in this city are manifest in the number of arrests and false imprisonment made where no shadow of criminality exists, while gangs of idle rebel soldiers and other dissolute rowdies insult, rob, and assault the helpless freedmen with impunity.

All hopes of equity and justice through the civil organization of this city is barred; prejudice and a vindictive hatred to color is universal here; it increases intensely, and the only capacity in which the negro will be tolerated is that of slave.

The fever of excitement, distrust, and animosity, is kept alive by incendiary and lying reports in the papers, and false representations of rebel detectives. The alarm is constantly abroad that the negroes are going to rise; this is utterly without foundation. The freedmen will not rise, though docile and submissive to every abuse that is heaped upon them in this city. If they are ragged and dirty, they are spurned as outcasts; if genteel and respectable, they are insulted as presumptive; if intelligent, they are incendiary; and their humble worship of God is construed as a designing plot to rise against the citizens who oppress them.

It is evident that General Swayne's good intentions are nugatory from the want of faith on the part of those to whom he intrusted his order.

These men have been recipients of office for years. Old associations, customs and prejudices, the pressure of public opinion, and the undying hostility to federal innovation, all conspire gainst impartiality to color. Such is the state of affairs in this city.

In the counties of this district above named there is no right of the negro which the white man respects; all is anarchy and confusion; a reign of terror exists, and the life of the freedmen is at the mercy of any villain whose hatred or caprice incites to murder. Organized patrols with negro hounds keep guard over the thoroughfares, bands of lawless robbers traverse the country, and the unfortunate who attempts escape, or he who returns for his wife or child, is waylaid or pursued with hounds, and shot or hung. Laborers on the plantations are forced to remain and toil without hope of remuneration. Others have made the crop and are now driven off to reach Mobile or starve; scarcely any of them have rags enough to cover them. Many who still labor are denied any meat, and whenever they are treated with humanity it is an isolated exception. Ragged, maimed, and diseased, these miserable outcasts seek their only refuge, the Freedmen's Bureau, and their simple tale of suffering and woe calls loudly on the mighty arm of our government for the protection promised them.

These people are industrious. They do not refuse to work; on the contrary, they labor for the smallest pittance and plainest food, and are too often driven off deprived of the small compensation they labored for.

The report of rations issued to destitute citizens on August 1, 1865, was 3,570 persons. Owing to the numerous impostures by those who had means of support, I erased the names of a large number and the list now stands 1,742 persons who are recipients of government alms. Of this number, 95 per cent. are rebels who have participated in some manner in this rebellion. Number of rations issued to destitute colored people is simply six (6).

The report of the freedmen's colony of this district to this date is (12) twelve men, (71) seventy-one women, and (88) eighty-eight children, and sick in hospital (105) one hundred and five; total (276) two hundred and seventy-six. Of this number many have been driven off of plantations as helpless, while many of their grown children are forcibly retained to hard labor for their masters.

I am, general, very respectfully, your obedient servant,

W.A. POILLON,*Captain, Assistant Superintendent freedmen, refugees, abandoned lands, &c.*

General CARL SCHURZ.

Freedmen's Bureau, *July* 29, 1865.

Sir: I have the honor to report some testimony I have received of the murders and barbarities committed on the freedmen in Clark, Choctaw, Washington and Marengo counties, also the Alabama and Bigbee rivers.

About the last of April, two freedmen were hung in Clark county.

On the night of the eleventh of May, a freedman named Alfred was taken from his bed by his master and others and was hung, and his body still hangs to the limb.

About the middle of June, two colored soldiers (at a house in Washington county) showed their papers and were permitted to remain all night. In the morning the planter called them out and shot one dead, wounded the other, and then with the assistance of his brother (and their negro dogs) they pursued the one who had escaped. He ran about three miles and found a refuge in a white man's house, who informed the pursuers that he had passed. The soldier was finally got across the river, but has not been heard of since.

At Bladen Springs, (or rather, six miles from there,) a freedman was chained to a pine tree and *burned to death*.

About two weeks after, and fifteen miles from Bladen, another freedman was burned to death.

In the latter part of May, fifteen miles south of Bladen, a freedman was shot *outside* of the planter's premises and the body dragged into the stable, to make it appear he had shot him in the act of stealing.

About the first of June, six miles west of Bladen, a freedman was hung. His body is still hanging.

About the last of May, three freedmen were coming down the Bigbee river in a skiff, when two of them were shot; the other escaped to the other shore.

At Magnolia Bluff (Bigbee river) a freedman (named George) was ordered out of his cabin to be whipped; he started to run, when the men (three of them) set their dogs (five of them) on him, and one of the men rode up to George and struck him to the earth with a loaded whip. Two of them dragged him back by the heels, while the dogs were lacerating his face and body. They then placed a stick across his neck, and while one stood on it the others beat him until life was nearly extinct.

About the first of May, near —— landing, in Choctaw county, a freedman was hung; and about the same time, near the same neighborhood, a planter shot a freedman, (who was talking to one of his servants,) and dragged his body into his garden to conceal it.

A preacher (near Bladen Springs) states in the *pulpit* that the roads in Choctaw county stunk with the dead bodies of servants that had fled from their masters.

The people about Bladen *declare* that *no negro* shall live in the county unless he remains with his *master* and is as obedient as heretofore.

In Clark county, about the first of June, a freedman was shot through the heart; his body lies unburied.

About the last of May, a planter hung his servant (a woman) in presence of all the neighborhood. Said planter had *killed* this woman's husband three weeks before. This occurred at Suggsville, Clark county.

About the last of April, two women were caught near a certain plantation in Clark county and hung; their bodies are still suspended.

On the 19th of July, two freedmen were taken off the steamer Commodore Ferrand, tied and hung; then taken down, their heads cut off and their bodies thrown in the river.

July 11, two men took a woman off the same boat and threw her in the river. This woman had a coop, with some chickens. They threw all in together, and told her to go to the damned Yankees. The woman was drowned.

There are regular patrols posted on the rivers, who board some of the boats; after the boats leave they hang, shoot or drown the victims they may find on them, and all those found on the roads or coming down the river are most invariably *murdered*.

This is only a few of the murders that are committed on the helpless and unprotected freedmen of the above-named counties.

All the cases I have mentioned are *authentic*, and *numerous* witnesses will testify to all I have reported. *Murder with his ghastly train stalks abroad at noonday and revels in undisputed carnage*, while the bewildered and terrified freedmen know not what to do. To leave is death; to remain is to suffer the increased burden imposed on them by the cruel taskmaster, whose only interest is their labor *wrung* from them by every device an inhuman ingenuity can devise. Hence the lash and murder are resorted to to intimidate those whom fear of an awful death *alone* causes to remain, while patrols, negro dogs, and spies (disguised as Yankees) keep*constant* guard over these unfortunate people.

I was in Washington county in the latter part of June, and there learned there was a disposition to *coerce* the labor of these people on plantations where they had always been abused. I was alone, and consequently could not go where my presence was most required, but I learned enough then to convince me there were many grievances which required military power to redress. Since my return I have been attentive to the recital of the horrors which these people suffer, and have carefully perused their statements, which receive corroborate testimony.

I have been careful in authenticity, and very much that has been related to me I have declined accepting as testimony, although I believe its truth.

The history of all these cases, besides others, I have in full, with all their horrible particulars.

Believing, sir, you required the earliest intelligence in this matter, I concluded not to await your arrival.

With much respect, I am, sir, your obedient servant,

W.A. POILLON,*Captain and Ass't. Sup't. Freedmen.*

Brig. Gen. SWAYNE.

A true copy of the original deposited in this office.

CHARLES A. MILLER,*Major and A.A.A. General.*

No. 23.

Vicksburg, Mississippi, *July* 8, 1865.

Captain: I have the honor to report that, in compliance with Special Orders No. 5, Headquarters Sub-district Southwest Mississippi, I proceeded to the counties of Madison, Holmes, and Yazoo, but that I did not reach Issaquena from the fact that the country between Yazoo City and that county has been so overflowed as to render the roads impassable.

I found a provost marshal of freedmen at Yazoo City—Lieutenant Fortu, who seemed to understand his duties well, and to have performed them satisfactorily. There was no officer of the bureau in either of the other counties. The whole country is in a state of social and political anarchy, and especially upon the subject of the freedom of the negroes, but very few who understand their rights and duties.

It is of the utmost importance that officers of the bureau should be sent to all the counties of the State to supervise the question of labor, and to insure the gathering of the growing crop, which, if lost, will produce the greatest suffering. In no case ought a citizen of the locality be appointed to manage the affairs of the freedmen: first, because these men will wish to stand well with their neighbors and cannot do justice to the negro; and secondly, because the negroes only know these men as oppressors of their race, and will have no confidence in their acts. The officers of the bureau should be especially charged to impress upon the freedmen the sacredness of the family relation and the duty of parents to take care of their children, and of the aged and infirm of their race. Where a man and woman have lived together as husband and wife, the relation should be declared legitimate, and all parties, after contracting such relations, should be compelled to legal marriage by severe laws against concubinage. Where parents have deserted their children, they should be compelled to return and care for them; otherwise there will be great suffering among the women and children, for many of the planters who have lost the male hands from their places threaten to turn off the women and children, who will become a burden to the community. The two evils against which the officers will have to contend are cruelty on the part of the employer, and shirking on the part of the negroes. Every planter with whom I have talked premised his statements with the assertion that "a nigger won't work without whipping." I know that this is not true of the negroes as a body heretofore. A fair trial should be made of free labor by preventing a resort to the lash. It is true that there will be a large number of negroes who will shirk labor; and where they persistently refuse compliance with their contracts, I would respectfully suggest that such turbulent negroes be placed upon public works, such as rebuilding the levees and railroads of the State, where they can be compelled to labor, and where their labor will be of benefit to the community at large.

It will be difficult for the employers to pay their laborers quarterly, as required by present orders. Money can only be realized yearly on a cotton crop, because to make such a crop requires an entire year's work in planting, picking, ginning, and sending to market. The lien upon the crop secures the laborer his pay at the end of the year, for which he can afford to wait, as all the necessaries of life are furnished by the planter, who could not pay quarterly except at a great sacrifice.

The present orders recommend that the freedmen remain with their former masters so long as they are kindly treated. This, as a temporary policy, is the best that could be adopted, but I very much doubt its propriety as a permanent policy. It will tend to rebuild the fallen fortunes of the slaveholders, and re-establish the old system of class legislation, thus throwing the political power of the country back into the hands of this class, who love slavery and hate freedom and republican government. It would, in my opinion, be much wiser to diffuse this free labor among the laboring people of the country, who can sympathize with the laborer, and treat him with humanity.

I would suggest that great care be taken in the selection of officers of the bureau to be sent to the various counties. The revolution of the whole system of labor has been so sudden and radical as to require great caution and prudence on the part of the officers charged with the care of the freedmen. They should be able to discuss the question of free labor as a matter of political economy, and by reason and good arguments induce the employers to give the system a fair and honest trial.

Nowhere that I have been do the people generally realise the fact that the negro is free. The day I arrived at Jackson *en route* for Canton, both the newspapers at that place published leading editorials, taking the ground that the emancipation proclamation was unconstitutional, and therefore void; that whilst the negro who entered the army *might* be free, yet those who availed themselves not of the proclamation were still slaves, and that it was a question for the State whether or not to adopt a system of gradual emancipation. These seem to be the views of the people generally, and they expressed great desire "to get rid of these garrisons," when they hope "to have things their own way." And should the care and protection of the nation be taken away from the freedmen, these people will have their own way, and will practically re-establish slavery, more grinding and despotic than of old.

Respectfully submitted:

J.L. HAYNES,*Colonel First Texas Cavalry*.

Captain B.F. MOREY,*Assistant Adjutant General*.

Official:

STUART ELDRIDGE,*Lieutenant and Acting Assistant Adjutant General*.

Colonel Haynes was born and raised near Yazoo City, Mississippi. He owns a plantation, and owned negroes before the war. He left the State in 1862, and went to New Orleans, where he received a commission to raise a regiment of Texas troops.

SAMUEL THOMAS,*Colonel*.

No. 24.

RAILROAD, *Camp near Clinton, Miss., July 8, 1865.*

Sir: I am induced by the suffering I daily see and hear of among colored people to address you this communication. I am located with my command four miles west of Clinton, Hines county, on the railroad. A great many colored people, on their way to and from Vicksburg and other distant points, pass by my camp. As a rule, they are hungry, naked, foot-sore, and heartless, aliens in their native land, homeless, and friendless. They are wandering up and down the country, rapidly becoming vagabonds and thieves from both necessity and inclination. Their late owners, I am led to believe, have entered into a tacit arrangement to refuse labor, food or drink, in all cases, to those who have been soldiers, as well as to those who have belonged to plantations within the State; in the latter case, often ordering them back peremptorily to their "masters."

One planter said in my hearing lately, "These niggers will all be slaves again in twelve months. You have nothing but Lincoln proclamations to make them free." Another said, "No white labor shall ever reclaim my cotton fields." Another said, "Emigration has been the curse of the country; it must be prevented here. This soil must be held by its present owners and their descendants." Another said, "The constitutional amendment, if successful, will be carried before the Supreme Court before its execution can be certain, and we hope much from that court!"

These expressions I have listened to at different times, and only repeat them here in order that I may make the point clear that there is already a secret rebel, anti-emigration, pro-slavery party formed or forming in this State, whose present policy appears to be to labor assiduously for a restoration of the old system of slavery, or a system of apprenticeship, or some manner of involuntary servitude, on the plea of recompense for loss of slaves on the one hand, and, on the other, to counterbalance the influence of Yankee schools and the labor-hiring system as much as possible by oppression and cruelty. I hear that negroes are frequently driven from plantations where they either belong, or have hired, on slight provocation, and are as frequently offered violence on applying for employment. Dogs are sometimes set upon them when they approach houses for water. Others have been met, on the highway by white men they never saw before, and beaten with clubs and canes, without offering either provocation or resistance. I see negroes almost every day, of both sexes, and almost all ages, who have subsisted for many hours on berries, often wandering they know not where, begging for food, drink, and employment.

It is impossible for me or any officer I have the pleasure of an acquaintance with to afford these people relief. Neither can I advise them, for I am not aware that any provisions have been, or are to be made to reach such cases. The evil is not decreasing, but, on the contrary, as the season advances, is increasing.

I have heretofore entertained the opinion that the negroes flocked into the cities from all parts of the country; but a few weeks' experience at this station has changed my views on the subject, and I am now led to believe that those who have done so comprise comparatively a very small part of the whole, and are almost entirely composed of those belonging to plantations adjoining the towns. However, those who did go to the cities have been well cared for in comparison with those who have remained in the country. A small proportion of the latter class are well situated, either as necessary house-servants, body-servants, or favorites by inclination, as mistresses, or by necessity or duty, as each master may have been induced to regard long and faithful service or ties of consanguinity. Throughout the entire country, from Vicksburg to the capital of the State, there is but little corn growing. The manner of cultivating is very primitive, and the yield will be exceedingly small. I estimate that in this country fully one-half of the white population, and a greater proportion of the colored people, will be necessitated either to emigrate, buy food, beg it, or starve. The negro has no means to buy, and begging will not avail him anything. He will then be compelled to emigrate, which, in his case, is usually equivalent to turning vagabond, or, induced by his necessities, resort to organized banding to steal, rob, and plunder. I am at a loss to know why the government has not adopted some system for the immediate relief and protection of this oppressed and suffering people, whose late social changes have conduced so much to their present unhappy condition, and made every officer in the United States army an agent to carry out its provisions. Were I employed to do so, I should seize the largest rebel plantation in this and every other county in the State, partition it in lots of suitable size for the support of a family—say ten acres each—erect mills and cotton gins, encourage them to build houses and cultivate the soil, give them warrants for the land, issue rations to the truly needy, loan them seed, stock, and farming utensils for a year or two, and trust the result to "Yankee schools" and the industry of a then truly free and proverbially happy people. Some other system might be better; few could be more simple in the execution, and in my opinion better calculated to "save a race" now floating about in a contentious sea without hope or haven.

I am, sir, very respectfully, your most obedient servant,

H.R. BRINKERHOFF,*Lieutenant Colonel 52d U.S. Colored Infantry, Commanding Detachment.*

Major General O. O. HOWARD, *Washington, D.C.*

Official:

STUART ELDRIDGE,*Lieutenant, Acting Assistant Adjutant General.*

No. 25.

EXECUTIVE OFFICE, *Jackson, August* 18, 1865.

Sir: Your order No. 16, disbanding police guard for Claiborne county, has been laid before me. I apprehend you are laboring under a mistake in regard to the character of this organization. I had express authority from the President himself to organize the militia if I thought it necessary to keep order in the country. This I did not do, but authorized the organization of patrol guards or county police, for the purpose of suppressing crime, and for arresting offenders. This organization is therefore part of the civil organization of the State, as much so as sheriff, constable, and justices of the peace, and I claim the right to use this organization for these purposes, and hope you will revoke your order.

Your obedient servant,

W.L. SHARKEY,*Provisional Governor of Mississippi.*

Colonel YORK.

Official copy:

J. WARREN MILLER,*Assistant Adjutant General.*

HEADQUARTERS POST OF PORT GIBSON,

Port Gibson, Mississippi, August 26, 1865.

General: I have the honor to state that my reasons for issuing the enclosed order, (No. 16,) was, that a party of citizens acting under authority from Captain Jack, 9th Indiana cavalry, and having as their chief C.B. Clark, was by their own acknowledgment in the habit of patrolling the roads in this section of the country, and ordering any one they came across to halt. If this was not promptly done, they were ordered to fire upon them. In this way one negro woman was wounded, and Union men and negroes were afraid to be out of their houses after dark. The company was formed out of what they called picked men, *i.e.*, those only who had been actively engaged in the war, and were known to be strong disunionists.

The negroes in the section of the country these men controlled were kept in the most abject state of slavery, and treated in every way contrary to the requirements of General Orders No. 129 from the War Department, a copy of which order was issued by me to C.B. Clark.

Hoping, general, to receive instructions as to the manner in which I shall regulate my action,

I have the honor to be, very respectfully, your obedient servant,

P. JONES YORK,*Lieutenant Colonel Commanding Post.*

Provost Major General DAVIDSON,*Commanding Southern District of Mississippi.*

Official copy:

J. WARREN MILLER,*Assistant Adjutant General.*

[Special Orders No. 16.]

HEADQUARTERS POST OF PORT GIBSON,

Port Gibson, Mississippi, August 10, 1865.

The permission given from these headquarters, dated July 3, 1865, by Captain Jack, provost marshal, is hereby revoked.

C.B. Clark, chief of police, under the permission, will notify the parties forming the said patrol to discontinue the practice of patrolling the roads and country armed. All arrests must be made by the proper military or civil authorities.

P. JONES YORK,*Lieutenant Colonel Commanding Post.*

Official copy:

J. WARREN MILLER,*Assistant Adjutant General.*

No. 26.

BUREAU REFUGEES, FREEDMEN, AND ABANDONED LANDS,

OFFICE ACTING ASSISTANT COMMISSIONER FOR WESTERN DIST. OF MISS.,

Vicksburg, Miss., September 28, 1865.

Colonel: I beg leave to call your attention to some of the difficulties we are still obliged to contend with, and some of the abuses still inflicted upon the freedmen, resulting from the prejudices which are still far from being eradicated. In the immediate vicinity of our military posts, and in locations that can readily be reached by the officers of this bureau, the citizens are wary of abusing the blacks; they are so because this bureau has arrested and punished people committing such offences; and the manner in which such cases have been dealt with has shown people that abuse and imposition will not be tolerated, and that such offences are sure to be punished in accordance with the enormity of the crime. But in remote localities, those that cannot well be reached by officers of the bureau, the blacks are as badly treated as ever; colored people often report themselves to the sub-commissioners with bruised heads and lacerated backs, and ask for redress, protection, to be permitted to live at their former homes, and some assurance that they will not be treated in a like manner again if they return. But nothing can be done if their homes happen to be twenty or thirty miles from any office that will protect them. A great many have thus learned that there is no protection for them, and quietly submit to anything that may be required of them, or, as is more frequently the case, they leave such places and crowd about the places where they can be protected.

A girl about twelve years of age, certainly too young to commit any serious offence, lies in No. 1 hospital now with her back perfectly raw, the results of a paddling administered by her former owner. Any number of such cases could easily be cited. In many cases negroes who left their homes during the war, and have been within our military lines, and have provided homes here for their families, going back to get their wives or children, have been driven off and told they could not have them. In several cases guards have been sent to aid people in getting their families, in many others it has been impracticable, as the distance was too great. In portions of the northern part of this district the colored people are kept in SLAVERY still. The white people tell them that they were free during the war, but the war is now over, and they must go to work again as before. The reports from sub-commissioners nearest that locality show that the blacks are in a much worse state than ever before, the able-bodied being kept at work under the lash, and the young and infirm driven off to care for themselves.

As to protection from the civil authorities, there is no such thing outside of this city. There is not a justice of the peace or any other civil officer in the district, eight (8) counties, of which I have charge, that will listen to a complaint from a negro; and in the city, since the adjudication of these cases has been turned over to the mayor, the abuse of and impositions upon negroes are increasing very visibly, for the reason that very little, if any, attention is paid to any complaint of a negro against a white person. Negro testimony is admitted, but, judging from some of the decisions, it would seem that it carries very little weight. In several cases black witnesses have been refused on the ground that the testimony on the opposite side, white, could not be controverted, and it was useless to bring in black witnesses against it. I enclose an affidavit taken on one such case. In the mayor's court, cases in which it is practicable to impose a fine and thereby replenish the city treasury, are taken up invariably, but cases where the parties have no money are very apt to pass unnoticed. One more point, and a serious one, too, for the colored people, is, that in the collection of debts, and a great many of a similar class of cases that are not taken cognizance of in the mayor's court, they have to go through a regular civil process, necessitating the feeing of lawyers, &c., which is quite a burden on a people whose means are limited. These cases have all formerly been handled by an officer of this bureau, and without any expense to the parties for fees, &c.

The prejudices of the citizens are very strong against the negro; he is considered to be deserving of the same treatment a mule gets, in many cases not as kind, as it is unprofitable to kill or maim a mule, but the breaking of the neck of the free negro is nobody's loss; and unless there is some means for meting out justice to these people that is surer and more impartial than these civil justice's courts, run by men whose minds are prejudiced and bitter against the negro, I would recommend, as an act of humanity, that the negroes be made slaves again.

I am, colonel, very respectfully, your obedient servant,

J.H. WEBER,*Captain and Acting Ass't. Com'r. Freedmen's Bureau for Western Dist. Miss.*

Colonel SAMUEL THOMAS,*Ass't. Com'r. Bureau Freedmen, &c., Vicksburg, Miss.*

No. 27.

OFFICE ASSISTANT COMMISSIONER BUREAU REFUGEES, FREEDMEN, AND ABANDONED LANDS FOR STATE OF MISSISSIPPI,

Vicksburg, Mississippi, September 28, 1865.

Dear Sir: In accordance with your request, I write the following letter, containing some of my views on the subject to which you called my attention—a subject worthy of great consideration, because a bad policy adopted now with reference to the administration of justice and the establishment of courts in the south may lead to evils that will be irreparable in the future.

You are aware that some time ago General Swayne, commissioner of the Freedmen's Bureau for Alabama, constituted the civil officers of the provisional government of that State commissioners of the bureau for hearing and deciding all cases in which freedmen were parties, provided no invidious distinctions in receiving testimony, punishment, &c., were made between blacks and whites. Governor Parsons, of Alabama, approved of the arrangement, and urged the State officials to comply with the condition, and thus do away with the necessity for military courts in connexion with freedmen affairs. I have no doubt I could have induced the governor of Mississippi to take the same action had I thought it the policy of the government. I was under the impression that General Swayne had made a mistake, and that he would defeat the very objects for which the bureau was laboring. I thought the citizens were not to be trusted with freedmen affairs until they had given some strong evidence that they were prepared to accept the great change in the condition of the freedmen. I had not the least idea that such a limited control as General Swayne now has would accomplish what the authorities desired. The protection he gives freedmen under his order is so limited, and will fall so far short of what the freedmen have a right to expect, that I did not think of bringing the matter before the government. Late orders and instructions from the President convince me that I was mistaken, and that the trial is to be made.

I have issued an order in accordance with these instructions, which I append:

[General Orders No. 8.]

BUREAU REFUGEES, FREEDMEN, AND ABANDONED LANDS, *Office Ass't.*
Commissioner for State of Miss., Vicksburg, Miss., September 20, 1865.

The following extracts from Circular No. 5, current series, Bureau Refugees, Freedmen, and Abandoned Lands, and General Orders No. 10, current series, headquarters department of Mississippi, in reference to the same, are hereby republished for the guidance of officers of this bureau:

["Circular No. 5.]

"WAR DEPARTMENT,

"Bureau Refugees, Freedmen, and Abandoned Lands, Washington, May 30, 1865.

"RULES AND REGULATIONS FOR ASSISTANT COMMISSIONERS.

"VII. In all places where there is an interruption of civil law, or in which local courts, by reason of old codes, in violation of the freedom guaranteed by the proclamation of the President and laws of Congress, disregard the negro's right to justice before the laws, in not allowing him to give testimony, the control of all subjects relating to refugees and freedmen being committed to this bureau, the assistant commissioners will adjudicate, either themselves or through officers of their appointment, all difficulties arising between negroes and whites or Indians, except those in military service, so far as recognizable by military authority, and not taken cognizance of by the other tribunals, civil or military, of the United States.

"O.O. HOWARD, *Major General, Commissioner Bureau of Refugees, Freedmen,& c.*

"Approved June 2, 1865.

"ANDREW   JOHNSON,
"President of the United States."

["General Orders No. 10.]

"HEADQUARTERS DEPARTMENT OF MISSISSIPPI,

"Vicksburg, Mississippi, August 3, 1865.

"VII. This order, (Circular No. 5, paragraph VII, Bureau Refugees, Freedmen, and Abandoned Lands,) however, must not be so construed as to give the colored man immunities not accorded to other persons. If he is charged with the violation of any law of the State, or an ordinance of any city, for which offence the same penalty is imposed upon white persons as upon black, and if courts grant to him the same privileges as are accorded to white men, no interference on the part of the military authorities will be permitted. Several instances have recently been reported in which military officers, claiming to act under the authority of the order above mentioned, have taken from the custody of the civil authorities negroes arrested for theft and other misdemeanors, even in cases where the courts were willing to concede to them the same privileges as are granted to white persons. These officers have not been governed by the spirit of the order. The object of the government is not to screen this class from just punishment—not to encourage in them the idea that they can be guilty of crime and escape its penalties, but simply to secure to them the rights of freemen, holding them, at the same time, subject to the same laws by which other classes are governed.

"By order of Major General Slocum:

"J. WARREN MILLER, "*Assistant Adjutant General.*"

In accordance with this order, where the judicial officers and magistrates of the provisional government of this State will take for their mode of procedure the laws now in force in this State, except so far as those laws make a distinction on account of color, and allow the negroes the same rights and privileges as are accorded to white men before their courts, officers of this bureau will not interfere with such tribunals, but give them every assistance possible in the discharge of their duties.

In cities or counties where mayors, judicial officers, and magistrates will assume the duties of the administration of justice to the freedmen, in accordance with paragraph VII, Circular No. 5, issued from the Bureau of Refugees, Freedmen, and Abandoned Lands, and approved by the President, and will signify their willingness to comply with this request by a written acceptance addressed to the assistant commissioner for the State, no freedmen courts will be established, and those that may now be in existence in such localities will be closed.

It is expected that the officers of this bureau will heartily co-operate with the State officials in establishing law and order, end that all conflict of authority and jurisdiction will be avoided.

By order of Colonel Samuel Thomas, assistant commissioner Freedmen's
Bureau for State of Mississippi.

STUART ELDRIDGE,*Lieutenant, Acting Assistant Adjutant General.*

I have written to Governor Sharkey, and explained to him how this order can be put in force in this State, and will do all I can to secure its success, and to aid the civil authorities to discharge their duties. I presume the legislature of this State, which is to meet in October, will take up this matter immediately, and arrange some plan by which the State authorities can take complete charge of freedmen affairs, and relieve the officers of this bureau. There is a jealousy of United States officers existing among the State officials that makes it disagreeable to perform any duty which is liable to conflict with their authority.

When General Howard's Circular No. 5 was issued, I thought it was the intention that military courts should be established for the purpose of taking the administration of justice among the freedmen out of the hands of their old masters, and placing it under the control of their friends for a short time—until the citizens of the south were reconciled to the change, and until their feeling of hatred for their former slaves had abated; that a complete restoration of rights, privileges, and property was to come after a period of probation, in which they should give some evidence of their changed feelings. I have thought much on this subject, have watched the development of feeling among the southern people, and am satisfied that the time for such a restoration has not yet arrived.

The order of General Swayne and the proclamation of General Parsons are unexceptionable in form. If justice to the freedmen can be secured by the means indicated in these documents, and if the process be not too expensive, and if ruinous delays be not allowed, then, it may be, all this movement will be good. But it seems to me that so delicate a matter cannot be smoothly managed in the present temper of Mississippi.

I am aware that it is the policy of the government; that we must trust these people some time; that the establishment of the Freedman's Bureau is (as soon as martial law is withdrawn) a violation of the spirit both of the State and federal constitutions; that the officers of the bureau have no interest in common with the white citizens of the State, and that the bureau is an immense expense to the general government, which should be abolished as soon as compatible with the public interest.

Yet, I feel that we are in honor bound to secure to the helpless people we have liberated a "republican form of government," and that we betray our trust when we hand these freed people over to their old masters to be persecuted and forced to live and work according to their peculiar southern ideas. It seems to me that we are forgetting the helpless and poor in our desire to assist our subjugated enemies, and that we are more desirous of showing ourselves to be a great and magnanimous nation than of protecting the people who have assisted us by arms, and who turned the scale of battle in our favor. We certainly commit a wrong, if, while restoring these communities to all their former privileges as States, we sacrifice one jot or tittle of the rights and liberties of the freedmen.

The mayor of this city has had complete charge of all municipal affairs since the issue of General Slocum's Order 10, (quoted in the order I have before given.) He has been compelled to admit negro testimony by the provisions of that order. In cases that come before him, when it is necessary to admit it he goes through the form of receiving it, but I have yet to hear of one instance where such evidence affected his decision. The testimony of one white man outweighs (practically) that of any dozen freedmen.

The admission of negro testimony will never secure the freedmen justice before the courts of this State as long as that testimony is considered valueless by the judges and juries who hear it. It is of no consequence what the law may be if the majority be not inclined to have it executed. A negro might bring a suit before a magistrate and have colored witnesses examined in his behalf, according to provisions of general orders and United States law, and yet the prejudices of the community render it impossible for him to procure justice. The judge would claim the right to decide whether the testimony was credible, and among the neighbors that would surround him, in many places, he would be bold, indeed, if he believed the sworn evidence of a negro when confronted by the simple assertion or opposed even to the interest of a white man. I recently heard a circle of Mississippians conversing on this subject. Their conclusion was, that they would make no objection to the admission of negro testimony, because "no southern man would believe a nigger if he had the dammed impudence to testify contrary to the statement of a white man." I verily believe that in many places a colored man would refuse, from fear of death, to make a complaint against a white man before a State tribunal if there were no efficient military protection at hand.

Wherever I go—the street, the shop, the house, the hotel, or the steamboat—I hear the people talk in such a way as to indicate that they are yet unable to conceive of the negro as possessing any rights at all. Men who are honorable in their dealings with their white neighbors will cheat a negro without feeling a single twinge of their honor. To kill a negro they do not deem murder; to debauch a negro woman they do not think fornication; to take the property away from a negro they do not consider robbery. The people boast that when they get freedmen affairs in their own hands, to use their own classic expression, "the niggers will catch hell."

The reason of all this is simple and manifest. The whites esteem the blacks their property by natural right, and however much they may admit that the individual relations of masters and slaves have been destroyed by the war and by the President's emancipation proclamation, they still have an ingrained feeling that the blacks at large belong to the whites at large, and whenever opportunity serves they treat the colored people just as their profit, caprice or passion may dictate.

Justice from tribunals made up among such people is impossible. Here and there is a fair and just man. One in a hundred, perhaps, sees the good policy of justice; but these are so few that they will not, at present, guide public sentiment. Other States may, in this matter, be in advance of Mississippi; I suspect they are. If justice is possible, I feel sure they are.

I fear such tribunals would be very expensive for the poor freedmen. Fees are heavy in this State. Unless they can get justice inexpensively, we might as well deny them all remedy before courts at once. Indeed, I think that would be rather more merciful than the arrangement proposed, as they would then trust nobody, and would be less defrauded. Long delays in the course of procedure would be ruinous to most of them. How could a freedman appeal a suit for wages, or respond adequately to an appeal, when he is starving for want of the very wages which are withheld from him?

It may be claimed that officers of the bureau can watch such cases and see that justice is done the freedman. I say they cannot do it. Political power is against him, and will destroy any officer who fearlessly does his duty in this way. He will be charged with interference with the civil authority, with violating some constitution or some code; his acts will be so twisted and contorted before they reach Washington, that he will get nothing for his pains but censure and dismissal.

I can say without fear of contradiction, that there has not occurred one instance of interference with civil authorities on the part of military officers in this State, unless they saw first that every law of justice was violated to such an extent as to arouse the indignation of any man born in a country where human beings have an equal right to justice before the tribunals of the land. Yet, if I am not mistaken, there is a growing impression, supported by this same political power in the south, that the officers in this State are tyrannical, meddlesome, and disposed to thwart the faithful efforts of the noble white people to reorganize the State.

Many delegations of the citizens of this State have visited Washington for the purpose of getting their property returned, or of obtaining some other favor. They, in order to accomplish their desire, represent the feeling of their friends at home as very cordially disposed toward the United States government, and say that they all acquiesce in the freedom of the negroes. A little examination into the condition of affairs in this State will show that this is not the case, and that what the people do is only done in order that they may be restored to power so as to change the direction in which affairs are tending. I am afraid the profuse loyalty of the delegations to Washington is being taken as the sentiment of the masses, and is directing legislation and policy.

It is idle to talk about these people working out this negro problem. People who will not admit that it is best, or even right, to educate the freedmen, are not the proper persons to be intrusted with the administration of justice to them. I have no hesitation in saying, that if the question of educating the colored people were to-day submitted to the whites of this State, they would vote against it in a body. Nine-tenths of the educated and refined class, who are supposed to have higher and nobler feelings, would vote against it.

I have been called on by persons of this class, and asked to suppress the religious meetings among the colored people because they made so much noise! When I remonstrate with them and talk of religious freedom, and of the right of all to worship God in the manner most suited to their convictions of right, these gentlemen hold up their hands in horror at the idea. What would magistrates selected from these people do in reference to such complaints? Suppress the meeting, of course.

A similar and much stronger prejudice exists against the establishment of schools for the negro's benefit. If federal bayonets were to-day removed from our midst, not a colored school would be permitted in the State. The teachers, perhaps, would not be tarred and feathered and hung, as they would have been in old times, but ways and means innumerable would present themselves by which to drive them out.

The white citizens both of Vicksburg and Natchez have requested me not to establish freedmen schools inside their city limits, yet over one-half the population of these cities is composed of freed people—the class who are doing the work, toiling all day in the sun, while the white employers are reaping the benefit of their labor through superior knowledge, and are occupying their elegant leisure by talking and writing constantly about the demoralization of negro labor—that the negro won't work, &c.

It is nonsense to talk so much about plans for getting the negroes to work. They do now and always have done, all the physical labor of the south, and if treated as they should be by their government, (which is so anxious to be magnanimous to the white people of this country, who never did work and never will,) they will continue to do so. Who are the workmen in these fields? Who are hauling the cotton to market, driving hacks and drays in the cities, repairing streets and railroads, cutting timber, and in every place raising the hum of industry? The freedmen, not the rebel soldiery. The southern white men, true to their instincts and training, are going to Mexico or Brazil, or talk of importing labor in the shape of Coolies, Irishmen—anything—anything to avoid work, any way to keep from putting their own shoulders to the wheel.

The mass of the freedmen can and will support themselves by labor. They need nothing but justice before the courts of the land, impartial judges and juries, to encourage them in well-doing, or punish them for the violation of just laws, a chance to own the land and property they can honestly obtain, the free exercise of their right to worship God and educate themselves, and—let them alone.

The delegates to Washington think that it is their duty, peculiarly, to see the President and arrange the affairs of the negro. Why don't they attend to their own business, or make arrangements for the working of the disbanded rebel army in the cotton fields and workshops of the south? There are to-day as many houseless, homeless, poor, wandering, idle white men here as there are negroes in the same condition, yet no arrangements are made for their working. All the trickery, chicanery and political power possible are being brought to bear on the poor negro, to make him do the hard labor for the whites, as in days of old.

To this end the mass of the people are instinctively working. They steadily refuse to sell or lease lands to black men. Colored mechanics of this city, who have made several thousand dollars during the last two years, find it impossible to buy even land enough to put up a house on, yet white men can purchase any amount of land. The whites know that if negroes are not allowed to acquire property or become landholders, they must ultimately return to plantation labor, and work for wages that will barely support themselves and families, and they feel that this kind of slavery will be better than none at all.

People who will do these things, after such a war, and so much misery, while federal bayonets are yet around them, are not to be intrusted with the education and development of a, race of slaves just liberated.

I have made this letter longer than it should have been, and may have taxed your patience, yet I do not see how I could have said less, and expressed my views on the subject.

I am, general, very respectfully, your obedient servant,

SAMUEL THOMAS, Colonel, Assistant Commissioner B.R.F. and A.L. for Mississippi and N.E. Louisiana.

General CARL SCHURZ.

No. 28.

Mobile, Alabama, *September* 9, 1865.

Colonel George D. Robinson, 97th United States colored troops, states as follows:

I was sent out to Connecuh, Covington, Coffee, Dale, and Henry counties, to administer the amnesty oath. I was at Covington myself, having officers under my orders stationed in the other four counties. I travelled through Connecuh and Covington; about the other counties I have reports from my officers. A general disposition was found among the planters to set the colored people who had cultivated their crops during the summer adrift as soon as the crops would be secured, and not to permit the negro to remain upon any footing of equality with the white man in that country.

In none of the above-named counties I heard of a justice of the peace or other magistrate discharging the duties of an agent of the Freedmen's Bureau, nor did I hear of any of them willing to do so. I deem it necessary that some officers be sent out there to attend to the interests of the freedmen, in order to avoid the trouble and confusion which is almost certain to ensue unless the matter is attended to and regulated.

I returned from Covington yesterday, September 8.

GEO. D. ROBINSON,*Colonel 97th United States Infantry*.

No. 29.

MEMORANDUM OF A CONVERSATION BETWEEN WILLIAM KING, ESQ., OF SAVANNAH, AND CARL SCHURZ.

Savannah, July 31, 1865.

Question by Mr. Schurz. What are the ideas of the people in this State as to the future organization of your labor system?

Answer. It is generally conceded that slavery is dead, but it is believed that the negro will not work unless compelled to. Money is no inducement that will incite him to work. He works for comfort, that is, he wants to gain something and then enjoy it immediately afterwards. He has no idea of the binding force of a contract, and it is questionable whether he ever will have.

Question. So you consider the contract system, as it is now introduced here and there, a failure.

Answer. In a number of cases that I know of it is a failure. The negroes are not doing the work they have contracted for. I know other cases in which they have remained with their former masters, work well, and produce fair crops.

Question. In what manner, then, can, in your opinion, the free-labor system be made to work here?

Answer. The negro must be kept in a state of tutelage, like a minor. For instance, he may be permitted to freely choose the master for whom he wants to work; he may bind himself for a year, and, for all practical purposes, the master must act as his guardian.

Question. You think, then, something more is necessary than a mere contract system by which the negro is only held to fulfil his contract?

Answer. Yes. The negro ought to be held in the position of a ward.

Question. Do you not think the negro ought to be educated, and do you believe the people of this State would tax themselves for the purpose of establishing a general system of education?

Answer. I think it would be well to have the negro educated, but I do not think the people of this State would tax themselves for such a purpose. The people are too poor and have too many other things to take care of. We have to look for that to the people of the North. The North having freed the negroes, ought to see to it that they be elevated. Besides, the poor whites are not in favor of general education at all. They are themselves very ignorant, and look upon education as something dangerous. For them we must have a system of compulsory education, or we cannot get them to send their children to school. A good many of the Hardshell Baptists among them look upon school-teachers as the emissaries of the devil.

Question. How far do you think the people of this State would be prepared to grant the negro equality before the law? Would they, for instance, give him the right to testify in courts of justice against white men?

Answer. I think not. It is generally believed that the negro has no idea of the sanctity of an oath.

Question. Do you not think such disabilities would place the negro under such disadvantage in the race of life as to deprive him of a fair chance?

Answer. This is the dilemma, in my opinion: either we admit the negro's testimony in courts of justice, and then our highest interests are placed at the mercy of a class of people who cannot be relied on when testifying under oath; or we deny the negro that right, and then he will not be in a position to properly defend his own interests, and will be a downtrodden, miserable creature.

Question. Do you not think vagrancy laws and police regulations might be enacted, equally applicable to whites and blacks, which might obviate most of the difficulties you suggest as arising from the unwillingness of the negro to work?

Answer. Perhaps they might; but the whites would not agree to that. The poor whites hate and are jealous of the negro, and the politicians will try and please the whites so as to get their votes.

Question. Do you think it would be advisable to withdraw our military forces from the State if the civil government be restored at an early date?

Answer. It would not be safe. There are a great many bad characters in the country who would make it for some time unsafe for known Union people, and for northerners who may settle down here, to live in this country without the protection of the military. The mere presence of garrisons will prevent much mischief. The presence of the military is also necessary to maintain the peace between the whites and blacks, and it will be necessary until their relations are settled upon a permanent and satisfactory basis.

This memorandum was read by me to Mr. King and approved by him as a correct reproduction of the views he had expressed.

C. SCHURZ.

No. 30.

What the planter wants before he embarks his capital and time in the attempt to cultivate another crop.—Suggestions submitted by a committee at a meeting of planters, November 24, 1864.

First.—Above all, he wants an undoubted guarantee that the labor and teams, corn and hay, with which he begins the cultivation of another crop shall be secured to him for at least twelve months. From past experience, we know that, to be reliable, this guarantee must come from the government at Washington.

Second.—Some mode of compelling laborers to perform ten (10) hours of faithful labor in each twenty-four hours, (Sundays excepted,) and strict obedience of all orders. This may be partially attained by a graduated system of fines, deduction of time or wages, deduction of rations of all kinds in proportion to time lost, rigidly enforced. But in obstinate cases it can only be done by corporal punishments, such as are inflicted in the army and navy of the United States. In light cases of disobedience of orders and non-performance of duty the employer should impose fines, &c. The corporal punishment should be inflicted by officers appointed by the superintendent of "colored labor," who might, from time to time, visit each plantation in a parish, and ascertain whether the laborer was satisfied with his treatment, and whether he performed his part of the contract, and thus the officer would qualify himself by his own information to correct any abuse that might exist, and award equal justice to each party. The plan of sending off refractory laborers to work on government plantations is worse than useless. A planter always plants as much land as he believes he has labor to cultivate efficiently, neither more nor less. If less, a portion of his laborers are idle a part of their time; if more, his crops must suffer from the want of proper cultivation. If the laborers do not work faithfully, and their work is not judiciously directed, either from want of skill on the part of him who directs the labor, or from the refusal or failure of the laborers from any cause to do the work as it ought to be done, the crops must suffer. If, then, a portion of labor necessary to cultivate a certain amount of land is abstracted by sending it to work anywhere else, the crop must fail in proportion to the amount of labor abstracted. It must therefore be apparent to all that the amount of prompt, faithful, and well-directed labor, necessary to cultivate a given quantity of land efficiently, must be available at all times, when the cultivator deems it necessary, or the crops must necessarily, to a greater or less extent, prove a failure.

Third.—The rate of wages should be fixed—above which no one should be allowed to go. There should be at least four classes of hands, both male and female. If the laborer should be furnished, as this year, 1864, with clothing, shoes, rations, houses, wood, medicine, &c., the planter cannot afford to pay any more wages than this year, and to some hands not so much. Wages should not be paid oftener than once a quarter. As long as a negro has a dime in his pocket he will go every Saturday to some store or town. Besides, if the men have money once a month they are constantly corrupting the women, who will not work because they expect to get money of the men. If the laborers are to pay for all their supplies, some think higher wages could be paid; but it would be necessary to require the negro to supply himself with at least two suits of clothes, one pair of shoes, a hat, and four pounds of pork or bacon, one peck of corn meal a week, vegetables at least twice a week, for a first-class hand. The laborer should pay for his medicine, medical attendance, nursing, &c.; also, house rent, $5 a month, water included; wood at $2 a cord in the tree, or $4 a cord cut and delivered. Instead of money, each employer should be required to pay once a week in tickets issued and signed by himself or agent, not transferable to any one off the premises of him who issues them, redeemable by the issuer quarterly in current funds, and to be received by him in the purchase of goods, provisions, &c., which he sold at current prices.

Fourth.—A law to punish most severely any one who endeavors, by offering higher wages, gifts, perquisites, &c., &c., to induce a negro to leave his employer before the expiration of the term for which he has engaged to labor without the consent of said employer.

Fifth.—Wages to be quarterly. One-half to be retained to the end of the year, unless it is found that more than half is required to maintain a man and his family.

Sixth.—Lost time to be deducted from wages daily; fines to be charged daily; rations, of all kinds, to be docked in proportion to the time lost during the week, if rations are to be supplied.

Seventh.—Fines to be imposed for disobedience of any orders.

Eighth.—During sugar-making the laborer should be required to work at night as well as during the day. For night-work he might be allowed double wages for the time he works.

Ninth.—The negroes should not be allowed to go from one plantation to another without the written permit of their employer, nor should they be allowed to go to any town or store without written permission.

Tenth.—That the laborers should be required to have their meals cooked in a common kitchen by the plantation cooks, as heretofore.

146

At present each family cook for themselves. If there be twenty-five houses on a plantation worked by one hundred hands, there are lighted, three times every day, winter and summer, for the purpose of cooking, twenty-five (25) fires, instead of one or two, which are quite as many as are necessary. To attend these twenty-five fires there must be twenty-five cooks. The extravagance in wood and the loss of time by this mode must be apparent to all. Making the negroes pay for the wood they burn, and for fencing lumber of any kind, would have a tendency to stop this extravagant mode of doing business. They should also be fined heavily or suffer some kind of corporal punishment for burning staves, hoop-poles, shingles, plank, spokes, &c., which they now constantly do.

Eleventh.—None but regularly ordained ministers should be allowed to preach. At present on every plantation there are a number of preachers. Frequent meetings are held at night, continuing from 7 or 8 p.m. until 1 or 2 o'clock a.m. The day after one of these long meetings many of the laborers are unfit to labor; neither are the morals of the negroes improved by these late meetings, nor the health. The night meetings should break up at 10 p.m., and there should be but one a week on a plantation. Some of the preachers privately promulgate the most immoral doctrines.

Twelfth.—A police guard or patrol should be established under the control of the superintendent of free labor, whose duty it shall be, under their officers, to enforce the rules and regulations that the superintendent of free labor may think best to adopt for the government of the laborers and their families on plantations and in private families.

Thirteenth.—The laborers are at present extremely careless of the teams, carts, wagons, gear, tools, and material of all kinds put in their possession, and should therefore be held accountable for the same. Parents should be held liable for things stolen or destroyed by their children not over twelve years of age.

Fourteenth.—Foremen should be fined whenever they fail to report any of the laborers under them who disobey orders of any kind. The foreman at the stable should be required especially to report neglect or ill treatment of teams by their drivers, and he should be held liable for all tools and halters, &c., put in the stable.

Fifteenth.—The unauthorized purchase of clothing or other property by laborers, or others domesticated on plantations, should be severely punished, and so should the sale by laborers or others domesticated on plantations of plantation products without a written permission be punished by fine, imprisonment, and obstinate cases by corporal punishment. The sale or furnishing of intoxicating liquor of any kind to laborers or others domesticated on plantations should be severely punished.

Sixteenth.—The possession of arms or other dangerous weapons without authority should be punished by fine or imprisonment and the arms forfeited.

Seventeenth.—No one, white or colored, with or without passes, should have authority to go into a quarter without permission of the proprietor of said quarter. Should any insist upon going in, or be found in a quarter without permission of the proprietor, he should be arrested at once by the proprietor.

Eighteenth.—Fighting and quarrelling should be prohibited under severe penalties, especially husbands whipping their wives.

Nineteenth.—Laborers and all other persons domesticated on plantations or elsewhere should be required to be respectful in tone, manner, and language to their employers, and proprietors of the plantations or places on which they reside, or be fined and imprisoned.

Twentieth.—The whole study, aim, and object of the negro laborer now is how to avoid work and yet have a claim for wages, rations, clothes, &c.

No. 31.

OAK FOREST, NEAR TIGERVILLE STATION,

N.O. and O. Railroad, December 1, 1864.

Dear Sir: The earnest desire you have manifested to make the negro laborer under the new order of things successful, makes me the more disposed to offer every assistance in my power to that end. I have no prejudices to overcome; I would do the blacks all the good in my power consistently with their welfare and the welfare of the country; I owe them no ill will, but I am well satisfied that it will demand the highest skill and the largest experience combined to make the new system work successfully, when hitherto all others, including our own two years' experience, have signally failed. No namby-pamby measures will do. We may have more psalm singing, more night preaching, greater excesses in the outward manifestation of religion, but depend upon it there will be less true morality, less order, less truthfulness, less honest industry. It is not the experiment of a few only, or of a day, but of an *institution*, if anything, for millions; the mixing in industrial association of separate races hitherto distinct; of systems fundamentally changed and not of mere individuals, and the man who does not rise to the height of the great argument fails before he starts. It is not to listen to babblers, to *professional* philanthropists, to quacks and demagogues: it demands a manly, masculine, vigorous exercise of executive power, adapted to the circumstances of the case. Nobody is absolutely free, white or black. I have been a slave all my life; you have been the same. We were subject to discipline from childhood, and the negro as well, and must continue to be subject to wholesome restraints all of us.

It is well to consider that the measures of the government have rendered labor scarce. It would be safe to say there is not *half a supply*; that every sort of inducement will be held out to get labor away from present situations; that the inclination of all who are unincumbered is, to get to the city and its neighborhood. Every planter has some already there, living most unprofitably. I have half a dozen, some under the agreement of the present year. Concentration is the order of the day, and none but those who can command the largest sum of money will be able to carry on plantations with any hope of success. I take leave to add some suggestions, believing you will receive them with the same friendly spirit in which they are offered. I am still surrounded by my own servants, and would like to see the system so ordered that they would still find it to their advantage to remain in their present comfortable homes.

Wages, rules, and regulations should be fixed and uniform: nothing left to discretion.

A penalty should be inflicted on every employer who deviates from the established rates, *maximum* rates.

No field crops should be raised by hired laborers. The evils attending this are numerous and insurmountable.

Wages should be extremely moderate on account of the unsteadiness of labor and exceeding uncertainty of crops of all sorts, but especially of cane and cotton.

Cooking for hands should be confined absolutely to one kitchen, and a charge made for all wood taken to their houses; a certain supply should be allowed, and no additional quantity permitted at any price: otherwise no plantation can long stand the enormous, wasteful consumption of fuel.

All necessary expenditures for the blacks, old as well as young, should be borne by themselves. White laborers are all liable to such charges, and why not wasteful and improvident blacks? They should be early taught the value of what they consume as well as the other costs of living.

About keeping stock the rule should be absolute.

No travelling about, day or night, without a written sanction from the proper person. The violation of this order by a commanding officer has brought the small-pox on my place and already eight grown hands have died with it, and there are not less than twenty invalids besides: this is one of the evils.

Medicine and professional attendance a charge to the patient, as well as all educational arrangements.

Every ploughman or woman, and teamster, to be obliged to feed and curry his or her team once at least every day.

Payments beyond proper and prescribed supplies to be small, the smaller the better, and still better if withheld till the crop is made and saved; but settlements by tickets should be made weekly. (A share in the crop is the best for both parties.) I do not perceive the utility of "home colonies;" they belong to the class of *theories* more than anything else. Families should be kept together and at the "homes" to which they have been accustomed, if possible, and *made* to support themselves, all who are able to do so. At present there are many who will not do this because they are made a charge on the master or employer. Vagrants should be punished; *work is a necessity*. But I only put down a few particulars to *impress* upon your mind as they occur to me.

I know the difficult task you have undertaken. You have a giant to manage, and you will have to exercise a giant's strength. You have no less than to revise the teachings of all past history. You have to accomplish what has never been accomplished before. Neither in the east nor in the west has the African been found to work voluntarily; but the experiment is to be tried anew in this country, and I shall lend my assistance, whatever it is, to help on in the road to success, if that be possible. I have tried it two years under the military without success, or the prospect of it. If, however, I can in any way assist you to gain the meed of success, both my own interest and my kind feelings towards you combine to prompt me to renewed efforts in the cause.

I remain, very respectfully and truly, yours,

T. GIBSON.

Hon. B.F. FLANDERS.

P.S.—The great desideratum in obtaining labor from free blacks is its*enforcement*. How is this to be done? Formerly the known authority possessed by the master over the slave, prevented in a great degree the exercise of it. The knowledge now, on the part of the blacks, that the military authority has forbidden any authority over them, increases the very necessity of the power which is forbidden. This is palpable to any one who sees with an experienced eye for a day. There can necessarily be no order, day or night, no fidelity, no morality, no industry. *It is so*, speculate and theorize as we may. I wish it were different; it is a great pity to witness these deplorable effects.

Disease is scattered broadcast; my own stock has been for some time consumed, except a few milch cows. The sugar from the sugar-houses has been sold in quantities in every direction. The cotton of one plantation has been sold to the extent of half the crop to a white man, and only by the merest accident discovered in time to be detected. My neighbor's hogs have been taken from the pen, killed and brought home for consumption; his cattle the same. These things are within my knowledge by the merest accident, but there is absolutely no remedy, because their testimony is as good, if not better than mine, and this they know perfectly well. In a case of sugar-selling, I had the oath of a disinterested white man to the fact, and the black and white man identified by the witness. When this witness was through with his testimony, the negro man, the interested party, *the accused himself*, was called up by the provost marshal, and of course he swore himself innocent, and so he was *cleared*. In the case of the cotton not a negro can be brought to confess, notwithstanding the confession of the white man and the surrender of the cotton. How, then, can good order, good morals and honest industry be maintained when immunity from punishment is patent to their understandings?

I know no remedy adequate to the circumstances but an always present power to enforce law and order, and this now requires the constant presence of the bayonet. Which is the best, a regular military government, or the quiet, humane exercise of just so much authority as the case demands, by the master, who has every motive, human and divine, to exercise humanity and protect his slave from injustice and injury?

The past, or rather the present year, we had nothing but blank orders, and these are of no avail whatever without enforcement; and this brings us back to the starting-point again, and the bayonet again, and so it is to the end of the chapter. Moral suasion will not do for whites who have had freedom as an inheritance, and education within their reach. How then can it be expected that he who has been predestined by the Almighty to be a servant of servants all the days of his life, shall be capable of at once rising to motives of human conduct higher than those possessed by the white man?

All that my reason teaches and the experience I have had, and the history I have read, bring me to the same conclusion: you must utterly fail unless you add the stimulus of *corporal punishment* to the admonitions of the law; but as this would be somewhat inconsistent with the freedom which our solons have decreed, I must only confess my inability to prescribe the orthodox remedies according to the received dogmas from the inspired sources of knowledge at the north above all the lessons I have learned heretofore, and entirely above everything I expect to learn hereafter.

No. 32.

FREEDMEN'S BUREAU,

Shreveport, La., August 1, 1865.

Sir: At the date of my last monthly report, (July 2d,) the free-labor system in western Louisiana was an experiment. No contracts between the planters and freedmen had then been entered into, and the difficulties to be met with and overcome by the contracting parties were new to each. The herculean task of removing the objections which the freedmen offered to signing a "contract," and of eradicating the prejudice existing among the planters against countenancing the employment upon their plantations as free men of those whom they had so long and firmly held in bondage, devolved upon the agents of the bureau.

The objection presented by the freedmen consisted chiefly in the fact that they had *no confidence whatever* in the word of their "old masters." Said they, in substance, "We cannot trust the power that has never accorded us any privileges. Our former oppressors show by their actions that they would sooner retard than advance our prosperity." While in nine cases out of ten the freedmen eagerly and readily acceded to fair terms for their labor when the matter was explained by a government agent, exactly in the same ratio did they refuse to listen to any proposition made by the planter alone.

Their readiness to comprehend their situation and to enter into an agreement to work when enlightened by an agent of the bureau, or, in exceptional cases, when the planters sought in a kind and philanthropic spirit to explain to them their relations to society and the government, is conclusive proof that the disposition to be idle formed no part of the reason for their refusing to contract with their former masters.

With these facts in view, it will be readily perceived that the only feasible mode of success was to send agents into the country to visit every plantation. This was undertaken; but with no funds to procure the services of assistants, and with the difficulty of obtaining the right class of men for these positions from the army, the progress made has not been as rapid or the work as effectual as it would have been under more favorable circumstances. Partial returns have been received, as follows:

From	Bienville	parish	248		contracts.
"	Bossier	parish		14	"
"	Caddo	parish		172	"
"	DeSoto	parish		246	"
"	Marion	county,	Texas	206	"
—-					
Total		received		886	"
===					

Returns are yet to be received from the parishes of Claiborne, Natchitoches, Winn and Sabine, and from Harrison county, Texas. These will all be given in by the 15th inst., and I shall then be able to determine the exact number employed upon each plantation and laboring under the new system. Regarding the average number employed upon each plantation in the parish of Caddo as a basis for an estimate, the returned rolls will foot up a list of 7,088 names, and the whole number of freedmen contracted with during the month of July in the district under my supervision will not probably exceed 20,000, or fall short of 15,000.

During the month a sufficient length of time has elapsed to render judgment to a certain extent upon the workings of the new system. That it has not satisfied a majority of the planters is a conclusion which, from their disposition at first, was evident would be arrived at. That the freedmen have accepted the arrangements devised by the government for their protection so readily and have worked so faithfully, is a matter for congratulation.

The planters at first expected that, though the power to "control" the persons of the laborers had been torn from them by the stern requirements of war, the agents of the bureau would, through the military, confine the negro to their plantations and compel him to labor for them. In this way it was thought that the same *regime* as pursued in times of slavery could be kept up, and it was this idea which prompted a planter, noted for his frankness, to remark "that the people of the south desired the government to continue this supervision for a term of years." Finding that their ideas of the policy of the government were erroneous, and that they could not exercise this "controlling power" either directly or indirectly, and that the freedman was to be placed, as nearly as the circumstances surrounding his situation would permit, upon the same grounds as the white laborer, it is but a logical sequence that the planters should be disappointed and dissatisfied with the work performed by the freedmen.

In this place it may be well to notice that the country is yet in a very unsettled condition. After a four years' war which has sapped it of all its resources, and after a life-long servitude for a hard taskmaster, the negro is liberated from bondage, and he finds the people of the country in no condition to offer him the most advantageous terms for his services. This, with the natural desire experienced by all mankind for a period of repose after that of incessant and forced labor, is one of the causes which have contributed to render the freedmen negligent and inconstant at their work.

Reports are constantly brought to this office by the negroes from the interior that freedmen have been kidnapped and summarily disposed of. These obtain circulation and credence among all classes, and, whether true or not, operate disadvantageously to the interests of both the planters and the freedmen.

Again, the threat of shooting the laborers, so frequently made by the planters, is very unwise, and usually has the effect of causing a general stampede from the plantation where the threat was made. The fact that the body of a negro was seen hanging from a tree in Texas, near the Louisiana line; and of the murder in cold blood, in the northern part of the parishof Caddo, of Mary, a colored woman, by John Johnson, the son of the proprietor of the plantation where the woman worked; and that instances have repeatedly occurred similar to a case presented at my office, where an old man had received a blow over his head with a shillalah one inch in diameter, which was so severe as to snap the stick asunder; and also the fracturing of the skull and the breaking of the arm of a helpless, inoffensive colored woman by a vindictive planter in the parish of Natchitoches; and the statement of one of my agents, who says that "upon half the plantations the freedmen are not well clothed and their rations are scanty;" and of another who has visited every plantation in ward No. —, parish of ——, who reports at the close of the month as follows: "The freedmen in my ward are very poorly clothed and fed, although no particular complaints have been made as yet;" should all be taken into consideration in arriving at conclusions in regard to the disposition of the freedmen to work, and before judgment is rendered upon the complaints of the major portion of the planters; and it is also useless to disguise the fact that among the freedmen, as among all classes of people, there are many ill-disposed as well as idle persons, and a few of these upon each plantation create dissatisfaction among the others.

Notwithstanding the complaints of the planters and the above-named facts, the existence of which would cause a disturbance among any class of laborers in the world, the majority of the planters have been eager to contract with their former slaves, for the reason that after their plantations had been visited by an agent of the government, and an agreement had been made upon the prescribed forms, the freedmen worked better than before. This is a matter of significance, and its bearing is readily seen. Having noticed the disapprobation of the larger portion of the planting community, and the causes which led to their complaints, I desire to call your attention in this connexion to the report of one of my most experienced agents. It is as follows:

"In all cases have the employees given satisfaction where their former masters are at all reasonable. I would mention the case of Jacob Hoss as an example: he contracted with his former slaves in the latter part of May for one-fourth of all his crops; they have been steady and industrious, and have decidedly the finest cotton and corn in the district." Mr. Hoss has 200 acres of cotton, 400 of corn, and 8 of potatoes. Your attention is also solicited to the testimony of the *liberal few* who have taken the amnesty oath with the intention to keep it. One says: "The freedmen in my neighborhood are laboring well where they are well paid." Another, a large land proprietor, states that "he could not ask his hands to work better." The same gentleman also states that "he would not have the freedmen upon his plantation made slaves again if he could."

The testimony is concurrent that, where liberal wages are paid and the freedmen are kindly treated, no difficulty is experienced with them, and that they labor honestly and industriously. The complaints which have been presented at the office for consideration are very nearly in a direct ratio of the two classes, but the wrongs of the freedmen are by far the most aggravated, as they suffer in almost every conceivable way. It has been necessary to fine and assess damages upon several planters for beating their laborers, and also to punish several freedmen for violating their contracts and for other misdemeanors. The following is a literal copy of a document brought to this office by a colored man, which is conclusive evidence that there *are* those who still claim the negro as their property:

"This boy Calvin has permit to hire to whome he please, but I shall hold him as my propperty untill set Free by Congress.

"July the 7, 1865. E.V. TULLY."

The spirit of the above also made its appearance in another form in the action of the police jury of the parish of Bossier, which was an attempt to revive at once the old slave laws, and to prevent the freedmen from obtaining employment from the plantations of their former masters. The gist of the enactment alluded to is contained in the paragraph directing the officers on patrol duty "to arrest and take up all idle and vagrant persons running at large without employment, and carry them before the proper authority, to be dealt with as the law directs."

As soon as this matter came under the observation of the bureau, the facts in the case were represented to Brevet Major General J.P. Hawkins, commanding western district of Louisiana, and at the same time a request was made that the restrictions imposed upon the freedmen in this section by General Orders No. 24, headquarters northern division of Louisiana, be revoked; and the general issued an order, dated July 31, which removes the said restrictions, and prohibits the parish police juries, established by the civil authorities, from arresting freedmen unless for positive offence against the law. This breaks down the last barrier to the enjoyment of liberty by the freedmen in western Louisiana, and I feel highly gratified that it has been accomplished without referring it to higher authorities, as our mail facilities are so irregular that at least two months would have been consumed by the operation.

Upon the 10th of July the freedmen's hospital was opened for the reception of patients, and enclosed please find a copy of the hospital report for July, marked 1. This is a necessary as well as a charitable institution, as the city authorities have as yet taken no measures to provide for the indigent sick.

Since the establishment of the bureau here, it has been found necessary to issue rations to freedmen, as follows:

To citizen employees 46 To helpless and infirm 236 To sick and hospital attendants 1,169 ——-Total issued 1,451 =====

The number fed by the government to-day is as follows:

Men	7
Women	6

Children   10
—

Total number infirm and helpless rationed 23

Number sick at hospital 40 Number hospital attendants 24 Number citizen employees rationed 1 —Total number supplied with rations 88
==

None but the helpless and infirm and sick have been fed at the expense of the government, and these only in cases of absolute necessity. Many planters who abandoned their homes on the Mississippi and carried away their slaves to Texas have returned to this city, and with a coolness amounting to audacity have demanded transportation for their former slaves to various points from the mouth of the Red river to Lake Providence. Finding that the officers of the government would not oblige them in this particular, they left behind the aged and infirm to provide for themselves as best they could. This and the abuses on plantations have caused the principal suffering among the freedmen, and have brought many to the city who otherwise would have remained upon the plantation, but, all things being considered, comparatively few have congregated about town. There has been such a demand for day labor in the city that I have deemed it a false philanthropy to feed those who temporarily sought refuge from oppression.

The permanent residents are orderly and industrious, and desire very much to have schools established for their children. I cannot here refrain from mentioning the fact that the presence of negroes in town possessing free papers is extremely disagreeable to the citizens.

The tax collected of planters has thus far been sufficient to defray office and printing expenses. The hire of a surgeon and nurses for the hospital, amounting in July to $204.46, is the only bill which it is necessary to refer to you for payment. All the property and money which has come into my hands on account of the bureau has been accounted for to the proper departments, according to regulations.

By Special Orders No. 140, dated at headquarters northern division of Louisiana, June 21, 1865, Chaplain Thomas Callahan, 48th United States colored infantry, was assigned to duty with me as my assistant, and he has had charge of the department of complaints. He is a very capable and efficient officer, and his services are very valuable to the bureau.

Again, I have occasion to return acknowledgments to Brigadier General J.C. Veatch for his cordial assistance in aiding me to carry out the measures of the bureau, and also to Colonel Crandal and

Lieutenant Colonel McLaughlin, post commandants, for valuable aid; and to Brevet Major General J.P. Hawkins we are indebted for that which makes the colored man in reality a *free* man.

Believing that with proper management and kind treatment the freedmen in western Louisiana will be found to be as industrious as laborers in other sections of the country,

I have the honor to be, with much respect, your obedient servant,

W.B. STICKNEY,*Lieutenant and Assistant Superintendent Freedmen.*

THOMAS W. CONWAY,*Assistant Commissioner Bureau of Freedmen. &c.*

No. 33.

FREEDMEN'S BUREAU,

Shreveport, Louisiana, August 26, 1865.

Sir: I have the honor to report, in accordance with orders, that in the district under my supervision, comprising eight parishes in Louisiana and two counties in Texas, and an area of about 13,764 square miles, 3,105 contracts have been made, and 27,830 laborers enrolled since the first of July. The work of making contracts is now nearly completed, but the returns for the month of August from the officers acting in the different parishes have not as yet been received. From the data already collected it will be safe to estimate the whole number of laborers working under the contract system in the district at not less than 32,000, 25,000 of whom are in Louisiana.

The experience of two months has demonstrated the fact that the negro will work well when he is well paid and kindly treated; and another principle in the nature of the contracting parties has been equally as clearly elucidated, *i.e.*, the planters are disposed to pay the freedmen the least possible sum for their labor, and that for much compensation the freedmen make an offset by making as little as possible. To acknowledge the right of the negro to freedom, and to regard him as a free man entitled to the benefits of his labor and to all the privileges and immunities of citizenship, is to throw aside the dogmas for which the south have been contending for the last thirty years, and seems to be too great a stride for the people to take at once, and too unpalatable a truth for the aristocratic planter to comprehend, without the interposition of the stern logic of the bayonet in the hands of a colored soldier. Duty to my government compels me to report the following well-authenticated facts:

1. Nineteen-twentieths of the planters have no disposition to pay the negro well or treat him well.

2. In the same proportion the planting aristocracy proffers obedience to the government, and at the same time do all in their power to make trouble.

3. The planters evince a disposition to throw all the helpless and infirm freedmen upon the hands of the government possible, in order to embarrass us and compel us to return them to slavery again.

4. A majority of the planters desire to prevent the success of the free-labor system, that they may force Congress to revive slavery, or, what is more, a system of peonage.

5. The belief is general among the planters that without some means of "controlling" the persons of the laborers they cannot succeed; and for this reason they desire to have the military force removed, and the privilege of enacting such laws as will enable them to retain this power.

6. To defraud, oppress, and maltreat the freedmen seems to be the principle governing the action of more than half of those who make contracts with them.

7. The lives of the freedmen are frequently threatened, and murders are not of uncommon occurrence.

8. The life of a northern man who is true to his country and the spirit and genius of its institutions, and frankly enunciates his principles, is not secure where there is not a military force to protect him.

About the 15th of July Corporal J.M. Wallace, of company B, forty-seventh Indiana Veteran volunteer infantry, was on duty with this bureau, and engaged in making contracts upon Red river, in the parish of Caddo. He visited Mr. Daniel's plantation, and, as it is stated, started for Mr. White's place, but never reached it. Being absent unaccountably, a sergeant and a detail of four men were sent to look him up, but could find no trace of him. Without doubt he was murdered. He was a young man of unexceptionable habits and character, and was highly esteemed by the officers of his regiment. The circumstances of the case are such as to lead to the belief that the planters in the vicinity connived at his death. Captain Hoke, another agent of the bureau, was stopped by a highwayman within eight miles of Shreveport. One of my assistants reports as follows: "In the northern part of this parish (Cuddo) there are men armed and banded to resist the law." These facts prove that the presence of a military force is needed in every parish. Instead of the present system of districts, I would recommend that the officer for each parish report direct to headquarters at New Orleans for instructions, and that each officer be furnished with at least twenty men, ten of whom should be mounted. I apprehend that at the commencement of the next year the planters will endeavor to load us down with the aged and infirm, and those with large families. To meet this and other difficulties that may arise, I recommend that at least five thousand acres of land be confiscated in every parish, and an opportunity given the freedmen to rent or purchase the land, and that every facility be afforded planters in the lower part of the State to obtain laborers from western Louisiana. Another remedy has been suggested, and as it meets with my approval I quote the recommendations of the officer in his own words: "Let the white troops on duty in this department be mustered out; they are greatly dissatisfied with remaining in the service after the close of the war; let black troops be mustered in their stead. In urging this matter, I suggest that the government has the first right to the services of the freedmen, and he needs the discipline of the army to develop his manhood and self-reliance. Such a course of recruiting black soldiers will act as a powerful restraint upon the abuses practiced by the planters on the freedmen, and will also compel the payment of better wages. If the planter wishes the services of a shrewd, enterprising freedman, he must out-bid the government. Lastly, the country needs the soldiers. Politicians may say what they may; western Louisiana is no more loyal now than when the State adopted the ordinance of secession."

The statistics given at the commencement prove that we have experienced less difficulty with the freedmen than could have been expected. At times it has been necessary to adopt stringent measures to stem the tide of freedmen that seemed to be setting in toward Shreveport, and many of them have such vague ideas of the moral obligations of a contract that it has been necessary to strengthen them by imprisonment and hard labor; but the great and insuperable difficulty which meets us at every step is, *that the planters and the freedmen have no confidence in and respect for each other*. The planters inform us that they are the best friends of the negro, but the freedmen fail to see the matter in that light. I am well assured that as a general rule the old planters and overseers can never succeed with the freedmen; that there must be an entire change in either laborers or proprietors before the country will again be prosperous. The plan of renting lands to the freedmen, as proposed by a few planters, I am of the opinion will prove very profitable to both parties. While, as a general rule, there is constant difficulty between the freedmen and their old masters and overseers, my agents and northern men have no trouble with them; and should the planters employ practical farmers from the north as business managers, it seems to be well demonstrated that the free-labor system, as it now is, with but slight modifications, would be a grand success. In this connexion I cannot refrain from noticing the assertion of a southern politician to the effect "that were the freedmen enfranchised, nine out of ten of them would vote for their old masters," which assertion every freedman will pronounce a wilful and malignant falsehood.

The country is full of arms, and their use upon the freedmen is so frequent, and the general disposition of the people such, that I would strongly recommend, as a measure to secure the safety of life and property, that all classes of arms be taken from the citizens, not to be returned until an entirely different disposition is evinced.

The system to be made binding for the next year should be published as early as the 15th of October, and the matter of contracting be commenced as soon thereafter as the parties desire to do so. I would respectfully suggest the propriety for calling of such statistical matter upon the back of the contract as will enable the officer in charge of the educational interests to determine the whole number of freedmen residing in the different parishes, and also the number of children of school age.

The establishment of schools will be met by the most venomous opposition, and a military force will be required to protect the teacher and scholars from insult and injury unless the tone of public sentiment improves very rapidly.

The civil authorities, so far as my knowledge extends, are not willing to grant the freedmen the rights to which their freedom entitles them. In fact it became necessary, as will be seen by a former report, for the military authorities to interfere to prevent their being virulently oppressed. In consequence of this I have kept an officer constantly on duty adjusting the difficulties arising between the whites and negroes, but important cases have been referred to the military authorities.

Chaplain Thomas Callahan, the officer referred to above, in his last report says:

"To many of the planters the idea of a negro's testimony being as good as a white man's is very unpleasant, and occasional attempts are made to bully and browbeat a colored witness upon the stand. The attempt is never made twice. Once I pitted a lawyer against a negro witness, held the parties on the cross-examination, and the lawyer was badly beaten. Some of the freedmen can conduct a case with uncommon shrewdness."

I cannot urge upon your attention too strongly the importance of keeping an officer in every parish and of providing him with a sufficient guard to command respect and enforce obedience to the laws. The presence of a military force, with judicious and discreet officers to command it, is the only means of securing to the freedmen their rights and of giving proper security to life and property.

With many thanks for that encouragement which has supported and cheered me through every difficulty, I have the honor to be, with much respect, your most obedient servant,

W.B. STICKNEY,*Lieutenant and Assistant Superintendent of Freedmen*.

THOMAS W. CONWAY,*Assistant Commissioner, &c.*

No. 34.

Ordinance relative to the police of recently emancipated negroes or freedmen within the corporate limits of the town of Opelousas.

Whereas the relations formerly subsisting between master and slave have become changed by the action of the controlling authorities; and whereas it is necessary to provide for the proper police and government of the recently emancipated negroes or freedmen in their new relations to the municipal authorities:

SECTION 1. *Be it therefore ordained by the board of police of the town of Opelousas*, That no negro or freedman shall be allowed to come within the limits of the town of Opelousas without special permission from his employers, specifying the object of his visit and the time necessary for the accomplishment of the same. Whoever shall violate this provision shall suffer imprisonment and two days' work on the public streets, or shall pay a fine of two dollars and fifty cents.

SECTION 2. *Be it further ordained*, That every negro freedman who shall be found on the streets of Opelousas after 10 o'clock at night without a written pass or permit from his employer shall be imprisoned and compelled to work five days on the public streets, or pay a fine of five dollars.

SECTION 3. No negro or freedman shall be permitted to rent or keep a house within the limits of the town under any circumstances, and any one thus offending shall be ejected and compelled to find an employer or leave the town within twenty-four hours. The lessor or furnisher of the house leased or kept as above shall pay a fine of ten dollars for each offence.

SECTION 4. No negro or freedman shall reside within the limits of the town of Opelousas who is not in the regular service of some white person or former owner, who shall be held responsible for the conduct of said freedman; but said employer or former owner may permit said freedman to hire his time by special permission in writing, which permission shall not extend over twenty-four hours at any one time. Any one violating the provisions of this, section shall be imprisoned and forced to work for two days on the public streets.

SECTION 5. No public meetings or congregations of negroes or freedmen shall be allowed within the limits of the town of Opelousas under any circumstances or for any purpose without the permission of the mayor or president of the board. This prohibition is not intended, however, to prevent the freedmen from attending the usual church services conducted by established ministers of religion. Every freedman violating this law shall be imprisoned and made to work five days on the public streets.

SECTION 6. No negro, or freedman shall be permitted to preach, exhort, or otherwise declaim to congregations of colored people without a special permission from the mayor or president of the board of police under the penalty of a fine of ten dollars or twenty days' work on the public streets.

SECTION 7. No freedman who is not in the military service shall be allowed to carry firearms, or any kind of weapons, within the limits of the town of Opelousas without the special permission of his employer, in writing, and approved by the mayor or president of the board of police. Any one thus offending shall forfeit his weapons and shall be imprisoned and made to work for five days on the public streets or pay a fine of five dollars in lieu of said work.

SECTION 8. No freedman shall sell, barter, or exchange any articles of merchandise or traffic within the limits of Opelousas without permission in writing from his employer or the mayor or president of the board, under the penalty of the forfeiture of said articles and imprisonment and one day's labor, or a fine of one dollar in lieu of said work.

SECTION 9. Any freedman found drunk within the limits of the town shall be imprisoned and made to labor five days on the public streets, or pay five dollars in lieu of said labor.

SECTION 10. Any freedman not residing in Opelousas who shall be found within the corporate limits after the hour of 3 p.m. on Sunday without a special permission from his employer or the mayor shall be arrested and imprisoned and made to work two days on the public streets, or pay two dollars in lieu of said work.

SECTION 11. All the foregoing provisions apply to freedmen and freedwomen, or both sexes.

SECTION 12. It shall be the special duty of the mayor or president of the board to see that all the provisions of this ordinance are faithfully executed.

SECTION 13. *Be it further ordained*, That this ordinance to take effect from and after its first publication.

Ordained the 3d day of July, 1865.

E.D. ESTILLETTE,*President of the Board of Police*.

JOS. D. RICHARDS,*Clerk*.

Official copy:

J. LOVELL,*Captain and Assistant Adjutant General*.

No. 35.

An ordinance relative to the police of negroes recently emancipated within the parish of St. Landry.

Whereas it was formerly made the duty of the police jury to make suitable regulations for the police of slaves within the limits of the parish; and whereas slaves have become emancipated by the action of the ruling powers; and whereas it is necessary for public order, as well as for the comfort and correct deportment of said freedmen, that suitable regulations should be established for their government in their changed condition, the following ordinances are adopted, with the approval of the United States military authorities commanding in said parish, viz:

SECTION 1. *Be it ordained by the police jury of the parish of St. Landry*, That no negro shall be allowed to pass within the limits of said parish without a special permit in writing from his employer. Whoever shall violate this provision shall pay a fine of two dollars and fifty cents, or in default thereof shall be forced to work four days on the public road, or suffer corporeal punishment as provided hereinafter.

SECTION 2. *Be it further ordained*, That every negro who shall be found absent from the residence of his employer after 10 o'clock at night, without a written permit from his employer, shall pay a fine of five dollars, or in default thereof, shall be compelled to work five days on the public road, or suffer corporeal punishment as hereinafter provided.

SECTION 3. *Be it further ordained*, That no negro shall be permitted to rent or keep a house within said parish. Any negro violating this provision shall be immediately ejected and compelled to find an employer; and any person who shall rent, or give the use of any house to any negro, in violation of this section, shall pay a fine of five dollars for each offence.

SECTION 4. *Be it further ordained*, That every negro is required to be in the regular service of some white person, or former owner, who shall be held responsible for the conduct of said negro. But said employer or former owner may permit said negro to hire his own time by special permission in writing, which permission shall not extend over seven days at any one time. Any negro violating the provisions of this section shall be fined five dollars for each offence, or in default of the payment thereof shall be forced to work five days on the public road, or suffer corporeal punishment as hereinafter provided.

SECTION 5. *Be it further ordained*, That no public meetings or congregations of negroes shall be allowed within said parish after sunset; but such public meetings and congregations may be held between the hours of sunrise and sunset, by the special permission in writing of the captain of patrol, within whose beat such meetings shall take place. This prohibition, however, is not intended to prevent negroes from attending the usual church services, conducted by white ministers and priests. Every negro violating the provisions of this section shall pay a fine of five dollars, or in default thereof shall be compelled to work five days on the public road, or suffer corporeal punishment as hereinafter provided.

SECTION 6. *Be it further ordained*, That no negro shall be permitted to preach, exhort, or otherwise declaim to congregations of colored people, without a special permission in writing from the president of the police jury. Any negro violating the provisions of this section shall pay a fine of ten dollars, or in default thereof shall be forced to work ten days on the public road, or suffer corporeal punishment as hereinafter provided.

SECTION 7. *Be it further ordained*, That no negro who is not in the military service shall be allowed to carry fire-arms, or any kind of weapons, within the parish, without the special written permission of his employers, approved and indorsed by the nearest or most convenient chief of patrol. Anyone violating the provisions of this section shall forfeit his weapons and pay a fine of five dollars, or in default of the payment of said fine, shall be forced to work five days on the public road, or suffer corporeal punishment as hereinafter provided.

SECTION 8. *Be it further ordained*, That no negro shall sell, barter, or exchange any articles of merchandise or traffic within said parish without the special written permission of his employer, specifying the articles of sale, barter or traffic. Anyone thus offending shall pay a fine of one dollar for each offence, and suffer the forfeiture of said articles, or in default of the payment of said fine shall work one day on the public road, or suffer corporeal punishment as hereinafter provided.

SECTION 9. *Be it further ordained*, That any negro found drunk within the said parish shall pay a fine of five dollars, or in default thereof shall work five days on the public road, or suffer corporeal punishment as hereinafter provided.

SECTION 10. *Be it further ordained*, That all the foregoing provisions shall apply to negroes of both sexes.

SECTION 11. *Be it further ordained*, That it shall be the duty of every citizen to act as a police officer for the detection of offences and the apprehension of offenders, who shall be immediately handed over to the proper captain or chief of patrol.

SECTION 12. *Be it further ordained*, That the aforesaid penalties shall be summarily enforced, and that it shall be the duty of the captains and chiefs of patrol to see that the aforesaid ordinances are promptly executed.

SECTION 13. *Be it further ordained*, That all sums collected from the aforesaid fines shall be immediately handed over to the parish treasurer.

SECTION 14. *Be it further ordained*, That the corporeal punishment provided for in the foregoing sections shall consist in confining the body of the offender within a barrel placed over his or her shoulders, in the manner practiced in the army, such confinement not to continue longer than twelve hours, and for such time within the aforesaid limit as shall be fixed by the captain or chief of patrol who inflicts the penalty.

SECTION 15. *Be it further ordained*, That these ordinances shall not interfere with any municipal or military regulations inconsistent with them within the limits of said parish.

SECTION 16. *Be it further ordained*, That these ordinances shall take effect five days after their publication in the Opelousas Courier.

Official copy:

J. LOVELL,*Captain and Assistant Adjutant General*.

At a meeting of the citizens of the parish of St. Mary, held at the court-house in the town of Franklin, on Saturday, the 15th instant, P.C. Bethel, Esq., was called to the chair, when a committee was appointed to report upon certain matters submitted to the consideration of the meeting, which committee reported by their chairman the following, which was unanimously adopted:

REPORT OF THE COMMITTEE.

The committee appointed for the purpose of embodying the views and objects of the meeting of the citizens of the parish of St. Mary, assembled at the court-house of said parish on the 15th day of July, A.D. 1865, to deliberate concerning the discipline of colored persons or freedmen, respectfully report that they recommend to the town council of the town of Franklin the adoption of the ordinance of the board of police of the town of Opelousas, passed on the third day of the present month, with such alterations and modifications as may suit the wants and necessities of this locality; also the ordinance of the same board of police passed on the same day, relative to the town of Opelousas; which ordinances are herewith presented for reference. And they furthermore recommend to the police jury of the parish of St. Mary, whenever convened, to make such regulations with regard to the discipline and management of the freedmen or colored population for the entire parish as may be most conducive to the quiet, tranquillity, and productiveness of said parish generally. The committee further recommend to all well-disposed citizens to co-operate with the authorities and with each other in producing a return to civil rule and good order within the shortest delay possible, that the State of Louisiana may be restored to her proper condition as regards internal political stability and tranquillity, as well as the representation she is entitled to in the councils of the nation, which representation is more important to her now than at any previous period of her history.

W.T. PALFREY, Chairman.

Proceedings of the Mayor and Council of the town of Franklin.

Friday, *July* 28, 1865.

Pursuant to call of the major commanding, the mayor and council met this day. Present: A.S. Tucker, mayor; Wilson McKerall, Alfred Gates, John C. Gordy, and J.A. Peterman, members of the council.

The following was unanimously adopted, viz:

ORDINANCE relative to the police of negroes or colored persons within the corporate limits of the town of Franklin.

SEC. 1. *Be it ordained by the mayor and council of the town of Franklin*, That no negro or colored person shall be allowed to come within the limits of said town without special permission from his employer, specifying the object of his visit and the time necessary for the accomplishment of the same. Whoever shall violate this provision shall suffer imprisonment and two days work on the public streets, or shall pay a fine of two dollars and a half.

SEC. 2. *Be it further ordained. &c.*, That every negro or colored person who shall be found on the streets of Franklin after ten o'clock at night without a written pass or permit from his or her employer, shall be imprisoned and compelled to work five days on the public streets or pay a fine of five dollars.

SEC. 3. No negro or colored person shall be permitted to rent or keep a house within the limits of the town under any circumstances; and any one thus offending shall be ejected and compelled to find an employer, or leave the town within twenty-four hours. The lessor or furnisher of the house kept as above shall pay a fine of ten dollars for each offence:*Provided*, That the provisions of this section shall not apply to any free negro or colored person who was residing in the town of Franklin prior to the 1st January (1865) last.

SEC. 4. No negro or colored person shall reside within the limits of the town of Franklin who is not in the regular service of some white person or former owner, who shall be held responsible for the conduct of said negro or colored person; but said employer or former owner may permit said negro or colored person to hire his or their time by special permission in writing, which permission shall not extend to over twenty-five hours at any one time. Any negro or colored person violating the provisions of this section shall be imprisoned and forced to work for two days on the public streets: *Provided*, That the provisions of this section shall not apply to negroes or colored persons heretofore free.

SEC. 5. No public meetings or congregations of negroes or colored persons shall be allowed within the limits of the town of Franklin, under any circumstances or for any purpose, without the permission of the mayor. This prohibition is not intended, however, to prevent negroes or colored persons from attending the usual church service, conducted by established ministers of religion. Every negro or colored person violating this law shall be imprisoned and put to work five days on the public streets.

SEC. 6. No negro or colored person shall be permitted to preach, exhort, or otherwise declaim to congregations of colored people without a special permission from the mayor, under the penalty of a fine of ten dollars or twenty days' work on the public streets.

SEC. 7. No negro or colored person who is not in the military service shall be allowed to carry fire-arms or any kind of weapons within the limits of the town of Franklin without the special permission of his employer in writing, and approved by the mayor. Any one thus offending shall forfeit his weapons and shall be imprisoned and made to work five days on the public streets, or pay a fine of five dollars in lieu of said work.

SEC. 8. No negro or colored person shall sell, barter, or exchange any articles of merchandise or traffic within the limits of Franklin, without permission in writing from his employer or the mayor, under the penalty of forfeiture of the said articles and imprisonment and one day's labor, or a fine of one dollar in lieu of said work.

SEC. 9. Any negro or colored person found drunk within the limits of the town shall be imprisoned and made to labor five days on the public streets, or pay five dollars in lieu of said labor.

SEC. 10. Any negro or colored person not residing in Franklin who shall be found within its corporate limits after the hour of three o'clock p.m. on Sunday without a special written permission from his employer or the mayor, shall be arrested and imprisoned and made to work two days on the public streets, or pay two dollars in lieu of said work.

SEC. 11. All the foregoing provisions apply to negroes or colored persons of both sexes.

SEC. 12. It shall be the special duty of the town constable, under direction of the mayor, to see that all the provisions of this ordinance are faithfully executed.

SEC. 13. Whoever in Franklin shall sell or give to any negro or colored person any intoxicating liquors, or shall exchange or barter for the same with any such negro or colored person, without special permission from the mayor or employer of said negro or colored person, shall, on conviction thereof before the mayor or justice of the peace in and for the seventh ward of the parish of St. Mary, pay a fine of twenty-five dollars and costs of prosecution, and in default of the payment of said fine and costs the person thus offending shall suffer imprisonment in the parish jail for ten days.

A.S. TUCKER, *Mayor.*

R.W. McMILLAN, *Clerk.*

Approved: GEO. R. DAVIS,*Major Third Rhode Island Cavalry, Commanding Post.*

[Telegram.]

New Orleans, *August* 10, 1865.

The ordinance relative to the "Police of negroes or colored persons within the corporate limits of the town of Franklin," dated Friday, July 28, 1865, and signed by A.L. Tucker, mayor, being in violation of the emancipation proclamation, the orders of the War Department, and the orders of these headquarters, you will prevent their enforcement and arrest any person attempting to carry them out. The negroes are as free as other people. This ordinance, if enforced, would be slavery in substance, which can never be. Attend to this matter with all the vigor at your command. I have consulted General Canby, who concurs with me in the matter.

THOMAS   W.   CONWAY,
Ass't. Comm. Bureau of Refugees, Freedmen, &c., State of Louisiana_.

Lieutenant S.E. SHEPARD,*Provost Marshal, Parish of St. Mary, Brashear City, or Franklin, La.*

Official copy:

D.V. FENNO,*First Lieutenant and A.A.A. General.*

No. 36.

BUREAU REFUGEES, FREEDMEN AND ABANDONED LANDS, OFFICE ASSISTANT COMMISSIONER FOR STATE OF MISSISSIPPI,

Vicksburg, Miss., September 28, 1865.

General: I enclose a copy of the city ordinances. You will see that negroes who sell vegetables, cakes, &c., on the street are required to pay ten dollars ($10) per month for the privilege of doing so.

To illustrate the workings of this ordinance I will give you an actual occurrence in this city.

About a year ago an old negro man named Henderson, crippled with over-work, about seventy years of age, was sent to me for support by the military authorities. I issued him rations for himself and wife, an old negro woman, incapable of doing anything but care for herself. I continued this till about January 1, 1865, when the old man came to me and informed me that if I would allow him to sell apples and cakes to the soldiers on a corner of the street near my office, under a large tree that grew there, he thought he could care for himself and make enough to support himself and wife. I immediately gave him permission and an order to protect him. I had but little faith in his being able to do it, as he was compelled to go on crutches and was bent nearly double, owing to a severe whipping his old master had given him some years ago.

He commenced his work, and, much to my surprise, made enough to support himself, and asked for no more assistance from me.

When the city authorities took charge of the city matters the marshal of the city ordered him to pay the ten dollars per month for the privilege of supporting himself or desist from such trade.

The old man told him that all his profits would not amount to ten dollars per month, and that in some months he did not make that amount of sales, but, as Colonel Thomas provided him with a place to live, he could barely support himself by such trade. The marshal of the city informed him that the tax must be paid by all, and that Colonel Thomas could take care of him, as it was his duty to do so.

The old man came to my office and told me the whole affair. I wrote a letter to the mayor setting forth the whole case, and that the collection of this tax on such old cripples would compel me to support them, as they could not pay the city ten dollars per month and make their support. In fact, ten dollars per month is the common wages for negro labor. The mayor refused to allow the negro to continue his sales, and I was compelled to take charge of him. I would have refused to allow the city authorities to interrupt him had it not been for General Orders No. 10, from headquarters department of Mississippi, allowing the mayor to take charge of such matters.

You will see by the city ordinance that a drayman or hackman must file a bond of five hundred dollars in addition to paying for his license. The mayor requires that the bondsmen shall be freeholders. The laws of this State do not, and never did, allow a negro to own land or hold property. The white citizens refuse to sign any bonds for the freedmen.

The white citizens and authorities say that it is for their interest to drive out all independent negro labor; that the freedmen must hire to white men if they wish to do this kind of work.

I am, general, very respectfully,

SAMUEL THOMAS,

Colonel, Assistant Commissioner Freedmen's Bureau, State of Mississippi.

Major General C. SCHURZ.

Proceedings of the City Council.

At a regular meeting of the board of mayor and council of the city of Vicksburg, held at the City Hall, on Monday, August 7, 1865: Present—T.J.
Randolph, mayor; Messrs. Stites, Royall, Johnson, Bender, Spengler, Manlove, and Porterfield, councilmen.

Mr. Stites introduced the following ordinance, which was read; and, on motion of Mr. Bender, the rules were suspended, the ordinance read a second time; and, on motion of Mr. Manlove, the rules were again suspended, the ordinance read a third time by its title, and passed.

Mr. Johnson called for the ayes and noes on the passage of the ordinance, which were taken:

Ayes—Stites, Royall, Bender, Spengler, Manlove, and Porterfield—6.

Nay—Johnson—1.

AN ORDINANCE to raise revenue for the city of Vicksburg.

SEC. 1. That there shall be assessed, levied, and collected upon the landholders, freeholders, and householders of the city of Vicksburg, for the year commencing July 9, 1865, upon the *ad valorem* worth of all houses, lots and parts of lots, and lands, and on all goods, wares, and merchandise, on all moneys loaned at interest in said city, whether by a resident or nonresident or a corporation, a general tax of fifty cents on every one hundred dollars' value thereof; that said valuation or assessment shall be assessed from the 9th day of July, A.D. 1865, and shall be for one year, but the tax so assessed shall be payable in advance.

SEC. 2. That on all goods, wares, and merchandise, produce, &c., contained or sold on board any flatboat, or other water craft, there shall be assessed, levied, and collected upon the *ad valorem* worth a general tax of fifty cents on every one hundred dollars' value thereof.

SEC. 3. That there shall be assessed, levied, and collected a poll tax of two dollars upon every male inhabitant of said city over the age of twenty-one years.

SEC. 4. That the rate for license for the houses, business, &c., be assessed as follows, payable as set forth in section 1: On all family groceries, porter-houses, eating-houses, oyster houses, and restaurants, per year $40; on all auction stores, per year, $200; on all public auctioneers, $50; on all banks, brokers, and exchange offices, $500; on all insurance companies having agents in this city, $100; on all express companies, $200; on all wholesale and retail stores and commission houses, $50; on all drays and carts, $20; on all hacks, $25; on all private boarding-houses having ten or more boarders, $20; on all hotels, $100; on all rooms where billiard tables are kept for playing, $200; on all rooms where bagatelle or pigeonhole tables are kept for playing, $25; on all alleys known as ten-pin or nine-pin alleys, $200; on all livery stables, $50; on all wagon yards, $40; on all barber shops, for each chair, $40; on all manufactories of ale, porter, or soda-water per year, $75; on all bakeries, $25; on all theatres, circuses, animal shows, or any public performance or exhibition where compensation is paid in money, each day, $25; on all bar-rooms, or other places where vinous or spirituous liquors are sold in less quantities than one gallon, per year, $500; on all confectionary, fruit or ice cream, soda water or vegetable stores, $50; on all cigar stores, $50; on all shops where fresh meat is sold, $50; on all street peddlers of goods, wares, or merchandise, fruit& c., except from market carts from the country, per month, $10; on all live stock sold in this city, one-half of one per cent, *ad valorem*.

SEC. 5. That all ordinances in any way conflicting with the provisions of this ordinance be, and the same are hereby, repealed.

SEC. 6. That this ordinance take effect from and after its passage.

Vicksburg, Mississippi, *August* 7, 1865.

Mr. Stites introduced the following ordinance, which was read; and, on motion of Mr. Bender, the rules were suspended and the ordinance read a second time; and, on motion of Mr. Manlove, the rules were again suspended, the ordinance read a third time by its title, and passed.

AN ORDINANCE to regulate the mode of obtaining licenses within the city of Vicksburg.

SEC. 1. That, before license shall be granted to any one to keep a family grocery, porter-house, oyster-house, eating-house, or restaurant in this city, the person or persons so applying shall execute a bond in the penal sum of $500, with one or more securities, payable to the mayor of the city of Vicksburg and his successors in office, conditioned that he, she, or they will keep an orderly and well-conducted house, and will not permit any riotous or disorderly conduct, or any gaming in or about the same, and will not sell any vinous or spirituous liquors to any one in less quantity than one gallon during the continuance of his or her license.

SEC. 2. That before any person or persons shall be licensed to retail vinous or spirituous liquors within this city, he, she, or they shall produce before the board of mayor and council of said city the written recommendation of five freeholders of his or her neighborhood, setting forth that he or she is of good reputation and a suitable person to receive such license.

SEC. 3. That no license to sell vinous or spirituous liquors as aforesaid shall be delivered to any person until he or she shall have first produced the receipt of the treasurer of the city for the amount of tax assessed for such license, and shall also have executed a bond in the penal sum of $1,000, with one or more good and sufficient sureties, payable to the mayor of the city of Vicksburg and his successor in office, conditioned that he, she, or they will keep an orderly and well-conducted house, and will not permit any riotous or disorderly conduct, or any gaming, in or about the same.

SEC. 4. That the bonds provided for in this ordinance shall be submitted to, and approved by, the board of mayor and council before said license shall be issued.

SEC. 5. That if any person shall retail any vinous or spirituous liquors within this city in less quantity than one gallon without first having procured license to do so, pursuant to the provisions of this ordinance, or in any way violate the provisions of this ordinance, he shall, upon conviction before the mayor of the city, be fined in a sum not less than one hundred nor more than five hundred dollars.

SEC. 6. That before issuing license to any person or persons for the privilege of running a public dray, cart, or hack in this city, the party so applying shall first file with the mayor of the city a bond, with good and sufficient security, to be approved by the mayor, in the penal sum of $500, conditioned for the faithful performance of their duties as public carriers.

SEC. 7. That all ordinances in any way conflicting with the provisions of this ordinance be, and the same are hereby, repealed.

SEC. 8. That this ordinance take effect from and after its passage.

Vicksburg, Mississippi, *August* 7, 1865

Mr. Johnson introduced the following ordinance, which was read; and on motion of Mr. Manlove, the rules were suspended and the ordinance read a second time; and on motion of Mr. Bender, the rules were again suspended, the ordinance read a third time by its title, and passed:

AN ORDINANCE to amend the market ordinance.

SEC. 1. That from and after the passage of this ordinance it shall not be lawful for any person or persons to sell or expose for sale in the market-house of Vicksburg, after the hour of 9 o'clock a.m., any lemonade, ice-cream, cakes, pies, fruit, or vegetables, or other articles usually sold in market, under the penalty of $10 for each and every offence.

SEC. 2. That it shall not be lawful for any person or persons trading in the market to buy or bargain for, during market hours, or receive from any person or persons not renting a stall in the market, any meat, fish, poultry, butter, eggs, vegetables, or fruits, and offer the same for sale in the market again within ten days, under a penalty of $10 for each and every offence.

SEC. 3. That it shall not be lawful for any person or persons to buy from any person on their way to market, within the city, during market hours, any of the articles named in the second section, or prevent such person from going to market with aforesaid articles, under a penalty of $10 for each and every offence.

SEC. 4. That it shall be the duty of the day police of each ward to arrest and bring before the mayor all persons found violating any section of the above ordinance.

SEC. 5. That all ordinances or parts of ordinances conflicting with this ordinance be, and the same are hereby, repealed.

Mr. Porterfield introduced the following ordinance, which was read; and on motion of Mr. Manlove, the rules were suspended and the ordinance read a second time; and on further motion of Mr. Manlove, the rules were again suspended, the ordinance read a third time by its title, and passed:

AN ORDINANCE regulating ferry-boats, &c.

SEC. 1. That all ferry-boats crossing the Mississippi river and landing in the city limits shall pay the sum of $25 per week.

SEC. 2. That this ordinance shall be in force from and after its passage.

On motion of Mr. Manlove, the following resolution was adopted:*Resolved*, That hereafter it shall be lawful for the city marshal to charge for prisoners committed to workhouse for board, per day, sixty cents.

On motion of Mr. Spangler, the following resolution was adopted:*Resolved*, That the city marshal notify the owners of property to have their side-walks and gutters repaired on Washington street, between second corner of East to Depot street, in thirty days; and if not done, the city marshal have it done, at the expense of the property.

On motion of Mr. Manlove, the following resolution was adopted:*Resolved*, That the mayor be authorized to pay the policemen the amounts due them respectively to date, according to the report by the city marshal.

On motion of Mr. Spangler, the following resolution was adopted:*Resolved*, That the overseers of street hands' pay shall be $100 per month.

On motion of Mr. Manlove, the following resolution was adopted:*Resolved*, That the salary of the city marshal shall be $1,200 per annum, the salary of the deputy marshal be $900 per annum, and the salary of the policemen $60 per month, all of which shall be paid monthly.

On motion of Mr. Manlove, the following resolution was adopted:*Resolved*, That a committee of two be appointed to receive proposals to publish the proceedings of the city council to the third Monday in March next, and also inquire on what terms the city printing can be done, and report to next meeting of this council.

The mayor appointed Messrs. Manlove and Bender on said committee.

On motion of Mr. Bender, the board adjourned till Thursday evening, August 10, at six o'clock.

T.J. RANDOLPH, *Mayor.*

No. 37.

FREEDMEN'S BUREAU, STATE OF MISSISSIPPI,

_Office State Superintendent of Education,

Vicksburg, Miss., September_ 28, 1865.

General: At the request of Colonel Thomas, I beg your attention to a few considerations touching the turning over of the care of the freedmen in Mississippi to the State authorities, so far as the transfer bears upon the religious and educational privileges of the colored people. Perhaps no one who has been less engaged in caring for the education and the moral interests of these people can fully appreciate the facts that I intend to lay before you, or understand them as having the intensity of meaning that I see in them.

I have seen a good deal of the people of Mississippi, and have purposely sounded them as to their feelings with regard to the effort to educate the blacks. The general feeling is that of strong opposition to it. Only one person resident in Mississippi before the rebellion has expressed himself to me as in favor of it, and he did not propose to do anything to aid it; and, to show how much his favor was worth, he said he regretted that he was not able to prevent the negroes from having shouting meetings, and that he would keep them from going off the plantation to meeting now if he could, as he formerly did. Aside from this gentleman, every native Mississippian and Irishman with whom I have conversed opposes the instruction of freedmen. Some disguise their opposition by affected contemptuous disbelief of the negro's capacity. All the facts that we can give them, however rich and suggestive, are received with sneering incredulity and the assurance that they know the negroes better than we do. A little persistence in giving this class of men facts disproving their assertions usually makes them angry, and leads them to declare that if the negroes can learn, the greater the damage that will be done them, for the education will do them no good, and will spoil them. Others take this last-mentioned ground at first, and say that a learned negro is a nuisance; for, while he is ignorant, stupid, and loutish, he may be compelled to labor; but as soon as he comes to know something the white people cannot make so profitable use of him.

Some manifest great spite when this subject is mentioned. They say we are trying to make the negro equal with them. Many do not hesitate to say that he ought to be kept uneducated in order that he may not be superior to ignorant white men.

I have discovered that many object to the negro women's being educated lest they should be led to respect themselves, and not so easily be made the instruments of the white man's lust.

The people of Vicksburg have asked Colonel Thomas to prevent the establishment of colored schools within the city—they would probably say, to preserve the peace of the city; but I feel sure it is because the sight of them gives pain. And if their removal ever becomes necessary to the peace of a place, the fact will illustrate public feeling sufficiently.

I have heard more than one person say that he would kill a colored teacher if he ever saw one.

The children of a community generally express the public feeling, and we may usually learn from them what the feeling is, even when the parents, from prudence, seek to conceal it. Children often exaggerate, but they get their bias at home. The children of Mississippi throw stones at colored scholars, and are only restrained by fear from mobbing colored schools.

My memorandum book contains such information as to points in the interior of the State as I can gather from officers, and from any reliable source, to guide me in locating teachers. Some of these memoranda are: "Garrison withdrawn; school impossible." "No resident federal officer; a teacher could not be protected." "People much prejudiced; protection cannot be guaranteed." Such things are said in regard to every place not under northern protection. I think I do not overstate in saying that I do not know a single northern man in Mississippi who supposes a colored school possible where there is no federal sword or bayonet. Some northern men do not regret this fact, perhaps; and this makes their testimony on this point more valuable.

White churches recover their houses of worship which the blacks helped to build, and which they have repaired extensively during the last two years, and remorselessly turn the blacks out without any regard to their rights in equity, their feelings, or their religious interests.

I may state here that there is such a general expression of contempt for negro religion, and such a desire to suppress it, if possible, that it seems as if the whites thought it a piece of terrible impertinence for the blacks to worship the same God that we do. The white people also fear, or affect to fear, that opposition to their plans, and even insurrection, will be hatched at the meetings of colored people. The Nemesis of slavery still holds her whip over them. From this source arise the occasional reports of intended insurrections; and these reports are intended, often, to cause the prevention of meetings, at which the colored people may consult together, and convey information important to them.

In view of all these things, I have no doubt but that, if our protection be withdrawn, negro education will be hindered in every possible way, including obstruction by fraud and violence. I have not the smallest expectation that, with the State authorities in full power, a northern citizen would be protected in the exercise of his constitutional right to teach and preach to the colored people; and shall look for a renewal of the fearful scenes, in which northerners were whipped, tarred and feathered, warned off, and murdered, before the war.

I meant to make this letter shorter, but could not. I hope I need not assure you, general, that I am not conscious that any part of the above comes of enmity to the south. I certainly should rejoice to see my opinion of the state of feeling in Mississippi falsified by patent facts.

I have the honer to be, general, your obedient servant,

JOSEPH WARREN,*Chaplain, State Superintendent of Education*.

Major General CARL SCHURZ.

No. 39.

OFFICE ASSISTANT COMMISSIONER BUREAU REFUGEES, FREEDMEN AND ABANDONED LANDS FOR STATE OF MISSISSIPPI,

Vicksburg, Mississippi, September 30, 1865.

General: I see by the papers of a late date that Dr. Murdoch, of Columbus, Mississippi, has made a speech at General Howard's office, in which he makes strong promises of the hearty co-operation of his fellow-citizens in the education of the freedmen in the State.

The officer of this bureau at that place, Captain Hubbard, writes that "the citizens of the place are so prejudiced against the negroes that they are opposed to all efforts being made for their education or elevation; that the people will not give rooms, or allow the children of their hired freedmen to attend the schools; that the citizens of the place have written a letter to the officer saying that they would respectfully ask that no freedmen schools be established under the auspices of the bureau, as it would tend to disturb the present labor system, and take from the field labor that is so necessary to restore the wealth of the State." This is signed by half a dozen citizens purporting to represent the people, and certainly gives us a different idea of the case from that stated by Dr. Murdoch.

I am, general, very respectfully,

SAMUEL THOMAS,*Colonel, Assistant Commissioner for Mississippi*.

Major General CARL SCHURZ.

No. 40.

To the Voters of Wilkinson county:

Fellow-Citizens: When I consented, some days ago, to be a candidate for the State convention, I confess that, with some of my personal friends, I was vain enough to believe that I was sufficiently well known to the people of Wilkinson county to make it unnecessary for me to publish my political creed. But, to my surprise, it is rumored, to the prejudice of my humble claim upon your suffrage, that I am an "*unconditional, immediate emancipationist—an abolitionist.*"

In the freedom of casual, friendly conversation, it is certainly not unreasonable that I may, as any other man, be misunderstood. I cannot think any of my fellow-citizens capable of misrepresenting me purposely. But certain it is I am misunderstood if any man believes me to favor the policy that wrongs and impoverishes my country. It does occur to me, fellow-citizens, that the *charity*, at least, if not the good sense of those who know me, would contradict any such insinuation. True, I only claim to have done my duty, but my record for the last four years, I trust, is sufficient proof of my fidelity to the interests of the south and all her institutions. Can any man believe me now in favor of, and ready to advocate, the abolition of an institution for which I have contended so long, and which I am as fully persuaded to-day, as ever, was the true status of the negro? Surely not.

But, fellow-citizens,—what I may, in common with you all, have to submit to, is a very different thing. Slavery has been taken from us. The power that has already practically abolished the institution threatens totally and forever to abolish it. But does it follow that I am in favor of this thing? By no means. And, certainly, you who know me will not demand of me any further assurance than my antecedents afford that I will, as your representative, should you elect me, "do all and secure all" I could for the best interest of the State, and the rights and interests of a free people.

I have thought, and have said, and do now repeat, that my honest conviction is, we must accept the situation as it is until we can get control once more of our own State affairs. We cannot do otherwise and get our place again in the Union, and occupy a position, exert an influence, that will protect us against further and greater evils which threaten us. I must, as any other man who votes or holds an office, submit, for the time, to evils I cannot remedy.

I want it distinctly understood that *I do not run on "Mr. Burruss's platform," or any other man's, save my own.*

Should you send me to the convention I will go committed, as I think an honest man can only commit himself, i. e., according to my best judgment, and with an intention to guard all the blessings we now enjoy, to the extent of my ability, exert myself, as I have said, to secure all I can for the interest of our State. If I cannot be trusted, then choose some other man, who may have shown himself hitherto, and is now, more truly your friend, and who is, in your judgment, more capable of representing you.

W.L. BRANDON.

Wilkinson County, *August* 6.

No. 41.

OFFICE ACTING ASSISTANT COMMISSIONER BUREAU FREEDMEN, &c., FOR SOUTHERN DISTRICT OF MISSISSIPPI,

Natchez, Miss., September 25, 1865.

General: In obedience to your request, I have the honor to submit the following as the result of my observations during the past year among freedmen:

The opinion and feeling among the negroes throughout this district, comprising the counties of Claiborne, Copiah, Lawrence, Covington, Jones, Wayne, Jefferson, Franklin, Pike, Marion, Perry, Greene, Adams, Wilkinson, Amite, Hancock, Harrison, and Jackson, and Concordia and Teusas parishes, Louisiana, are almost unanimous on one point, viz: they will remain this year on their old places for a support, and such remuneration as the crop raised can give them, but next year they will leave and make other arrangements. They say that they have tried their old masters, know what they require, and how they will be treated, and that, as they are now free, they will try some other place and some other way of working. They take this view not because they are tired of work, or because they want to be idle, but because they are free, and want to find out in what their freedom consists.

To contend with the results of this opinion will be the great work flung upon the hands of some one next year. And not only will they have to see that the laborers are properly settled, but they must provide for the crippled, the helpless and the children. The planters cannot be made to support those who are too feeble to give any return, and who only remain because they are too old or too young to get away. What, then, is to become of them?

As to those who can labor, there will be no difficulty—the demand for laborers will far exceed the supply. The great trouble will be to keep the negro in the State, and to provide assistance for those who are unable to take care of themselves. Another want to be provided for is that of education. If we are to have good, industrious, and law-abiding people, we must provide some means for their education. It is intended to place a teacher in every town in which schools can be established and protected. From conversations with intelligent citizens, whom I feel assured, represent the feelings of a large class of people, I think that for some time the equality of negroes and whites before the law, as regards testimony, will be merely an equality in name.

Citizens say that their legislature may, and probably will, make laws receiving the testimony of negroes in all cases, as a means of inducing the government to re-admit them to a full exercise of their State jurisdiction and representation, but that no southern jury can ever be found that, when it comes to a case where twenty negroes testify one way, and two white men testify the other, will not decide in favor of the white, and virtually throw out the negro testimony. Of course this matter of testimony will settle itself with time, and a negro's word obtain the same credit from his individual character as among whites, for the whites, having cases that they are dependent upon negro testimony for, will in the course of time be brought by their own interests to take and demand the full benefit of the law; but for some time, although legally admitted, it will in fact be excluded.

The report of Captain Warren Peck, a copy of which I have the honor to enclose, gives a very fair view of what the result would be, were the officers of this bureau removed.

When I took charge here I found a perfect state of terror among whites and blacks; but now that officers are thickly distributed over the district, complaints are few, and the laborers are well, and, so far as possible, comfortably fixed for this year. Out of a negro population of over 75,000, only 649 receive rations from the government as destitutes.

I feel no hesitation in saying that it is imperatively necessary to give the system of free labor a fair trial, and to secure to the freedmen all the benefits contemplated by the emancipation proclamation; that officers or agents should be retained whose duty it is to look after the interests of this large class of people, and see that they are gradually accustomed to manage their own business and protect their own interests.

I have the honor to be, general, very respectfully, your obedient servant,

GEORGE D. REYNOLDS,*Major 6th United States Colored Heavy Artillery, and Acting Assistant Comm. Bureau of Freedmen, &c., Southern Dist. of Mississippi.*

Major General CARL SCHURZ.

No. 42.

HEADQUARTERS NORTHERN DISTRICT OF MISSISSIPPI,

Jackson, Miss., August 21, 1865.

Captain: I have the honor to enclose copies of a notice to form companies in this and a neighboring county, and of my letter to Governor Sharkey in reference to this matter. In a discussion which I had with the governor he told me that it was his intention to raise a company of militia in every county of the State, in accordance with the militia law of Mississippi, mainly for the purpose of suppressing any acts of violence which the negroes may attempt to commit during next winter. I called the attention of the governor to the fact that the docket, until this day, exhibits only the name of white criminals, and that all information proves that almost all the cases of robbery, murder, &c., were brought in connexion with young men in the country lately returned from military service—just the very same men who, in all probability, would join the intended meetings to form companies of militia.

The result of the organization of such companies, while the State is occupied by United States troops, mostly colored, cannot be doubted—the heterogeneous element must clash and bring about a state of affairs which certainly would prove detrimental to the peace and best interests of the State.

Governor Sharkey tells me that he has applied to President Johnson for authority to raise the militia, and that he would inform me of any decision he may receive from Washington; in the mean time I consider it my duty to take action as communicated in my letter, and respectfully request the approval of the major general commanding department. Very respectfully, your obedient servant,

P. JOS. OSTERHAUS,*Major General Volunteers.*

Captain J. WARREN MILLER, *A.A. General, Department of Mississippi.*

Official copy:

W.A. GORDON,*A.A. General.*

EXECUTIVE OFFICE, *Jackson, Miss., August* 19, 1865.

Information having reached me that parties of bad men have banded together in different parts of the State for the purpose of robbing and plundering, and for violating the law in various ways, and that outrages of various kinds are being perpetrated, and the military authorities of the United States being insufficient to protect the people throughout the entire State, I do therefore call upon the people, and especially on such as are liable to perform military duty, and are familiar with military discipline, to organize volunteer companies in each county in the State, if practicable, at least one company of cavalry and one of infantry, as speedily as possible, for the detection of criminals, the prevention of crime, and the preservation of good order. And I urge upon these companies, when formed, that they will be vigilant in the discharge of these duties. These companies will be organized under the law in relation to volunteer companies as contained in the Revised Code, and the amendment thereto, passed on the 10th of February, 1860, except that as soon as the proper number shall volunteer, the election for officers may take place immediately and without further order, and commissions will be issued as soon as returns are received, and the election may be held by any justice of the peace. I most earnestly call upon the young men of the State, who have so distinguished themselves for gallantry, to respond promptly to this call, which is made in behalf of a suffering people.

It will be the duty, as I hope it will be the pleasure, of these companies to pursue and apprehend all offenders against law, and by vigilance to prevent crime, to aid the civil authorities, and to contribute all in their power to the restoration of good order in the community. Arms will be procured, if possible, for such as may not have them, but I would advise an immediate organization with such arms as can be procured.

Given under my hand and the great seal of State affixed.

W.L. SHARKEY,*Provisional Governor of Mississippi.*

By the Governor:

JOHN H. ECHOLS,*Secretary of State.*

HEADQUARTERS NORTHERN DISTRICT OF MISSISSIPPI,

Jackson, Miss., August 22, 1865.

Captain: I have the honor to enclose copy of a letter received from Governor Sharkey in reply to my communication of yesterday, copy of which was sent you by last courier. The governor's proclamation, raising troops in the whole State, changes the status of things, as it no longer belongs to the limits of my district, but to the department; and, consequently, I desist from all further action in the matter until your instructions have come to hand.

In regard to the robberies, I will state that not a single *regular*stage, between Big Black and Jackson, has been earnestly interfered with; they were permitted to run, without molestation, while the "robbers" operated against a Massachusetts schoolmaster, some darkies, and the government messengers; not a house was entered in the vicinity of the field of operations, not an inhabitant robbed. All "home institutions" are apparently safe. The inference is natural that these

184

highway men are guerillas in the true sense of the word, and are waging a war against the "invaders." The governor admits, very candidly, that he knows that the people are reluctant to give aid to me by imparting information. Several persons who were halted by the "robbers," but released with the excuse that they were stopped by mistake, refused flatly to give any name, of the party they were stopped by, but declared to know them.

You know, captain, that certain parties have importuned the governor, from the beginning, to raise the militia; and, as there was no cause for such a measure before, it probably was thought expedient to get up some cause for the desired purpose. Now we have the "robberies"—they are very one-sided and extraordinary—but they furnished the cause so badly wanted. The governor is confident that a few squads of young men, armed with fowling-pieces and the omnipresent revolvers, can suppress all irregularities, which the utmost vigilance and constant exertion of a large number of United States troops failed to suppress!

I must state yet that the parties arrested under suspicion of participating in the described robberies are young men lately connected with the rebel army. There is no doubt on my mind that the young men "who steal the despatches from our messengers" will become good members of the intended militia.

With great respect, your obedient servant,

P. JOS. OSTERHAUS,*Major General Volunteers*.

Captain J. WARREN MILLER,*A.A. General, Department of Mississippi*.

Official copy:

W.A. GORDON,*A.A. General*.

HEADQUARTERS NORTHERN DISTRICT OF MISSISSIPPI,

Jackson, Miss., August 21, 1865.

Sir: A notice appears in yesterday's paper, over the signature of Lamar Fontaine, calling on the young men of Hinds and Madison counties to meet at Cooper Wells and at Livingstone, respectively, on the 22d and 24th instant, for the purpose of organizing companies and electing officers.

The notice creates the impression that some kind of military organization is intended, and in that event I would beg leave to call your attention to the fact that the State of Mississippi is under occupation, and that martial law is still in force, and that no military organizations can be tolerated which are not under the control of the United States officers. I am, therefore, in duty bound and compelled to prevent and prohibit all military organization not recognized as a portion of the United States forces, unless they are formed under special authority of the War Department, or the major general commanding the department of Mississippi.

I can assure your excellency that the number of troops in the counties of Hinds and Madison is amply sufficient to give the civil authorities all the assistance they may possibly need, and the means at my disposal are amply sufficient to stop all crime, provided the civil authorities will co-operate sincerely with the military commanders, and furnish information promptly and voluntarily, as the public peace and safety require them to do.

I respectfully request that you will communicate the tenor of this communication to Mr. Fontaine.

Believe me, with great esteem, your excellency's obedient servant,

P. JOS. O'STERHAUS,*Major General Volunteers*.

His Excellency Hon. W.L. SHARKEY,*Provisional Governor of Mississippi*.

Official copy:

W.A. GORDON, A.A.G.

EXECUTIVE OFFICE, *Jackson, Miss., August* 22, 1865.

General: I have the honor to acknowledge the receipt of your communication of yesterday, in which you call my attention to the fact that the State of Mississippi is still under military occupation, and that martial law is still in force, and that no military organizations can be tolerated which are not under the control of United States officers; and you add that you will feel bound to prevent such organizations, and you also assure me that you have sufficient troops in the counties of Hinds and Madison to aid the civil authorities. This last remark was made by you with reference to a particular organization which has been proposed in those counties. I have, however, issued a general order on this subject, a copy of which I hand you, regretting that you have felt yourself compelled to take this view of the subject, and I know you are prompted by a sense of duty. I beg to remind you that for twelve or fifteen consecutive nights passengers travelling in the stage between here and Vicksburg have been robbed, and these things have occurred within twelve or fifteen miles of your own headquarters. I would not be understood as reflecting in the slightest degree on you. I know you have every desire to prevent such occurrences, and will use every means in your power to do so, and to arrest the culprits. I know, too, that the people are reluctant to give you aid by imparting information to you, but, in addition to these robberies, information daily reaches me of the perpetration of outrages, committed in various ways in distant parts of the—State where you have no military force. The people are calling on me for protection, which I cannot give them under existing circumstances, and it was to give them relief that the military organizations have been ordered. If further justification be necessary, I may add in the last interview I had with the President, in speaking of anticipated troubles, he distinctly stated to me that I could organize the militia if it should become necessary. I think the necessity is now manifest, and therefore claim the authority of the President of the United States for my action. It was precisely under this authority that in my proclamation of the 1st of July I called upon the people in unprotected counties to organize for their security. I will also state that the President has been apprised of what I am doing in this respect, and when he shall change his instructions I will, of course, yield obedience; but until he shall do so, I shall feel it to be my duty to carry out the line of policy I have adopted. I need scarcely assure you, general, that this is not in any sense a hostile demonstration, and feel quite sure no evil can result from it. Mississippi has spoken too plainly in her convention to leave any doubt about her future purposes.

Believe me, with great respect, your most obedient servant,

W.L. SHARKEY,*Provisional Governor of Mississippi.*

Major General P. Jos. OSTERHAUS.

Official copy:

W.A. GORDON, A.A.G.

No. 43.

OFFICE ACTING ASSISTANT COMMISSIONER FREEDMEN'S BUREAU

FOR NORTHERN DISTRICT OF MISSISSIPPI,

Jackson, Miss., September 28, 1865.

Major: In compliance with your request desiring me to furnish you a list of crimes and assaults against freedmen, I have the honor to report that on or about the 18th day of August, 1865, Matilda, a colored woman, was murdered by one J.H. Kiley and son, in Newton county, in this State, for simply remonstrating against whipping her son. Lucinda, a colored woman, in Yalobusha county, was stripped naked, tied to a tree, and severely whipped by three men, names unknown. In the county of Holmes, between the 5th and 15th days of September, 1865, five negroes were murdered; names of the perpetrators unknown. In Simpson county, about the 1st of August, a father and his two sons cruelly whipped and abused a colored woman in their employ. Near Lauderdale Springs, Castwell Eads, a citizen, by his own statement, shot and wounded a colored man for simply refusing to obey his command, *halt*! while he was running from him after being cruelly whipped. In Smith county, S.S. Catchings, a citizen, followed a colored man, who had left his plantation, overtook him, knocked him down, and beat him brutally.

These are all the cases of which I have detailed accounts, none but general reports having yet been received from the agents. These indicate that cruelty is frequently practiced.

I am, sir, very respectfully, your obedient servant,

E.S. DONALDSON,*Lieutenant Colonel, Acting Assistant Commissioner.*

Major W.A. GORDON,*Assistant Adjutant General.*

No. 44.

Savannah, Ga., *August* 1, 1865.

General: In answer to your question with regard to free labor at the South, and particularly the way in which the contract system is viewed by persons who were formerly slaveholders, I would state that these persons accept the present condition of affairs as an alternative forced upon them, believing still that the emancipation of their slaves was a great blunder, and that slavery is the only system by which the colored laborer can be made profitable to his employer.

Within this district the plantation contracts now in force were entered into just subsequent to the arrival of the army, and when it was impossible for planters to undertake the care of their plantations. The negroes, therefore, planted for themselves, promising the owner a fair proportion of the crop as rent for the use of the land.

Now, however, the matter comes up in a different shape. Owners have returned, and it is necessary to make arrangements for the next season. Most of them complain and find fault with the government, and remain inactive. So long as the military form prevails they seem to submit and to conform to present requirements, but at heart they are unfriendly. Some few, however, ask of us what we are going to do with the negro, and what provision will be made with regard to labor. There is nothing in their conduct that betokens sympathy with our movements, or a desire to co-operate with us earnestly in our work. The rebel spirit is as bitter as ever in the minds of the southern people. To return to the old customs is now their effort, and step by step they would take us back to where we were when the war broke out. They will contract with the freedmen, not because they prefer to, but because they are obliged to, and so long as the authority of the United States is present for the protection of all parties, and to compel a faithful performance, the agreement will be carried out; but should the army be withdrawn, the freedmen would virtually be reduced to slavery, and freedom-loving men would find a southern residence unsafe.

I think the negro is disposed to fulfil his contract, and in cases where it has seemed otherwise, the other party has often been at fault.

While I have met a few planters who seem to realize that emancipation is a fixed fact, and that they must make the most of present circumstances, by resorting to the only means by which labor can now be obtained, (the contract system,) I have found scarcely one who will enter into the matter with any kind of sympathy, or with either the belief or the hope that our plans will eventually succeed, for they feel keenly that the success of those plans will prove the foolishness of slavery.

The coming year will produce a change of opinion at the South, I think, if by thorough supervision we secure protection to free labor.

I am, general, very respectfully, your obedient servant,

A.P.   KETCHUM.
Major General CARL SCHURZ.

LETTER OF GENERAL GRANT CONCERNING AFFAIRS AT THE SOUTH.

HEADQUARTERS ARMIES OF THE UNITED STATES,

Washington, D.C., December 18, 1865.

Sir: In reply to your note of the 16th instant, requesting a report from me giving such information as I may be possessed of coming within the scope of the inquiries made by the Senate of the United States in their resolution of the 12th instant, I have the honor to submit the following:

With your approval, and also that of the honorable Secretary of War, I left Washington city on the 27th of last month for the purpose of making a tour of inspection through some of the southern States, or States lately in rebellion, and to see what changes were necessary to be made in the disposition of the military forces of the country; how these forces could be reduced and expenses curtailed, &c.; and to learn, as far as possible, the feelings and intentions of the citizens of those States towards the general government.

The State of Virginia being so accessible to Washington city, and information from this quarter, therefore, being readily obtained, I hastened through the State without conversing or meeting with any of its citizens. In Raleigh, North Carolina, I spent one day; in Charleston, South Carolina, two days; Savannah and Augusta, Georgia, each one day. Both in travelling and whilst stopping I saw much and conversed freely with the citizens of those States as well as with officers of the army who have been stationed among them. The following are the conclusions come to by me.

I am satisfied that the mass of thinking men of the south accept the present situation of affairs in good faith. The questions which have heretofore divided the sentiment of the people of the two sections— slavery and State rights, or the right of a State to secede from the Union—they regard as having been settled forever by the highest tribunal—arms—that man can resort to. I was pleased to learn from the leading men whom I met that they not only accepted the decision arrived at as final, but, now that the smoke of battle has cleared away and time has been given for reflection, that this decision has been a fortunate one for the whole country, they receiving like benefits from it with those who opposed them in the field and in council.

Four years of war, during which law was executed only at the point of the bayonet throughout the States in rebellion, have left the people possibly in a condition not to yield that ready obedience to civil authority the American people have generally been in the habit of yielding. This would render the presence of small garrisons throughout those States necessary until such time as labor returns to its proper channel, and civil authority is fully established. I did not meet any one, either those holding places under the government or citizens of the southern States, who think it practicable to withdraw the military from the south at present. The white and the black mutually require the protection of the general government.

There is stick universal acquiescence in the authority of the general government throughout the portions of country visited by me, that the mere presence of a military force, without regard to numbers, is sufficient to maintain order. The good of the country, and economy, require that the force kept in the interior, where there are many freedmen, (elsewhere in the southern States than at forts upon the seacoast no force is necessary,) should all be white troops. The reasons for this are obvious without mentioning many of them. The presence of black troops, lately slaves, demoralizes labor, both by their advice and by furnishing in their camps a resort for the freedmen for long distances around. White troops generally excite no opposition, and therefore a small number of them can maintain order in a given district. Colored troops must be kept in bodies sufficient to defend themselves. It is not the thinking men who would use violence towards any class of troops sent among them by the general government, but the ignorant in some places might; and the late slave seems to be imbued with the idea that the property of his late master should, by right, belong to him, or at least should have no protection from the colored soldier. There is danger of collisions being brought on by such causes.

My observations lead me to the conclusion that the citizens of the southern States are anxious to return to self-government, within the Union, as soon as possible; that whilst reconstructing they want and require protection from the government; that they are in earnest in wishing to do what they think is required by the government, not humiliating to them as citizens, and that if such a course were pointed out they would pursue it in good faith. It is to be regretted that there cannot be a greater commingling, at this time, between the citizens of the two sections, and particularly of those intrusted with the law-making power.

I did not give the operations of the Freedmen's Bureau that attention I would have done if more time had been at my disposal. Conversations on the subject, however, with officers connected with the bureau, lead me to think that, in some of the States, its affairs have not been conducted with good judgment or economy, and that the belief, widely spread among the freedmen of the southern States, that the lands of their former owners will, at least in part, be divided among them, has come from the agents of this bureau. This belief is seriously interfering with the willingness of the freedmen to make contracts for the coming year. In some form the Freedmen's Bureau is an absolute necessity until civil law is established and enforced, securing to the freedmen their rights and full protection. At present, however, it is independent of the military establishment of the country, and seems to be operated by the different agents of the bureau according to their individual notions. Everywhere General Howard, the able head of the bureau, made friends by the just and fair instructions and advice he gave; but the complaint in South Carolina was that when he left, things went on as before. Many, perhaps the majority, of the agents of the Freedmen's Bureau advise the freedmen that by their own industry they must expect to live. To this end they endeavor to secure employment for them, and to see that both contracting parties comply with their engagements. In some instances, I am sorry to say, the freedman's mind does not seem to be disabused of the idea that a freedman has the right to live without care or provision for the future. The effect of the belief in division of lands is idleness and accumulation in camps, towns, and cities. In such cases I think it will be found that vice and disease will tend to the extermination or great reduction of the colored race. It cannot be expected that the opinions held by men at the south for years can be changed in a day, and therefore the freedmen require, for a few years, not only laws to protect them, but the fostering care of those who will give them good counsel, and on whom they rely.

The Freedmen's Bureau being separated from the military establishment of the country, requires all the expense of a separate organization. One does not necessarily know what the other is doing, or what orders they are acting under. It seems to me this could be corrected by regarding every officer on duty with troops in the southern States as an agent of the Freedmen's Bureau, and then have all orders from the head of the bureau sent through department commanders. This would create a responsibility that would secure uniformity of action throughout all the south; would insure the orders and instructions from the head of the bureau being carried out, and would relieve from duty and pay a large number of employees of the government.

I have the honor to be, very respectfully, your obedient servant,

U.S. GRANT,*Lieutenant General*.

His Excellency ANDREW JOHNSON,*President of the United States*.

End

Made in the USA
Lexington, KY
19 May 2018